D1234029

CATHOLIC CHURCHES

SINCE 1623

ALSO BY BRYAN LITTLE

The Building of Bath
Cheltenham
The Three Choirs Cities
Exeter
The City and County of Bristol
The Life and Work of James Gibbs
Portrait of Cambridge
    (with A. F. Kersting as photographer)
The Monmouth Episode
Crusoe's Captain
Cambridge Discovered
Bath Portrait
English Historic Architecture

Burrell

2.00

CATHOLIC CHURCHES

SINCE 1623

*A Study of Roman Catholic Churches
in England and Wales from Penal Times
to the Present Decade*

BRYAN LITTLE

Illustrated

ROBERT HALE · LONDON

© Bryan Little 1966

First published in Great Britain 1966

PRINTED BY C. TINLING AND CO. LTD,
LIVERPOOL, LONDON AND PRESCOT

FOREWORD

The task of putting together this account of Roman Catholic church-building in England and Wales has been made longer and harder by certain facts which have been borne in on me since I started the work. The astonishing, but complete, lack of comprehensive books on the buildings concerned has meant that facts have had to be accumulated piecemeal, and that despite much help from archive records, and from some books on individual churches, I have had to work on numerous and separated sources, and have paid many special visits all over the country, to gain a reasonably clear picture of a long, and unduly, neglected subject. Without much kind help from those mentioned in my list of acknowledgements my task could never have been attempted.

The churches and chapels of any denomination form part of the whole nation's corpus of religious architecture. I have therefore treated my subject as one of general and not merely of Roman Catholic interest, and I have tried to show how the buildings covered in these pages fit in to a wider stylistic and aesthetic whole. Catholic churches have for two centuries now been a slowly growing part, and are now a large proportion, of this country's religious architecture. Even in the early, immediately post-penal days they were (as one saw at Lulworth, Winchester, and Wigan) by no means lacking in aesthetic importance. As time went on they became a significant, but comparatively disregarded, element in Britain's nineteenth-century architecture; only Augustus Pugin and some of the Hansom dynasty escaped a more general oblivion. Yet no study of our Victorian churches can be complete if those built for Roman Catholic worship are left out. Leonard Stokes and Giles Scott were architects of great talent and renown, and such new churches as those at Harlow, East Acton, and Leyland suggest that this country's Catholic churchbuilding, with the Liturgical Movement now more widely accepted, and with the second

Vatican Council behind it, is nowadays more significant, within the whole subject of English and Welsh architecture, that it has been for a very long time.

Clifton, Bristol   B.D.G.L.
September, 1966

CONTENTS

ACKNOWLEDGEMENTS

My grateful thanks are due to many people without whose kind help the writing of this book would have been quite impossible; in many cases their assistance over literary research and the gathering of manifold facts has been accompanied by kind hospitality. Some of them are mentioned, where this is appropriate, in my reference notes. In addition, I have to thank those who kindly responded to my appeals, for example in the columns of the *Catholic Herald*, for written information and illustrative material.

My very special thanks are due to Prof. Stephen Welsh, M.A., of Sheffield, not only for his help over the members of the Hansom dynasty but for much other valuable information on architects who worked on Catholic churches in the nineteenth century. Mr. Denis Evinson has also helped me over Joseph Hansom and some other members of this important architectural family. I owe a special debt of gratitude to Mr. Peter Anson, not only for much written information but also for the loan of many newspaper cuttings, sketches, etc. Miss Rosemary Rendel, the Hon. Secretary of the Catholic Record Society, has given me constant help and encouragement.

My enquiries into the history and architecture of this country's Catholic cathedrals has been aided at Brentwood by the Very Rev. Canon T. C. Smith, Ph.D., at Cardiff by Rev. B. S. Cosulich, and at Clifton by the Very Rev. Mgr. Canon T. J. Hughes, V.G. The Rt. Rev. Mgr. Canon M. O'Sullivan sent me helpful information from Middlesbrough, and the Very Rev. Canon R. F. Thornhill greatly assisted me at Nottingham. At Wrexham I was helped by the Bishop's Secretary (Rev. M. Kelly) and Rev. H. Browne.

I am grateful, for research assistance or hospitality, or both, to the Abbots, members of their communities and lay library staffs at Ampleforth, Belmont, Douai (Woolhampton), Downside, Ealing, Worth, and Mount St. Bernard. I have had particular help from Rev. Dom

Hugh Aveling, O.S.B. and Rev. Dom Edward Corbould, O.S.B. at Ampleforth, from Rev. Br. Michael Oakley, O.S.B. at Belmont, from Rev. Dom Gregory Freeman, O.S.B. at Douai, from Rev. Dom Philip Jebb, O.S.B. at Downside, from the Abbot (Rt. Rev. Dom Rupert Hall, O.S.B.) at Ealing, and from the Abbot (Rt. Rev. Dom Victor Farwell, O.S.B.) and Rev. Br. Stephen Ortiger, O.S.B. at Worth. Rev. Dom Patrick Nuttgens helped me greatly at Mount St. Bernard. The Prior of Parkminster (Very Rev. Bonaventure Cretton O. Cart.) sent me valuable information on his monastery. Rev. Mark Brockle-hurst, O.P. and Rev. Bede Bailey, O.P. assisted me at Woodchester, and the Prior (Very Rev. Stanislaus Parker, O.P.) at Hawkesyard. Very Rev. Francis Etherington C.O. and Rev. the Hon. R. Addington, C.O. provided me with useful information and research facilities at the Birmingham and London Oratories, and the Very Rev. Anselm Cross C.R.P. helped me at Miles Platting.

Information on their convents has also been provided by the Abbesses, Prioresses, and members of their communities at Stanbrook, Colwich, and Teignmouth (Benedictine), Carisbrooke (Dominican) and Abbot-skerswell, Newton Abbot (Canonesses Regular of the Lateran). Sister Mary Alberic, of the Cistercian Abbey at Stapehill, Wimborne, has also helped me over Lulworth and Poole.

For details on seminaries and colleges I have to thank the Rt. Rev. Mgr. R. J. Foster, Rev. D. O'Shea, and Rev. C. Crawford (now in Northampton diocese) at Oscott, the Rt. Rev. Mgr. Paul Grant and Rev. David Milburn at Ushaw, and Rt. Rev. Mgr. M. Kelleher and Rev. J. Molloy, Ph.D., at St. Edmund's, Old Hall Green. At Cotton College I was greatly helped by Mr. Michael Hodgetts and Mr. F. G. Roberts, and Rev. H. Chadwick, S. J. sent me valuable particulars on Stonyhurst.

Among Diocesan Archivists I have to thank Rev. J. D. McEvilly of Birmingham, Rev. B. Eager of Liverpool, Very Rev. G. D. Sweeney of Nottingham, and Mr. P. J. Mowan of Plymouth. I have also to acknowledge kind help received from staff members of the County Record Offices at Chelmsford and Preston, and from Miss Margaret Holmes, M.A. of the County Record Office at Dorchester. Mr. N. Drinkwater, F.S.A., A.R.I.B.A., of the Royal Commission on Historical Monuments, gave me extra information on Lulworth, and Miss Dorothy Stroud of the Soane Museum, London, showed me the material there on Chillington.

Several architects have also been most helpful both with information and over material for illustrations. At Liverpool I have to thank Mr. A. G. Bullen, F.R.I.B.A., and members of the staff of Messrs. Weightman and Bullen, and Mr. Julian Velarde and others working in the F. X. Velarde Partnership. Mr. Anthony Rossi, A.R.I.B.A., has helped me over certain East Anglian matters, and I also owe a debt of gratitude to Mr. Gerard Goalen, F.R.I.B.A., of Harlow, Essex. I have also had help from Mr. D. R. Burles, A.R.I.B.A., and Mr. A. J. Newton, A.R.I.B.A., of Southend on Sea, from Mr. Peter Ware, A.R.I.B.A., of Bristol and Mr. Martin Fisher of Bath, and in London from Mr. F. G. Broadbent, F.R.I.B.A., and Mr. S. C. Kerr Bate, L.R.I.B.A.

Among the parish priests who have helped me by correspondence, or by information personally conveyed I have to thank the following: Very Rev. G. Catterall, D.D. (Bury), Very Rev. Canon B. C. George (Hathersage), Very Rev. Canon R. F. Meagher, D.D., Ph.D. (Ashton in Makerfield), Rev. Canon R. E. Scantlebury (Brockenhurst), Rev. Dom Dominic Allen, O.S.B. (Canton, Cardiff,) Rev. J. D. Crichton (Pershore), Rev. T. B. Croghan (Chorley), Rev. J. Dowd (Hassop), Rev. E. Dunn (East Greenwich), Rev. Dom Edmund Fitzsimons, O.S.B. (Leyland), Rev. J. Campbell, D.D., Ph.D. (Wigan), Rev. J. Gore (Wigan), Rev. T. Gore (Carlisle), Rev. E. McVicar, S.M. (Underwood Rd., London, E.1.), Rev. T. Marsh, Ph.D. (Hindley), Rev. G. Peulevé (Chipping Norton), Rev. F. Purcell, O.M.I. (Amlwch) Rev. Dom Martin Rochford, O.S.B. (Liverpool), Rev. H. Stapleton (Anglican, Everingham).

Among my other informants I wish to thank Sister Mary Catherine of the Ursuline Convent, Brentwood, Miss G. M. A. Beck of Guildford, Miss M. B. Carolan of Hampstead, Lady Crathorne of Crathorne, Lady Lawson of Brough, nr. Catterick, Miss Katherine Longley of Holme-on-Spalding Moor, Miss Pauline Roberts of Liverpool, and Miss E. M. Unsworth of Grantham. Capt. R. Berkeley kindly showed me the chapel at Spetchley, and Mr. and Mrs. Brian Whitlock-Blundell offered me the kindest of hospitality, and facilities for obtaining various information, at Little Crosby. I am also grateful, in varying ways, to Mr. W. Feeney of St. Helens, Lancs., to Lt. Col. Joseph Weld and Mrs. Berkeley at Lulworth, and to Mr. J. A. Williams, lately of Bath and now of Hull.

B.D.G.L.

ILLUSTRATIONS

SOURCES OF ILLUSTRATIONS

Many people have given invaluable help in the provision of
illustrations for this book, and to all of them I would express my
thanks. A number of the photographs had to be specially taken, and
many more, particularly among those supplied by the National Monuments Record, have only lately been taken and have never previously
been reproduced.

The complete list of sources is as follows:

The President, St. Mary's College, Oscott (1b, 13); Reverend
Mother Prioress, St. Augustine's, Newton Abbot (21); the President,
St. Cuthbert's College, Ushaw (24); the Prior, St. Hugh's Charter-
house, Parkminster, Sussex (25a); the Superior, Birmingham Oratory
(29b); the Rt. Rev. the Abbot of Downside (32a); the Rt. Rev. the
Abbot of Quarr (34a and b); the Rt. Rev. the Abbot of Douai (47a).

The Rector, St. James's, Spanish Place, London (23c); the Parish
Priests of Holy Rood, Watford (27b–photo by Leslie J. King, Watford),

St. Mary's, Canton, Cardiff (31a–photo by Robson, Cardiff), St. Joseph's, Penarth (31b), Our Lady of Lourdes, Ashby de la Zouch (31c–photo by Clive Jones).

Mr. Peter Fleetwood Hesketh (17a).

Mr. Hugh Bankart, Box (16b); Sir Giles Scott, Son, and Partners, London (35d, 36b); Stienlet, Son, and Partners, Newcastle on Tyne (36a); F. X. Velarde Partnership, Liverpool (37, 38); F. G. Broadbent, Son and Partners, London (now Twickenham) (39a, 42b, 47a); Burles, Newton and Partners, London and Southend-on-Sea (39b, 43); Weightman and Bullen, Liverpool (40, 41, 42a); F. R. Bates, Son, and Price, Newport (Mon.) and Cardiff (44, 46a); Gerard Goalen, F.R.I.B.A., Harlow, Essex (45a); Sir Percy Thomas and Son, Cardiff, Bristol and Shrewsbury (46b); Taylor Woodrow Construction Limited, London (48).

National Monuments Record (1a, 5, 6, 7, 8, 9, 10, 11, 12, 14, 17b, 19, 20, 25b, 26, 30b); British Museum (4a); Royal Institute of British Architects (35c); British Broadcasting Corporation (45b).

Mackenzie and Dent's *History of Newcastle* (4b); *The Builder* (now *Building*) (18, 22, 23a, 23b, 27a); *Building News* (23d).

Derwent Studios, Pocklington, Yorkshire (2a); Marcus (H. J. Marks), Weymouth (3a); Edwin C. Peckham, Stroud (15a); Marshall and Company, Nottingham (15b); W. Pegg, Leicester (16a); A. F. Kersting, London (28, 29a, 30a, 33); Harvey Barton, Bristol (32b); Britannia Colour Limited, Birmingham (34c); Radio Times Hulton Picture Library (35a); John R. Freeman (Photographers) Limited, London 35b); Ness Studios, Liverpool (47c).

BIBLIOGRAPHICAL NOTE

As no comprehensive book on the history and architecture of English and Welsh Catholic churches has yet appeared, one's booklist is inevitably short. Many works on individual churches, e.g. Norwich, Downside, etc., find their place, as may be appropriate, in my reference notes. There are, in addition, passages on churchbuilding in some general books on post-penal Catholicism, e.g. the volumes by Rev. (later Bishop) Bernard Ward on English Catholic history between 1780 and 1850, in Archbishop David Mathew's *Catholicism in England, 1535–1935*, 1935, and in *The English Catholics, 1850–1950*, ed. Bishop (now Archbishop) Beck, 1950. Valuable historical material, but comparatively little architectural comment, occurs in B. W. Kelly, *Historical Notes on English Catholic Missions*, 1907. Books on particular areas, e.g. Rev. George Oliver, *Collections Illustrating the History of the Catholic Religion in Cornwall, Devon, etc*, 1857, C. A. Bolton, *Salford Diocese and its Catholic Past*, 1950, and T. A. Burke, *Catholic History of Liverpool*, 1910 are also useful for their own districts, as also are the short diocesan histories produced by most dioceses for the Hierarchy Centenary of 1950.

Useful details can also be found in such early publications as the *Ordo*, the *Laity Directory*, the *Catholic Miscellany* (1822–28) and its successor the *Catholic Miscellany and Monthly Repository*, the *Orthodox Journal* and *Weekly Orthodox Journal*, and from such later periodicals as *The Tablet*, *The Rambler*, *The Dublin Review*, *The Catholic Herald*, and *The Universe* (especially, in the last named, from the articles and sketches of Mr. Peter Anson).

Works of more specially architectural interest include the volumes of such professional publications as *The Builder*, *Building News*, the *Architect and Building News*, and *The Architectural Review*. For the years since 1953 the Northern and Southern editions of the *Catholic Building Review* are an indispensable source.

B

The architects of some Catholic churches are mentioned by Rev. Basil Clarke in his *Churchbuilders of the Nineteenth Century*, 1938, and Mr. Peter Anson has covered much ground in *Churches, their Plan and Furnishing*, 1948, and *Fashions in Church Furnishing*, 1959.

Published works have so far come out on very few Catholic architects. But see Michael Trappes-Lomax, *Pugin*, 1933, and Denis Gwynn, *Lord Shrewsbury, Pugin, and the Catholic Revival*, 1946.

Chapter I

THE PENAL BACKGROUND

On the night of November 26th, in the year 1689, the Protestant rabble of Birmingham lit bonfires and shot off muskets to mark an anniversary. The occasion which called for this zealous usage of powder and combustibles was not some national victory on land or at sea. It was the utter destruction, just a year before and in the heady weeks of the Glorious Revolution, of the Catholic church and house of Franciscans lately built in this decidedly un-Anglican industrial town. This venture had been made, while James II still reigned, by Fr. Leo Randolph, well known in the English Province of the Franciscans as Brother Leo of St. Mary Magdalene.[1]

The year of this Midland bonfire had been that when William III and Mary II established their position as Britain's joint rulers. It had seen the passing of the Toleration Act which made it legally possible for Protestant Nonconformists (except those professing Unitarian beliefs) to build and frequent places of public worship. Catholics, however, were cut off from the benefits of the new law. The celebrations in Birmingham threw lurid light on the differences, in this matter of the non-Anglican contribution to this country's religious architecture, between the majority and the minority of those who refused to conform to the Established Church.

It was clear, well before 1701 when James II died and when the Act of Settlement barred his Catholic son, the "Old Pretender", from the Crown, that one of the assumptions underlying the Church of England's position was a statistical farce. When Henry VIII "reordered" England's religious affairs, and when the Anglican settlement was consolidated under Elizabeth I, the theory had been that the country was uniform in its religious practice, and that the laity of the Established Church and the whole unordained population were one and the same. Under Henry VIII the system had corresponded well enough to reality. For the king was more successful than either of his daughters in ensuring his Supremacy both in secular and church affairs; the axes of Tower Hill were more effective than the fires of Smithfield or the gallows of Tyburn in discouraging those whose consciences forbade them to conform.

Yet during the rest of the sixteenth century, and still more in the Puritan period of religious and intellectual ferment, many Englishmen organised themselves into religious bodies quite distinct, in their doctrines and modes of worship, from the Anglican *Via Media*. By 1700 some of the smaller sects of the Civil War era had disappeared or dwindled to insignificance. But others, most notably the Independents, the Quakers, and the Baptists, were entrenched as large, respected religious bodies, with firm traditions and now with their legalised Chapels or Meeting Houses. The country was overwhelmingly Protestant, and staunchly anti-Papal in its emotions. James II, like Queen Christina of Sweden, had found that it did not answer, in those days of strongly held religious views, for a sovereign to profess a faith which was not that of nearly all his subjects. Yet the fact remained that some Englishmen (and in some areas a substantial minority) still held to the religion of the King over the Water. How was it, when the fierce controversies of the Reformation were receding in time, and when toleration and religious indifference were increasingly in the air, that Englishmen of the Roman obedience were at least on paper denied what was now openly given to the Jews and to nearly all their non-Anglican compatriots?

The answer lay largely in dynastic politics. William III, himself of no strong religious convictions, was not personally against the public exercise of their religion by his English Catholic subjects; in his other realm, the United Provinces, the large Catholic minority enjoyed much freedom of worship. But such was the English political climate that nearly a century passed before Parliament formally allowed the building of Catholic churches. The long delay is easy to understand. Popular sentiment was most of it anti-Catholic. The Catholic religion was thought (and not without reason) to be deeply bound up with Jacobitism, and with the continuing efforts of the Stuarts to upset the Whig settlement and the peaceful Hanoverian Succession. Should the Catholic claim to freedom of worship, and freedom for priests, be legally recognised new strength and assurance would surely come to what was, from the Hanoverian standpoint, a leading subversive force. Only when a Stuart restoration was no longer a danger was it politically possible for public Mass to be heard by a diminished Catholic remnant. For most of the eighteenth century the English and Welsh Catholics (along with their fellows in Ireland and Scotland) had to rest content with the fact that they no longer faced the gallows for their faith. They also enjoyed more safety for their private worship, and in some places for the virtually public performance of their rites.

Yet the post-Reformation Catholic architecture of England had not started with its timid, technically illegal Georgian attempts; earlier on there had been something more to show than the rooms in houses in which most Catholic services had to be held. For in the Stuart era three Catholic Queens, and a Catholic King, had caused a few interesting ventures. Some of their buildings set patterns which later reappeared, and were in their own right of architectural and decorative note.

The Stuart sequence of Catholic royal marriages was preceded, in 1623, by the future Charles I's courtship of a Spanish Infanta. So certain was James I that he would welcome a Catholic Princess of Wales that practical provision was made for her to hear her Mass. So in May, while Charles still besieged the Princess in Madrid, the Spanish Ambassador laid the foundation stone of what is now the Chapel of Marlborough House.[2] It then formed part of the complex of St. James's Palace, but was not in tune with its late Gothic surroundings. Though an ornate Baroque façade was held politically unwise, and though tact required that its exterior should be restrained and "unchurchlike", its classical idiom marked it as a building of architectural significance. It was, indeed England's first place of worship with no medieval traces, built in a wholly classical style. Inigo Jones designed this novel chapel, with its Renaissance and Palladian detail, and a splendidly coffered ceiling. Through nothing came of the Spanish match, the chapel was soon finished for Henrietta Maria, the French Catholic princess whose marriage made her the Queen Consort of Charles I. An old print shows that originally it had large statues of saints in arched niches along its side walls. Below its "Venetian" East window an elaborate composition backed the High Altar. The chapel's status was royal and private, but here, as in other royal chapels of the Stuart age, the more socially select of London's Catholics could hear Mass as freely as they did in the chapels kept by the Ambassadors of some Catholic powers.

Queen Henrietta Maria was not content with a single chapel in London. In her residence at Somerset House Inigo Jones designed her one of great splendour. It was built in the 1630s. Like many other English Catholic chapels of the next two centuries this building was unremarkable from outside. But it was over a hundred feet long, with two small transepts for the private altars of the Queen's chaplains. The nave was of the favoured Palladian shape of a double cube, while on the West wall a gallery gave secluded accommodation to the Queen and her retinue. The interior displayed a richly coffered ceiling, pedimented or round-headed niches, and an assortment of detail from the Italian Renaissance—from Vignola, Domenico Fontana, and Palladio.[3] A drawing also shows how splendid were the fluted Doric columns, the herms, and the Baroque cresting of Inigo Jones's screen.[4] Here again a Catholic chapel was free and public to those who frequented the Court, and we hear how the King himself, despite the sincerity of his Anglicanism, came to see it a few days after its opening.[5]

The Civil War and the Commonwealth interrupted these activities and caused the sacking of the chapels themselves. Under King Charles II his consort Queen Catherine of Braganza at first heard Mass in the chapel at St. James's, and a small convent was built for her retinue of Portuguese Franciscans.[6] She later moved to the refitted chapel at Somerset House. James II's short reign saw an ambitious display of Baroque art as applied to the apparatus of Counter-Reformation Catholic worship. The private chapel at Windsor Castle had already been transformed, by Grinling Gibbons as the sculptor and by Antonio Verrio the South Italian painter of walls and ceilings, into a brilliantly ornate interior whose whole ceiling was a whirling, tempestuous fresco of the Ascension.[7] Then in 1685 and 1686 Gibbons, Verrio, and the youngest Arnold Quellinus of Antwerp worked together to make a splendid interior in a royal chapel which James II built in the Palace at Whitehall. Wren designed its unassuming fabric in brick and stone. He too planned the splendid, towering altarpiece whose statues and reliefs were by Gibbons and Quellinus. Verrio painted the ceiling of the Assumption, with its "world of figures" which astonished John Evelyn the diarist when he went to hear the Italian singers, finding himself puzzled and somewhat horrified at the "divers cringes" and other ritual of a pontifical High Mass.[8] Once James II had fled to France in 1688 the chapel was dismantled, and its fabric perished when the Palace was burnt in 1698. But most of the altarpiece was stored at Hampton Court, and then under Queen Anne it was set up again to adorn the sanctuary of Westminster Abbey. Here, however, it did not outlast a Regency Gothic refurnishing. A Dean of Westminster, who was also Bishop of Rochester and vicar of the Westminster living of Burnham on Sea in Somerset, took two splendid angel figures, and some charming reliefs of cherubs acting as acolytes at the Offertory of the Mass, to beautify his West Country church, where they can still be admired.

But royal chapels were not the only buildings in which, during the later part of James II's reign, the public worship of the Catholic minority gained a brief new lease of life. In several places the Romanist congregations got their chance to worship more openly and splendidly than they had done for over a century. At York, the Institute of the Blessed Virgin Mary established the Bar Convent in a private house in 1686; its career on that site has been uninterrupted to this day. This was also the period when, in 1688, the country was divided into the four vicariates apostolic whose bishops (holding titular sees *in partibus infidelium*) laid the foundations of what is still the ecclesiastical organisation of Catholic England.

For obvious reasons the Catholics of England and Wales had long been unable to make any show in their country's religious architecture. Their priests, whether secular clergy or members of the religious orders and congregations, came to England from their time of training abroad, and could only say their secret Masses in the seclusion of trusted adherents' homes. Under James I and Charles I there had been times when the nominally illegal worship of the Roman obedience was virtually undisturbed. Yet it had to remain in the houses of the more prominent Catholics. Though we sometimes hear of fairly elaborate candlesticks and other "church stuff" there was, as a rule, no question of permanently fitted chapels.[9] Ordinary tables were put out in ordinary rooms. They were furnished for the occasion with portable altar stones and the bare essentials for the quiet saying of Low Mass. They were then dismantled so that no visitors could tell the use to which the relevant garret or living room had been put. Chalices were often of pewter, like ordinary cups or so contrived that they could be unscrewed into sections for easier hiding. The chapel at Abergavenny, said by "Popish Plot" informers in 1679 to have been distinguished outside by the monogram of the Jesuits who then served that flourishing mission, and to be fitted with "all the formalities and ornaments belonging to a chapel" was rare in its time. This chapel, in a long attic whose house was later split into four dwellings, was rediscovered in 1907. Its ceiling had remains of a painting which showed the Adoration of the Magi, while the Jesuit monogram (IHS with a cross above its central letter) survived above a window.[10] Yet even here there was no separate building, like Nonconformist Meeting Houses, for public Catholic worship.

The grim terrors of Titus Oates, and of the mob frenzy aroused by what people believed about a Popish Plot, were soon followed by three years of respite. For under James II, and in particular after his politically tactless first Declaration of Indulgence in 1687, the Protestant and Catholic Non-Conformers could alike avail themselves of a freedom of worship which both parties had been denied in the last few years of Charles II. Though the Penal Laws and the Conventicle Acts remained on the Statute Book it was clearly understood that they would not be enforced, and that Quaker Meetings and Masses could alike be held in public and unpunished. The Catholics thus felt that now at last they could emerge from their private chapels, and worship in buildings put up for no other purpose than that of permanently furnished "Mass Houses".

Several public chapels were therefore built in the second half of James II's short reign. Two at least were in London, and the one near the bottom of the present-day Kingsway had an adjacent house of Franciscan Friars. In a staunchly Catholic district of Lancashire, a new church was built by the Jesuits at Wigan. At Newcastle a "sufficiently spacious chapel" existed in the back buildings of the White Hart Inn; in January, 1688, the Mayor and Corporation went there to a Mass of thanksgiving for the Queen's pregnancy.[11] We know nothing of the style or appearance of these buildings. But for Birmingham we are more happily placed. For Fr. Leo Randolph was careful to leave a full account of the church whose foundation stone he had laid in March, 1687. He also gives useful details on the financing of this Midland Catholic venture.[12] The king, closely following the frequent generosity to the friars of his medieval forbears, gave 180 tons of timber from Needwood Forest in Staffordshire. This was sold for £180. The Dowager Queen Catherine gave £10 15s. od., while Sir John Gage gave timber worth £190. A Mrs. Ann Gregg gave £250, the largest monetary sum, and among many smaller contributions some came from Protestant friends, and some from four members of the Penderel family who had helped to save Charles II's life in the early stage of his flight from Worcester.

No less interesting are Fr. Leo's particulars of the church itself; one could almost rebuild it from his precise account. Such was, indeed, his purpose. For after the mob had destroyed his church in 1688, he optimistically left his account so that it could be recreated "when Catholick times are settled, which I doubt not will bee ere long".

Like Henrietta Maria's chapel at Somerset House, this Birmingham building was cruciform. It had two small transepts which provided side chapels 15 feet square. Its total interior length was 95 feet, the nave being 80 feet by 33, and the sanctuary 23 feet across and 15 deep. The nave had no pillars, giving all the worshippers a clear view of the High Altar; the basic interior plan was that of the much later, still existing, Bristol church of St. Mary on the Quay. The principal altarpiece, flanked on each side by two Corinthian pillars or half-columns, showed the risen Christ appearing to Fr. Leo's patron St. Mary Magdalene. The two side altars, with their paintings of the Virgin and St. Francis, were backed by simpler compositions with two Corinthian columns apiece. All the altars had "other carved works answerable". The pictures, one imagines, were in the Baroque tradition, and they certainly contained imagery uncongenial to Anglican taste. Yet the general style of the chapel and of its altarpiece must have been as soberly English as were the provincial Catholics of England. High Baroque, with all the elaboration that Continental artists like Verrio or Quellinus could produce, was left to the Court chapels. Here in Birmingham, and probably in the other out of town Catholic centres, these buildings put up between 1686 and 1688 were closer in spirit to Wren than to the Fontanas or Borromini. They set a pattern for later, politically safer ventures.

One other building does seem, from its own stylistic evidence, to date in part from the short Catholic respite under James II. At Hathersage, in the lovely hill country of North Derbyshire, a large Catholic community existed throughout penal times. The Norfolks, and the Eyres of Hassop, were neighbouring families of influence. Yet in Hathersage itself no important mansion existed to house a private chapel for the local Catholics. For a time they frequented the ruins of a much older chapel at North Lees not far away. But with the coming of what they hoped to be a durable freedom of worship some more lasting and convenient Mass House would obviously be preferable. It is said, and seems likely from the visual evidence, that the rectangular nave which now forms most of the Catholic church in the village centre of Hathersage is a chapel first built under James II. In the tumults of November, 1688 it was unroofed and sacked. But the solidity of these stone-built walls could easily have defied total demolition. In 1806 it was restored with money left by Mr. Thomas Eyre of Hassop;[13] with a poor Victorian Gothic sanctuary it has been a church ever since. The heavy rustication of its quoins suggests a period much older than 1806, while the bold edging of its elliptically-headed side windows, the style of its round West window, the bolection moulding round its doorway, and the heavily bracketed cornice above that doorway all point to a date soon after 1685.

Once William and Mary were secure in their rule the chances for new Catholic building all but vanished for another hundred years. Yet it is from about this time, and from the Birmingham Franciscan Fr. Leo Randolph, that we have one of the best penal Catholic architectural documents. We have seen how he closely recorded the details of his demolished church. He soon went further. For his manuscript at Oscott gives full ground plans and specifications not only for a new church, but also for a well thought-out, quadrangular Friary. The plans were optimistically made for use "when it shall please God to convert the hearts of this Nation and grant such times that decayed and destroyed Churches, Monasterys, and Convents shall be repaired and rebuilt". Fr. Leo must have made the designs himself; he is not the last priest-architect of whom I shall speak in this book.[14]

Fr. Randolph's church and friary were to have been of brick, with water tables, quoins, and window dressings of stone. The public part of the church was planned on very similar lines to that destroyed in 1688. The nave, with its shallow transeptal chapels, was to have had a main altarpiece exactly as before. The sanctuary was to have been less wide than the nave, while the church was to have been paved with brick tiles as these were warmer to kneel on. An oval window was planned above the West doorway, and each gable of the church was to have a cross. Where the new church would have differed from the first one was in its careful provision for a properly planned Friary choir. Behind the High Altar a narrow retrochoir was to have supported a steeple, in the manner of medieval English friaries like the Franciscan one at King's Lynn. East of that, a compartment 30 feet long and 24 across would have housed the stalls. The whole length of the church is given as 134 feet. A neat stylistic point comes in the drawing of the windows in the church's side and eastern walls. For they were to have been round-headed, with a transom high up and two vertical mullions; the pattern is that of Wren's windows in Trinity College Library at Cambridge. The Friary buildings were to have been most compactly laid out, in three storeys with semicircular arches round a central cloister. Sixty feet were allowed for the refectory, a large Chapter House was to be on the western side, the Parlour is designated as the "Speak House", and separate buildings were to contain the Infirmary and the Brew House.

But nothing so ambitious was politically possible for many years. As the eighteenth century wore on the Catholic body, no longer exposed to death on the gallows, instead experienced political complications, social pressures, and a numerical decline rarely relieved by conversions or newly founded missions.* Yet from the building point of view the picture was less gloomy than one might suppose from the written law.

As the eighteenth century progressed it was seen that a Catholic minority could safely be allowed to worship in a mainly Protestant State. Mob violence, of the type that occurred at Preston in 1768, was more dangerous to Catholics than the closure of Mass Houses by zealous magistrates. There were, moreover, some places ruled by Britain where facilities for Catholic worship could not be denied. When Gibraltar fell the terms of surrender laid it down that Catholicism should keep its freedom. After nearly all the local Spaniards had decamped the newcomers brought in by Queen Anne's Government were mostly Catholics from Malta, Genoa, and elsewhere. In 1713 the Treaty of Utrecht provided that the people of Gibraltar were to have *el uso de la religión Catolica;* a similar clause applied to Minorca. At least one Gibraltar church was continuously in Catholic use, and by about 1750 over half the Gibraltar civilians were listed as "Roman Catholics".[15] George I, as ruler of Hanover, allowed a public church for the racially mixed Catholic community of his German capital; for him it was as probable Jacobites, not as Romanists, that Catholics were vexatious. Soon before England's Catholics saw the beginnings of Parliamentary relief the Quebec Act of 1774 declared that George III's

---

* Dodding Green near Kendal, and Shortwood and Shepton Mallet in Somerset were exceptions to this rule of stifled development.

French Canadian subjects who professed "the Religion of the Church of Rome" could freely do so provided they accepted the King's temporal supremacy.

The '15 and the '45 meant a setback for the English Catholics. Each rising meant some riotous damage to their simple chapels. We see vividly what happened, in the winter of 1715–16, at Fernyhalgh near Preston. After the town itself had surrendered some of George I's soldiers came out. Though they spared the fabric of "the chapel-house" they plundered its furniture and "church stuff". Worse still were the discomforts and dangers endured by Christopher Tuttell the priest. While the troops were out at Fernyhalgh he lay nine hours in a "haymow in a noisome barn" where the cold, the noise of owls, and the "bustling and squeaking of mice" disturbed his rest. For five months the chapel stood empty, and "playing at Boh-Peep was all that winter's pastime".[16]

But in 1766 an event eased the way to greater toleration. The Old Pretender (James III to Jacobites) died that year. Bonnie Prince Charlie was no longer edifying or promising as a Stuart claimant. As his brother Henry had followed an ecclesiastical career the main line of the Stuarts was no longer dynastically credible. George III, a moral and religious sovereign, and the first Hanoverian king to live a respectable private life, was a more suitable object of his Catholic subjects' loyalty. The Pope gave him *de facto* recognition, and ordered the Church to pay no royal honours to "Charles III". At the highest religious level, the divorce between Popery and Jacobitism was complete. So far as the Government and the magistrates were concerned the churchgoing restrictions of the Penal laws were but lightly enforced, and for upper class Catholics exclusion from politics was a worse hardship than in-ability to hear Mass. If one looked carefully at the England of 1766 it was reasonably clear that Catholic architecture had modestly started its rebirth.

A Guide to Bath of 1753 makes open mention of the Catholic chapel which had long existed in a room at Bell Tree House.[17] This house was the residence of the Benedictines who served the chapel, and was used for lodging by some of the numerous Catholic gentry and nobility who came to take the Bath waters.* Then in July of 1766

* Bath Abbey has several Catholic mural monuments among the hundreds which line its walls. The letters R.I.P. are apt to appear below their inscriptions, and they are the only Georgian ones whose iconography includes a cross.

a London newspaper listed the public Catholic chapels in London and elsewhere; it also gave figures of the priests supposed to be serving them.[18] The chapels of the Sardinian, Neapolitan, French, Bavarian, Spanish, and Portuguese embassies are naturally mentioned, along with one in Virginia Street off Ratcliff Highway which was maintained by the Portuguese and served the Catholic seamen and poor immigrants of the East end. The convent chapel at Hammersmith, said to have been "continued by Charles II's Queen", is among the "Country Chapels". So too are those at Bath, Worcester, Preston, Lancaster, York, and elsewhere. The London journalist goes on to say that several existed in Wales, Monmouthshire, and various English counties, but makes the valid point that in Lancashire there were "as many as in all England put together". From now onwards, and for many decades, the story of England's Catholic worshipping places is largely that of Lancashire and the Rest.

The Catholic chapels timidly built in Georgian England, or fitted out within mansions or smaller private houses, were the settings for a crabbed, restricted version of the liturgy of the Counter Reformation. The buildings were rectangular, without screens between the sanctuaries and the congregations. Except in the London Embassy chapels, with their numerous foreign and English priests, and their elaborate music under such directors as Dr. Arne and the Novellos, the services were usually quiet and simple. Though altars in the more important mansion chapels would have sets of six candlesticks, Low Masses with instruction were the general rule. Altar plate was more apt than before to be made in England. During much of the eighteenth century the Austrian or South German immigrant family of the Kandlers made much plate for these late Recusant chapels. It was, moreover, much safer now to employ English goldsmiths and for the resulting plate to be fully hallmarked, as few pieces had been in the seventeenth century. Benjamin Pyne was a silversmith in particular demand.[19]

Despite the bringing over of some Continental adornments these Catholic chapels of Georgian England were as native in character as were the squires who largely sustained them. One wonders what might have happened had penal times ended a century earlier, and had the English Catholics been free to employ a London architect of the first eminence who was actually their cautious and secret co-religionist. James Gibbs had been brought up as a Scottish Catholic, and learnt his architecture in Rome under the Pope's head architect Carlo Fontana.[20]

But back in England he eventually kept his religion and his Jacobitism so quiet that he gained a wide patronage and was actually assumed to have turned Protestant. Had Gibbs been able to build Catholic churches between 1710 and 1750 they might have recalled the Rome of Bernini and Fontana, or they might have given London a foretaste of Brompton Oratory. Yet I think it likely that only in their altarpieces, and in the subjects of their plasterwork by Gibb's Italian *stuccatori* Artari and Bagutti, would they have displayed some repetition of what James II had ventured in Whitehall. Their exteriors, one suspects, would have been closer to Wren or St. Martin's in the Fields than to Baroque Rome.

We know little of the fabrics of the London Embassy chapels as they were before the Gordon Riots of 1780. Some, like those of Naples and France, moved about as the Ambassadors themselves changed their addresses. The Portuguese Chapel in Mayfair was upstairs over the stables. The chapel attached to the Embassy of the rising kingdom of Sardinia and Piedmont seems likely to have been the most imposing among them.[21]

Outside London the few Catholic chapels which could be classed as separate structures were mostly the close adjuncts of privately owned houses. Where in some strongly Catholic areas, as at Thropton in Northumberland and in several Lancashire villages, they were more isolated buildings they were discreet and simple, of an unassuming, vernacular charm. In the towns they often lay up alleyways or were concealed behind a frontage of houses.

A Georgian map of Worcester shows that there the Catholic chapel of 1764 had a house between itself and Sansome Walk. An old print of Liverpool shows that the first chapel in that town was simple, rectangular, and with round-headed side windows. Anti-Jacobite rioters destroyed it in 1746, and Liverpool's numerous Catholics then worshipped in a garret, with the house's stairs and lower storeys also crammed with the congregation. A little later they used the top storey of a secluded building erected (and described) as a warehouse. Its lower floor contained lumber, and the outside of the chapel storey had folding doors to lend it a commercial appearance; these were, however, bricked up inside.[22] At Lancaster Mass in houses gave way, in 1767, to a special chapel which lasted some thirty years.[23] In York the nuns of the Bar Convent completed a new chapel, by the local builder Thomas Atkinson, in 1769.[24] But in towns like Wolverhampton and Sheffield, where special conditions caused large Catholic congregations, no move was yet made to erect special and separate buildings. Yet in many towns a fair degree of freedom did exist for Catholic worship. Defoe could say, of Durham as he saw it about 1710, that the city was "full of Roman Catholicks, who live peaceably and disturb nobody, and nobody them, for we . . . saw them going as publickly to their Mass as the Dissenters . . . to their meeting-house".[25]

In the country, in Yorkshire for example where small Catholic groups were numerous and widely spread in penal times, most chapels were still in ordinary rooms of large farmhouses and mansions. Here and there they resembled specially built churches, yet even so they were often said to be stables or other out-buildings. At Llanarth in Monmouthshire the charming *sacellum* of 1750 was said, implausibly in view of its small area of glass, to be a conservatory. It is in the Georgian Nonconformist manner, with round-headed windows, boldly rusticated quoins, low benches and "Gothick" altar rails, and an apse added about 1930 by its Dominican users.[26] In the East Riding of Yorkshire, at Holme on Spalding Moor, the Catholic congregation grouped round the mansion of the Langdales long used a garret high up in the house, "a dark low room greatly inconvenient—both to Ye family and People". When in 1766 Mr. Marmaduke Langdale built the present chapel, nearly fifty feet long and far more convenient both to his family and those from outside who came to "prayers" (as Mass was then cautiously called) the new building had the outward appearance of a stable. But its interior was permanently fitted as a chapel, and it has been suggested that the designer may have been the well-known John Carr of York. The altarpiece, with its paired Corinthian pillars and its round-arched picture recess rising up between garlands to an open pediment, is of no mean splendour and on its smaller scale recalls the larger altarpiece set up by Bentley in Trinity College chapel at Cambridge.*[27]

The more splendid chapels of late penal times were those permanently furnished in the more important Catholic mansions. At East Hendred in Berkshire George Eyston, in 1687, fitted out the projecting medieval chapel in some style. Though in the next year some desecration was caused by "some loose fellows" who straggled from Dutch William's invading army there was no demolition of the Birmingham type and

* It was damaged, and its picture and some other decorations were lost, in an accidental fire in the 1940s.

the damage was soon made good.[28] At Cowdray the apsed late medieval chapel of the Montagues was made splendid, about the same time, by a Baroque altarpiece whose towering dignity and swan's neck pediment would not have disgraced some refurnished Gothic church in Bruges or Antwerp. It survived the conversion of its owners to Anglicanism, and was there for J. H. Grimm to draw not long before the fire of 1793. At Hazlewood in Yorkshire an excellent altarpiece, in the Wren manner of about the 1680s, survives in the Vavasours' old chapel of 1296 whose religious use has only lately ceased.

The house chapel in the Weld family's Jacobean Gothic castle at Lulworth had been threatened in 1688, and again in 1690, by the rabble in Wareham.[29] For a time it was wise for this important Catholic family to lie low. But when in 1774 Edward Weld became the first husband of the lovely young Mary Anne Smythe of Acton Burnell, who later became famous as Mrs. Fitzherbert, the opportunity was at hand for the Georgian redecoration of the mansion's interior. Among the Weld family papers are three alternative designs for the handsome fitting out of the long, four-windowed room which now served as a splendid domestic chapel.[30] Rococo-Gothic and Adamesque touches abound in these sumptuous, unsigned plans, while a photograph of the castle's dining room as it was before the fire of recent times shows that one, with a rococo hood above a doorway at the original altar end, was actually adopted. Edward died the year after his marriage, but Thomas his brother completed the work. He used the chapel till the fulfilment, a few years later, of much more ambitious ideas.

By now, moreover, the time had come for a fine private chapel whose placing, in relation to the main bulk of its mansion, almost made it a separate building. This was at Thorndon Hall in southern Essex, the main estate of the Petre family and the scene, from 1764, of an ambitious piece of building by the ninth Baron Petre. The young noblemen chose a new, more elevated site for the vast new mansion and its chapel. Since Gibbs had died in 1754 no important English Catholic architect was available for commissions so ambitious as this one in Essex. But James Paine, Lord Petre's actual choice, had already worked for the Duke of Norfolk at Worksop. The new Thorndon Hall was laid out on Palladian lines, with its central block connected to the wings by gracefully curved vestibules. Most of it is now a gutted, mournful shell, and its stupendous Corinthian portico looks out, a masterpiece in silvery stone, away across the Thames tidewater to the distant downs of Kent. But the eastern wing survives as the club house of a Golf Club. There, in a portion of a building as large as many medium-sized country mansions, Lord Petre fitted out the splendid chapel which was opened in 1770.[31]

The one-time chapel at Thorndon is of the height of two storeys; the remainder of the wing, including the storey above the fine curved brackets and the square or rectangular panels of its ceiling, contained servants' quarters and "domestic offices". One side of the chapel has two tiers of domestic-looking windows; the other has four niches once nobly filled by statues of saints. At the altar end four Ionic half-columns left a space for a permanent altarpiece, while above them some Corinthian pilasters, and a shallow arch, completed the altar's fixed backing. Still greater splendour adorns the liturgical West end. For six fluted Ionic half-columns support the floor of a fine gallery; above them two pairs of fluted pilasters, and two pairs of columns of the same order, screen off the private space, with its gracefully curved back wall and its ceiling shaped as an elliptical half dome, from which the noble family could look down on this highly elegant setting for the ceremonies of the Mass. Lord Petre and his family would approach their devotions unseen, strolling easily through the superb Adamesque library in the hall's eastern vestibule.

Henry, the eighth Baron Arundell of Wardour was a Catholic nobleman of prestige and eminence in Wiltshire and all the western counties. His family had gained in wealth from development on their London property round Wardour Street and elsewhere. Lord Arundell had little to fear from the hostile intentions of his neighbours, or from the nominal penalties of the law. In 1774 he commented on his "happiness of living under the British Constitution". By then he had already started to replace the shattered medieval castle at Wardour by a great classical mansion not far away. In this he provided another permanently furnished private chapel of unusual splendour.

The new Wardour Castle, another work for a Catholic by Paine, was designed in 1769. Like many Georgian country mansions it has a central block and flanking wings. One of these wings contains the chapel finished in 1776. From the outside it could be mistaken for a kitchen or stable block. But the interior of Lord Arundell's rectangular chapel was of a sober yet unfurtive magnificence. Corinthian pilasters lined the walls; above them a boldly modillioned cornice led up to a shallow-arched vault with rich plasterwork by an Italian named

C

Quarenghi. The fine marble altar, with its shallow-domed tabernacle upheld by dainty pillarets, came from Rome where its designer was Giacomo Quinenza.[32] Lord Arundell soon enlarged and still further adorned his chapel. But even as it stood in 1776 this gorgeous Catholic interior, set by its protecting mansion in the parkland beauty of rural Wessex, suggested that at least so far as their worship was concerned happier things might not be far distant from the small remnant of England's Catholics.

The 1770s saw the Catholics of England and Wales on the eve of their first small measure of legal relief. The Penal Laws, as they stood on the Statute Book, were not in fact completely enforced; had the full rigour of their provisions against Catholic property and worship been carried out one may reasonably doubt that English Catholicism would have survived except, perhaps, in Lancashire and the larger towns. But in 1788, ten years after the first instalment of legal relief and very shortly before the Act which finally legalised the public celebration of Mass, Bishop Walmsley the Vicar Apostolic of the Western District could admit that no Judge or Jury would fully enforce the measures against Catholicism, that so far as the old Penal Laws were concerned the Catholics of England had little to fear, and that the laws themselves "may be almost considered as not existing".[33] In the 1770s there was no real Government or legal persecution of the English Catholics. Mob violence and social prejudice were the dangers to be feared.

By 1778 the Catholics of England were no more to be reckoned as a dynastic danger. It was now good politics, if only for the recruiting of Scottish Catholic Highlanders to serve against American colonists, to make some first gesture of legal conciliation. For nearly a century they had been ruled, in a somewhat loose but not ineffective way, by the four bishops *in partibus* who served as the Vicars Apostolic of the four Districts of penal Catholic England. The London District covered the capital and the South-Eastern counties. The large Midland District stretched right across from the Welsh border to the East Anglian coast. Staffordshire was its most strongly Catholic county, and the Vicars Apostolic had for some time tended to live near Wolverhampton. The Northern District, with more Catholics in Lancashire than in all the rest of provincial England, stretched north to the Scottish border. The whole of Wales, and all the South-Western counties, made up the large and virtually unmanageable Western District, in Catholic numbers the Cinderella of them all with Charles

Walmsley its Benedictine bishop in residence at Bath. The Catholics of England may now have passed their lowest numerical point, for Irish immigration had started in some of the towns. Statistics, based on returns by the Anglican clergy and reckoned diocese by diocese, were regularly sent to the House of Lords. Those presented in 1781 gave a total of 69,373; of these over 27,000 were in the diocese of Chester which then included Lancashire.[34] For London, Bristol and some other towns such figures seem to be too low, but the Catholics of England are unlikely to have exceeded 100,000 in 1778. Most people reckoned, with some reason, that they were a declining, or at most a static force.

The Catholic Relief Act of 1778[35] freed bishops, priests, and schoolmasters from the risk of arrest and prosecution. The clergy were thus enabled to perform their priestly duties, and the Act gave security to private Catholic Academies like those at Sedgeley Park near Wolverhampton, Tudhoe in Co. Durham, and in Hertfordshire at Old Hall Green near Ware. No less important, for the chapels known to exist, in country mansions and elsewhere in private buildings, were the measures which allowed Catholics to own and inherit (as in large measure they already did) their houses and lands. Provided they, like the French Canadians in Quebec, swore allegiance to George III, and so long as they renounced the idea that the murder or deceit of heretics was lawful, the English and Welsh Catholics could now assume that their private chapels, and the lay education in their own country of their children, were no longer at the legalised mercy of the petty informer. Yet in another two years they were rudely made aware of another danger to their modest show in the field of public worship and church architecture.

Chapter II

EARLY REVIVAL

At ten o'clock on the night of Friday, June 9th, 1780, an agitated resident of Bath sent a letter to a friend in Bristol.[1] As he wrote a mob was gathered, in St. James's Parade, before the new Catholic chapel where the first Mass was due on the coming Sunday. They started its destruction, and whether or not they were urged on by anti-Catholic emissaries from London they were certainly inspired by the Gordon riots which had just disgraced and terrified the capital. As the horrified Bathonian put it, religion had been "the stalking horse for these dreadful scenes in London; but why should it approach this peaceful place?" In another six hours the chapel, the priest's lodging, and three adjoining houses had been sacked and gutted to their bare walls. Bath, and likewise Hull, had been caught up in a wave of anti-Papal and anarchist frenzy.

Bath's Catholics had built their property as a result of the Relief Act of 1778. The city's Catholic residents, and still more the Catholic visitors who resorted to the Spa, had indeed anticipated the new law. For in 1777 the Benedictines who served the Bath mission started a subscription for building a new chapel and a house, and for the buying of three houses in St. James's Parade whose rents would partly finance the chapel. The English Benedictines gave £200, the Duke of Norfolk sent £100, and local Catholic residents contributed.[2] Money came from many famous Catholic families who regularly took the Bath waters; the patronage by these families of spas and seaside resorts was long important for English Catholic churchbuilding. Lord Arundell gave fifty guineas, so helping to serve his own local interest. For one gathers that the priest's house was "very elegantly finished and furnished for the occasional residence, it is said, of Lord Arundell."[3] Donations, and a loan from the English Benedictines, soon reached over £2,000. So a new chapel, "more spacious and convenient" than that contrived in Bell Tree House, was built and stood ready for the rioters.[4]

Their ringleader, we hear, was one John Butler, a liveried footman from one of the new houses in the Royal Crescent. The local volunteers, who arrived with bayonets fixed but without powder and shot, were driven off. Only when dragoons and militiamen came from Devizes and Wells was the tumult suppressed.[5] It was rumoured that the rioters would go on, for the joint purpose of anti-Catholic demolition and plunder, to Bristol. But there the Corporation took preventive measures. Volunteers were put effectively under arms, and the Duke of Beaufort stood by with the Monmouthshire Militia. Trouble was avoided, but the owner of the humble Catholic chapel in St. James's Back dismantled part of the building, converting it to other purposes and so removing "the pretence of evil-disposed persons to destroy it".[6]

Far worse than the trouble at Bath had been the great mob outburst in London. Lord George Gordon's blue-cockaded followers had not confined themselves to gutting and looting the Catholic Embassy chapels, and others lately established at Moorfields and elsewhere. They sacked the houses of many peaceable Catholics, and forced the aged Bishop Challoner, Vicar Apostolic of the London District, to flee for safety to friends at Finchley. They burnt the house and library of Lord Mansfield the Lord Chief Justice; they likewise outraged the home of Sir George Savile, the Yorkshire Member of Parliament who had introduced the Relief Bill of 1778. They plundered the premises of Mr. Langdale, a Catholic distiller whose stock of spirits inflamed their ardour past the point of control. The rioting soon slipped from purposeful anti-Popery to sheer anarchy. Only when George III himself ordered the troops to fire, and when many had been shot or died besotted in the flames, could London recover from a terror which had gone far beyond diplomatic outrage and the smashing of a few simply furnished chapels. For the Catholics there was the immediate task of restoration; in Bath they were aided by over £3,000 in compensation and encouraged by the hanging of John Butler from a gallows specially

elevated near the scene of his riotous exploit.[7] But the lesson was that
authority could often be helpless against mob violence; among the
Catholics of England the trauma of the Gordon Terror superseded the
memory of Tyburn. It was some decades before the English Catholic
leaders, not least among them another Benedictine missioner in Bath,
could coax them out of a catacomb reticence towards the building of
chapels less furtive and unassuming than some which they erected in
the next thirty years.

By 1786 the Bath Catholics had spent their compensation money.
They had rebuilt their houses, and a simple but spacious new chapel
had arisen in Corn Street, near the site of that gutted by the rioters.
With its plain exterior, and with a simple classical doorway, it is now
used by the People's Mission. It has elliptically-headed side windows
and a shallow apse. It resembles many Georgian Nonconformist
chapels. In this, it is like many which Catholics put up in England
between the 1780s and the early Victorian age. For Catholic architecture at that time was in fact Nonconformist architecture. Its buildings
were often quietly tucked away up alleys and in courtyards (as one still
sees when one glimpses the Regency frontage of St. Mary's at Preston).
It was no surprise that these "chapels" had much in common with those
of the Baptists and Methodists. Only in the crosses which some had in
their pediments or on their gables, and in the design of their altars and
reredoses did they differ from the Protestant Nonconformist chapels,
though not, in those pre-Victorian days, from Anglican churches
which had been graced by classical compositions behind their Communion tables. These Georgian Catholic churches had no aisles; their
rectangular interiors, with or without side galleries, made it possible
for all to see the altar at Mass. They were closer to present-day liturgical
planning than most of those built by the Gothic enthusiasts whose
apostle was Augustus Pugin.

In London, the Catholic powers were compensated for the loss of
their Embassy chapels, and the buildings were replaced. Two of the
new structures were on "Nonconformist" rather than Continental
neo-classical lines. One was the simply fronted Bavarian Chapel, still
in use as Our Lady of the Assumption in Warwick Street near Piccadilly
Circus. The Sardinian Chapel's interior is well known from Ackermann's aquatint, and indeed from photographs. It had seats in galleries
as well as on its ground floor level. Only the altar, of Baroque "sarcophagus" shape like some others surviving from about this time,

combined with its reredos to give a more North Italian impression. But the new Spanish Chapel near Manchester Square* was far more sophisticated and ambitious. We now come to a Catholic architect at work in England, who was of some note in his own right, had interesting artistic connections, and founded an important architectural dynasty. Joseph Bonomi was an architect from Rome who had known the Adams and came to London at their invitation. He fitted easily into the capital's international artistic fraternity. In 1775 he married Rosa Florini, a young cousin of the devoutly Catholic artist Angelica Kauffmann. He later worked, at Towneley Hall near Burnley, on a sculpture gallery for the famous Catholic collector Charles Towneley. Now, in the years just after the next great measure of Catholic Relief he got his chance to build a Catholic chapel more consciously "architectural" than anything seen in London since Whitehall Chapel. The building was an attractive little basilica, aisled and barrel-vaulted, with a handsome row of Corinthian columns on each side.[8]

Despite their dire discouragements in 1780 some prominent Catholics had little hesitation, so far as privately owned buildings were concerned, in availing themselves of their new legal relief. Lord Arundell was a fearless pioneer. In 1786 he was one of the Trustees who bought the site for a new chapel to serve the numerous Catholics of Bristol.[9] The spacious building, with "Gothick" side windows and a shallow apse, was opened, still nominally illegal if reckoned as a public chapel, in 1790. By now Lord Arundell had splendidly extended his chapel at Wardour. His architect was Soane, and here, on the eve of easier times for this country's Catholics, we find Lord Arundell employing a Georgian architect of national importance in England's architectural history.

The new sanctuary and the shallow transepts of the chapel at Wardour are among their designer's fairly early achievements; as Miss Dorothy Stroud has pointed out the straightforward Corinthian classicism of the new work is that of Henry Holland (Soane's architectural master) and James Wyatt.[10]

Paine's chapel was lengthened by a square, shallow-domed sanctuary. Beyond it, Quinenza's marble altar was moved eastwards, being backed by a gently curving wall and two stately fluted Corinthian columns. The two transepts are filled by pillared galleries; from one of these Lord Arundell and his household could proudly look down on

* Built in the 1790s and the pastoral predecessor of St. James's, Spanish Place.

England's most sumptuous space for the worthy rendering of the Mass.

Nor was Wardour the only place for which Soane designed a dignified Catholic chapel. Between 1785 and 1789 he built a neo-classical mansion at Chillington in Staffordshire for the ancient Catholic family of the Giffards. A fine new chapel, separate from the house but fairly "domestic" in character, was also designed, but never built. The Vicars Apostolic of the Midland District had lived, for some decades, at Long Birch not far away; had these designs of 1786 been carried out the chapel could have served them as a quasi-cathedral. The main chapel was planned for a length of sixty feet, with a pedimented porch, a lunette-shaped window, and an upper pediment to crown its simple, sophisticated façade. A sacristy, and rooms for the chaplain and the family steward, were to complete a T-shaped group; the whole plan implied escape from the penal atmosphere of attic chapels and churches masked as stables.[11]

Far nobler were the plans made in 1785 for a new chapel in the Welds' grounds at Lulworth. Though it stands close to the gutted shell of the Jacobean castle this lovely church is a free-standing building. Strictly speaking, it was of somewhat doubtful legality. So when George III, who was a friend of the Welds, was specially asked for his sanction he advised that it should as little as possible resemble a chapel; it was, indeed, first described as a *mausoleum* of the type with which many Georgian landlords embellished their parks. In 1789, on one of his regular summer sojourns at Weymouth, the King visited the chapel, which was finished in the next year. In its structure, and in its internal decorations, it was, and is, a remarkable building.

The designer was a comparatively unknown London architect named John Tasker; I have been unable to find if he was related to a large Catholic family of that name in York or to the late Victorian Catholic architect of the same name.

The foundation stone was laid in February, 1786. Stone for the chapel came from various sources, among them from the nearby ruins of the Cistercian abbey of Bindon which stood on Weld property.*[12]

This "mausoleum" at Lulworth has a "centrally planned" main worshipping space. Two drawings by Tasker survive for a chapel with a longer nave, and planned as a Latin Cross.[13] But the actual chapel measures 76 feet by 61. A graceful dome covers the square central space, while a western vestibule, two transepts, and a sanctuary have

* This is the ruined abbey which grimly features in Hardy's *Tess of the Durbervilles.*

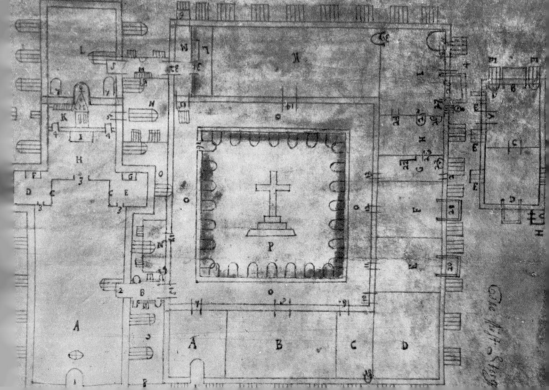

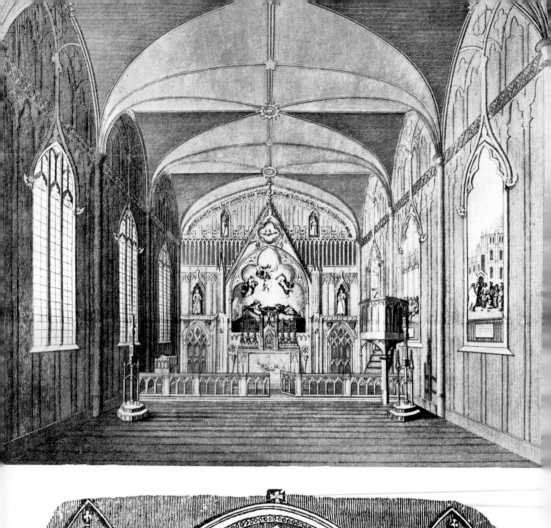

end walls which are curved on the inside and on the outside too except for the sanctuary end. Here, a squared projection contains the sacristy and the priest's rooms. This side towards the castle has an exterior, with its Doric doorway and niches with fine flaming urns, more ornate than that by which the villagers approach the chapel. Inside, the segmental transepts and vestibule are filled by galleries on dainty Doric columns. From these galleries, and from the gentle curvature of the walls behind them, one can guess Tasker's inspiration for this remarkable building. For the chapel at Lulworth is basically a miniature version of James Wyatt's much admired London Pantheon of 1772; Fanny Burney, who was there in 1789, saw this point when she called it "a Pantheon in miniature". At Lulworth, as at Wardour, much trouble was taken to set up a fine marble altar, with six candlesticks made in Rome by a craftsman who had started as a Papal soldier; Pius VI personally admired them before their shipment to England.[14]

Though secluded and 'privately built (for not less than £2,380) the Welds' new chapel was finer, and more suitable for ceremonies, than most buildings then used by England's Catholics. It was as a ceremonial setting that it soon gained fame. For in the summer of 1790 John Carroll, appointed to Baltimore and the first bishop to hold a Catholic see in the United States, came to England to get consecration. The chapel at Lulworth was his chosen spot. So Thomas Weld asked Bishop Walmsley, the elderly Vicar Apostolic of the Western District, to preside at the ceremony. He added that "the more private it can be done the better".[15] On the Feast of the Assumption the rite was duly performed, and then in Advent the new Vicars Apostolic of the London and Northern Districts were likewise consecrated at Lulworth. It was Bishop Carroll, in a letter from Baltimore sent to Bishop Walmsley in the spring of 1791, who neatly expressed the glory which John Tasker's domed masterpiece had attained. For he put it that "the chapel of that noble castle will be remembered in the future ecclesiastical history of the United States; it will be still more so in that of England."[16] It is good to know that after the ham-handed "Byzantinising" of some sash windows in the 1860s, the Lulworth chapel has recently had its late Georgian fenestration restored, and that its whole interior has been appropriately redecorated.

By the late 1780s more moves towards Catholic relief were in the air. The Catholic Committee, which played a large, though not an exclusive part in the coming negotiations was formed in 1782. In 1788

3 *Lulworth Castle, Dorset*
  (a) *The Chapel, 1786*
  (b) *Interior: "a Pantheon in Miniature"*

4 *Georgian Gothic*
  (a) *Winchester, 1792*
  (b) *Newcastle on Tyne, 1798*

William Pitt the Younger agreed to the introduction of more relieving legislation. The controversies which followed among English Catholics, and which partly caused another three years' delay, have been fully described elsewhere, and are outside the scope of a work whose concern lies mainly with church fabrics.* One notes, however, that the years which saw the erection of the Lulworth chapel also included the building of other, less assuming churches whose sponsors must have anticipated a time in which, however they might dread mob violence, they need fear little from the law.

In Birmingham, a Franciscan named Fr. John Nutt built St. Peter's in 1786. It is a humble brick structure, set amid some pleasing late Georgian terraces; it is said to have purposely resembled a workshop or a small factory. Some Epistle side windows have glazing bars which intersect to form "churchwarden Gothic" tracery. Inside, with a modillioned cornice, a fine roundel for a chandelier and a classical altarpiece there is a more religious effect. The gallery, round three of the chapel's sides, is particularly deep at the West end; this substantial duplication of floor space did much, in many pioneering Catholic chapels, to ease the problem of accommodation. Two years later, in Liverpool, the oldest part of the Benedictines' chapel in Seel Street was made plain and unassuming with two tiers of windows to allow for a gallery. Then in 1811, as one tells from a rainwaterhead, a large transeptal porch was built, with a Greek Doric doorway whose metopes spell out the older date of 1788; the ornately pilastered sanctuary is early Victorian Corinthian of 1845.

Very naturally Lancashire saw much early building work on plain "Non-Conformist" Catholic chapels. At Hindley near Wigan "Mr." (i.e. Dom Edmund) Duckett's chapel, commenced in 1789, was a barnlike structure of a Methodist character. Its building accounts give some nice glimpses of homespun Lancashire life. For a sum of £697 7s. 8½d. the chapel was very cheaply built, and prices were certainly low in Hindley. Softwood timber was bought in Liverpool, and shipped to the site by the canal which also serves the comically famed Wigan "pier". But some wood was also obtained on the cheap, for one John Bailey was paid six shillings for "snigging" two dozen balks of it "out of the navigation". Bricks were the main building material, and late in 1789 the sum of 2s. 8d. bought a pair of clogs which had been promised to Thomas Hayes "if he trod the mortar well". When all

* See Bernard Ward, *The Dawn of the Catholic Revival in England, 1781–1803*, Vol I.

was done the Hindley Singers were hired to perform an oratorio at the chapel's opening. £1 7s. 4d. was laid out, on the great day, for forty-one dinners for them and the doorkeeper.[17]

The Catholic Relief Act of 1791 took effect in the summer of that year.[18] So far as most aspects of churchbuilding were concerned it ended penal times. Provided they took a suitably worded oath the Catholics of England and Wales were no longer liable to prosecution for their religion, for hearing Mass, or for not attending their Anglican parish churches. They could now build churches (without bells or steeples) provided those places of worship were certified by the Justices of the Peace. Their services were not to be held (as often in penal times) behind locked, barred, or bolted doors, and provision was made against the disturbance of the Masses celebrated within the chapels. It was still illegal, within the Realm or Dominions of George III, for Catholics to found Schools, Academics, or Colleges, nor could they "found, endow, or establish" any religious order or convent; the politics of France soon made a dead letter of these last provisions. But English Catholics were now free to continue the widespread building of their simple, still unobtrusive buildings for the public, legally unfettered offering of Mass.

Lancashire was predictably an area where much use was made of the newly granted relief. Many simple Catholic chapels were built there in the years just after 1791. Congregations were often large, so that some were of fair size. But as architecture they were still improvised and unambitious, of a sturdy, vernacular simplicity; their builders were the local masons and carpenters who also ran up Baptist and Methodist chapels. More homely details come from papers covering the building, in 1794, of a new chapel at Claughton on Brock between Preston and Lancaster. An earlier one had stood nearby, its roof and other materials being reused for the building put up by Fr. John Barrow the parish priest. The new chapel (which cost nearly £700) was of stone, fifty-six feet long and thirty-six across. Its ceiling was to be plastered white, with a bold cornice, and a ventilating "flower" four feet across. The windows, eleven feet tall, were to be edged with a masonry frame like those which many chapels of this period could boast; their glazing was to be with "second-best" glass. The western half of the building was to be flagged with stone, no doubt for convenience in washing; the more "genteel" part of the chapel, and the vestry had boarded floors.[19] Some of the benches were to come from the temporarily disused St. Mary's at Preston, while Fr. Barrow, being a pastor of tough determination, insisted that no nails, "on any consideration", were to be allowed "for hats in the wall".[20]

Priests' houses were often built continuously with the altar ends of chapels. Yet even in largely Catholic Lancashire the penal period, and still more the Gordon and more local riots, were so traumatic a memory that concealment and reticence were still thought wise; one recalls that no properly effective police yet existed to prove that mob fury was less powerful than the law. So some chapels were hidden, from the road, by the façades of their late Georgian presbyteries. One finds it thus at Netherton near Liverpool, where in the 1790s a new chapel replaced that which had continued in Sefton Hall even after the Molyneux family had conformed. A neat little villa in the Adam manner, with a pedimented doorway and a fanlight, is what one sees from the road. But behind it, the simple chapel has a delightfully intact Georgian interior, with delicate joinery to adorn its gallery, a "sarcophagus" altar, and a pilastered and pedimented altarpiece which has winged cherubs' heads, a *gloria* of rays, and Adamesque urns and garlands of the type that many churches of the Establishment could boast before the zealous efforts of "ecclesiological" restorers.

Elsewhere in the North, and in the Midland District, other chapels of this modest pattern were widely erected. Ribchester in Lancashire got a chapel about 1790, with a boldly rusticated West doorway and "edged" windows like those at Claughton and elsewhere.[21] At Leeds a hired room had for some years succeeded several chapels in houses. Then in 1793-4 the Dominican missioners spent some £1,500 on a good-sized oblong building by Thomas Johnson. It had two-dozen pews; as in several contemporary Catholic chapels they were arranged (precluding processions) in a continuous block divided down the middle by a solid partition.[22] In the Lincolnshire Wolds an upstairs chapel at Osgoodby joined another like it at Market Rasen, while in the gentle Staffordshire countryside North of Lichfield the western part of the brick chapel at Wood Lane, with a balustraded gallery and a Georgian priest's house against its *western* end, is a simple structure of the mid-1790s.*

Before 1790 Oxford's tiny Catholic congregation, containing "scarcely a person of any property" had been served, every other

---

* The eastward extension, making the church cruciform and attractively "Churchwarden" Gothic, is probably of about 1825.

Sunday, by a Jesuit named Fr. Leslie who lived out at Waterperry. In 1793 he moved into the city, and in ten years spent nearly £1,000 on a chapel, with a fairly deep sanctuary and an alterpiece flanked by Corinthian half-columns and pilasters, which was said to be "solemn and handsome", and "in a style of elegant simplicity". Lord Petre had given £100 and Thomas Weld of Lulworth £30.[23] This was the building which later gained fame when Newman went there from Littlemore to his first Mass as a Catholic in a public Catholic church.

In South London, a house in Bandyleg Walk, Southwark, had been taken in 1786, and a room had been fitted as a chapel. This was soon too small, so another, of a plain late Georgian character with an Ionic altarpiece was built in the 1790s near the Elephant and Castle.[24] Its designer, of whom one soon heard more, was a young Catholic builder of Islington named James Taylor. The chapel, like that at Leeds, was the direct pastoral forbear of a modern cathedral.

More notable were two allied, and surviving, Catholic churches in the Isle of Wight. They are worth description, for there are none better from this immediately post-penal era.

Mrs. Elizabeth Heneage was a well-to-do convert lady, the daughter and heiress of John Browne of Gatcombe. She had married James Windsor Heneage, a Catholic landlord in Lincolnshire.[25] A daughter was the wife of one of Mrs. Fitzherbert's Swinnerton relatives, another married William Brockholes of Claughton.[26] Mrs. Heneage found much scope for the pious benevolences of her widowhood. She gave much money to churches, and towards the supply of priests, in the Western District.[27] She sent a little to the funds at Oxford and Winchester and £200 to her son-in-law's new chapel at Claughton.[28] Her main endeavour was the building of the two charming late Georgian churches in her native island.

The chapel at Newport was certified, in accordance with the Relief Act, in April, 1792. Bar its boldly projecting Roman Doric porch, and the crosses there and on the main gable, its red brick, pedimented exterior has little to mark it off from the almost contemporary Methodist Chapel down the street. The altar is in a shallow apse. The side galleries, with a sacristy and a confessional below their eastern ends, are upheld by delicately fluted Ionic pillars; the western one curves out in the middle like that in the slightly later Pump Room at Bath. Here in this chapel, when Mrs. Heneage died in 1800, William Brockholes put up the marble tablet whose neat lettering informs us that the good lady was "munificent in erecting sacred edifices, and bountifully assisting others in like works".

The chapel built by Mrs. Heneage in West Cowes lies parallel to the street; its priest's house abuts onto its liturgical East end. It is dated 1796, is of yellow brick, and has a boldly modillioned cornice and a good pedimented Ionic porch. Its windows, round-headed late Georgian but unhappily made Romanesque in Victorian times, are all on the Gospel side.* The church's designer was its priest, Fr. Thomas Gabb. He had been trained at the English College in Douai; it is said that the altar tabernacle copied that which stood, before the French Revolution, on its chapel's High Altar. The altar composition is this church's main inner glory, a work of much dignity with fluted pilasters, and above them rich Palladian Doric trabeation. An arched recess, with grapevine carving and winged cherubs' heads, encloses a picture of the Deposition, while on the white and yellow marble altar the brass candlesticks are miniature Corinthian columns.

But fear of riots still caused the quasi-concealment of some Roman Catholic chapels of the 1790s. The Navy of Nelson's time enlisted many Catholics from Ireland and elsewhere. So by 1796 a new chapel existed among the humble streets near Portsmouth Dockyard. A plain arch-way led up an alley, between two late Georgian houses, to a little courtyard before the chapel's façade.[29] The "simple and plain" chapel at Greenwich for Hospital pensioners and "poor sailors" was similarly placed, behind a pair of houses. Its builder, and main financier, was the architect-builder James Taylor;[30] grim events in France soon gave him chances for much more ambitious work.

In 1792 and 1793 the fear of the guillotine drove hundreds of French bishops and lesser clergy, and some thousands of the gentry, to refuge in England. Hospitality, blending pity and political sympathy, was given by high and low. Mrs. Fitzherbert, since 1785 the illegal and morganatic wife of the Prince of Wales, was not without her influence in the highest of circles. Catholicism, in the persons of these refugees from the Terror, gained a new respectability, and while Catholics lost their danger as Jacobites they gained respect as anti-Jacobins.

---

* Throughout this book, references to a church's Epistle and Gospel side relate to the old practice whereby the "Liturgy of the Word" was conducted, at the altar, with the priest's back to the people. The Epistle and Gospel, and indeed the collects and other introductory matter, are now read from a lectern put at some tactically convenient point in the sanctuary.

Some hundreds of refugee French clergy lived in a community in the Palace at Winchester while others did little, during their stay in England, by way of pastoral work. Yet many, once they had learnt English, were more zealous, so that numerous missions were founded, and many chapels (as at Hampstead, Chelsea, and in Liverpool along Scotland Road) were built by these pious *Abbés*. No less important, for the eventual building in England of conventual establishments which contravened one section of the Act of 1791, were the religious communities which now reached England from towns in France and what is now Belgium. A few were French in their membership. But most of them were English, recruited from the gentle Catholic families of penal times.

Most of these religious communities first found new quarters in the country mansions or town houses of their English benefactors. But thanks to Thomas Weld's generosity the French Cistercian monks of La Trappe were differently placed. Late in 1794 they came to Lulworth. They first lived in the chaplain's house, but the observance of their strict rule demanded something more enclosed. So in 1795-6 the new monastery of St. Susan was built. Thomas Weld could claim that these simple buildings on his Dorset estate were the first in post-penal England to be specially designed and erected for monastic use. Their quadrangle contained all the basic elements needed in an austere, simple monastery. They were plain, with cob walls, and their style was said to be "Early English"; one cannot tell now whether this was really the lancet Gothic later given that designation by Thomas Rickman.[31]

Legality apart, a full-blown monastery in Georgian Wessex was a major phenomenon. Many visitors came to explore these coenobitic mysteries; the second edition of Hutchins's great work on Dorset history has much on the builders, and on visitors' reactions. Catholics, very naturally, were full of enthusiasm. But not all the others could happily view this reversal of Henry VIII's achievement. One commentator referred, with horror, to a "gloomy abode of ignorance and nastiness".[32] Mr. Weld got his share of the Protestant attack, so that early in 1796 he wrote complainingly to the Anglican Bishop of Bristol whose diocese then included Dorset. Dr. Courtenay was all sympathy, and at a meeting of the Governors of Queen Anne's Bounty he spoke, to the Archbishop of Canterbury and his other colleagues, about the verbal onslaught made on Mr. Weld's "Establishment for the unfortunate objects" he had mentioned. A truly "ecumenical" spirit prevailed, for all present agreed in lamenting that this Catholic squire "should have suffered any causeless uneasiness on this subject".[33] Till 1817, when their community went back to France, the Cistercians stayed on in the safe seclusion of Lulworth.

More durable than the Lulworth monastery were two endeavours to recreate, in its inmates' own country, the English College at Douai which had trained many of the secular clergy. The staff and students in time reached England. Their traditions were soon carried on in Hertfordshire and in County Durham. The first of the new seminaries was small at first but speedily grew. It was at Old Hall Green, a Catholic centre where a Jacobean manor house contained the school originally started, not far away in 1749, in the Tudor mansion of Standon Lordship which belonged to the staunchly Catholic Astons of Tixall in Staffordshire.[34] The time soon came for buildings specially designed for this educational purpose. The architect of the severe, pedimented range put up between 1796 and 1799 was James Taylor of Islington.

Drawings kept at St. Edmund's College show that Taylor presented some plans other than those actually used. All presuppose a large, rectangular main block, more akin to some early College buildings in the United States than to the campus conception or the quads and courts of Oxbridge. One design is a notably fine late Georgian work, a refined composition of recessed arches and varied windows. It has dainty cupolas above pavilion ends, vermiculated rustication blocks of Coade stone above some ground-floor arches, and a cross in the pediment. Other drawings show a central block like that which exists, but with five-bay flanking vestibules leading to admirable balancing wings in the Wardour manner. Both of these were to be eighty feet long, one for the refectory, the other containing the chapel.[35] What was actually built was no more than the unflanked central block, of yellow London brick in fifteen "elements", with plain stone platbands to part its storeys, and with the Coade stone vermiculation from Taylor's most ambitious design. A wide passageway, or *ambulacrum* in Douai parlance, links the downstairs rooms, and the chapel was in a large first-floor room. Despite its falling short from its architect's fuller conceptions this austere range was the most ambitious Catholic building put up in England since the ending of penal times.

Progress on a lasting northern seminary was slower than at Old Hall Green. Some Douai students did, indeed, move to Co. Durham in

5 *Netherton, Lancashire*
   (a) *St. Benet's church and house, c. 1793*
   (b) *Altar composition*

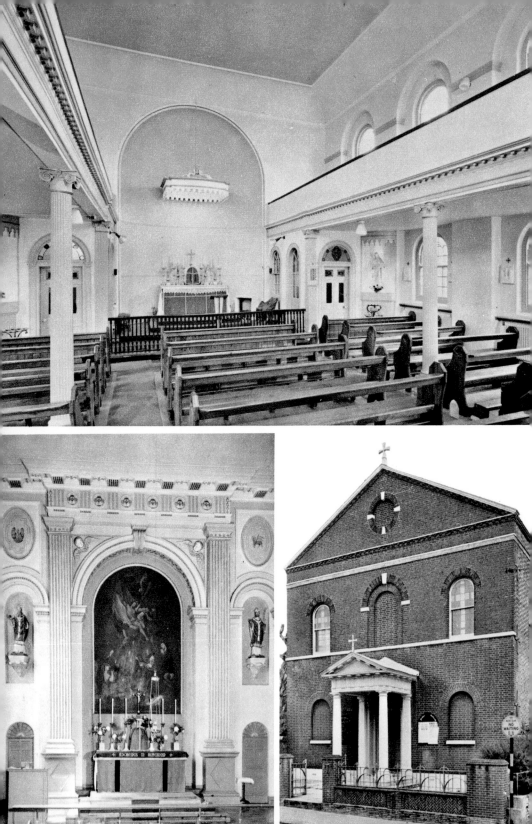

1793. Next year, and for fourteen years to come, they settled in the early Georgian mansion of Crook Hall. Then in 1799 Bishop William Gibson, Vicar Apostolic of the Northern District, bought an upland property, at Ushaw near Durham, from Mrs. Fitzherbert's relative Sir Edward Smythe of Acton Burnell. But no building was done till after 1800.[36]

Meanwhile, in 1792, a chapel had been built at Winchester which brought England's Catholic architecture into the embattled conflict of taste. Roman Catholics were numerous in the city, and had long worshipped in a building sited in the garden of a house. A new and larger Catholic chapel was not unremarkable in this particular town What made it unusual was the enthusiastic choice of its priest, John Milner, for "antiquarian" Gothic.

As a priest, as a man of taste, as a controversialist, and later as a bishop John Milner was prominent among the English Catholics of his time. His antiquarian tastes found ample scope at Winchester, and the best account of his new chapel is a long appendix to his own two-volume history of the Wessex capital.[37] The antiquarians of the late eighteenth century, like the early Victorian "ecclesiologists", held the view that in England at all events a place of Christian worship should really be Gothic. John Milner, anticipating Pugin, complained of the "more modern" Catholic chapels, "with small sashed windows and fashionable decorations hardly to be distinguished . . . from common assembly-houses". So his new chapel, a plain rectangle 75 feet long, followed Gothic "as closely as funds would allow". It was a deliberate reaction from the "Methodist" idiom of other Catholic chapels of that time. Its designer was the supremely suitable man for such an attack on the classical tradition. For John Carter, never prolific as an architect, was unchallengeable as an antiquarian draughtsman; from his many drawing excursions he had the whole gamut of Gothic at his fingertips. What he produced for Milner was an amazing *capriccio* of medieval bits and pieces derived from Winchester itself, from the Coronation chair at Westminster, from York Minster and elsewhere.* The winged cherubs' heads which acted as corbels for the hoodmoulds of the windows struck a discordant note, the chiaroscuro paintings (after Raphael and others and by the local painter William Cave) were hardly Gothic in their inspiration, and prints make it clear that the

---

* The tabernacle, with two tiny flanking towers, was a reasonably close version of the West end of York Minster.

6 (a) *Newport, Isle of Wight: interior, 1792*
  (b) *West Cowes, Isle of Wight: altar composition, 1796*
  (c) *Newport: a "Methodist" frontage*

interior ensemble was not really medieval in flavour. But the exterior gave a more convincing impression of an early Tudor chapel of the college or chantry type, and as a religious and cultural demonstration the whole building, with its saintly figures and lavish sacred symbolism, was deeply significant. As one now saw in such towns as Norwich and Lancaster the building of larger and more public Catholic chapels was at last much more a matter of course. Their sponsors' attention could now be turned, more self-consciously than before, to the contest between the two great provinces of style. The "romantic" Gothic doorways and panelling of the large new chapel which was opened, in 1798, by Fr. James Worswick at Newcastle also suggested that the choice need not be the pilasters and pediments of neo-classicism.[38]

Chapter III

AESTHETIC EMANCIPATION

The southern end of the small town of Shepton Mallet stretches out towards the rolling, pastoral countryside of central Somerset. That part of the parish was once more placid and secluded than it is nowadays; it was there, between 1801 and 1804, that the L-shaped block which comprises the Catholic church and its priest's house was built. The charming group looks out on to the road, with a "domestic" façade which is mainly that of the house. The unaisled, unobtrusive church runs back to complete the L. Inside, and along the façade, the idiom is the homely, vernacular Georgian Gothic of some contemporary Nonconformist chapels; the two-light windows resemble those in the somewhat earlier Unitarian chapel elsewhere in the town. This Catholic outpost in rural Wessex proved that the instinct for concealment, and the use of humble, unassertive building idioms still persisted among Englishmen of the lately proscribed religion.

It was, indeed, many years before the "priesthole and garret" mentality disappeared from the minds of England's Catholics. Despite considerable Catholic strength in some towns their vernacular Gothic, "barnlike", or "Methodist" chapels still arose in such places; while lofts and upper rooms did duty as the first worshipping places of many new or poverty-stricken congregations. Outside the private chapels of the leading Catholic gentry the time had hardly come for sophistication or stylish assertion. So although the large chapel opened in York about 1802 was "of modern architecture and much admired for elegance" it was probably a somewhat unremarkable building,[1] while at Hedon near Hull the church of 1803 is unambitious though charming.[2] At Coventry, the first chapel of 1807 was a "simple structure of brick-work, without any of the graces of architecture."[3] It was so badly built that it almost collapsed in less than forty years. The first St. Chad's, in Shadwell Street, Birmingham also dated from this first decade of the nineteenth century; though it was valuably large and roomy it seems to have been gaunt and unattractive. Its interest lay largely in its steeply sloping site, with Bath Street running for forty-four yards along its southern edge, and a south to north length of 163 feet 5 inches.[4] For this comprised most of the plot on which the present St. Chad's had later to be built; the nature of the ground bought in 1806 explains the need for a crypt below the sanctuary of Pugin's church, and the modest length of the building which has now to serve as an archbishop's cathedral.

At Sheffield, where the Norfolks had important estates, a much larger Catholic body existed than in most West Riding towns. They had used various house chapels, and then one attached to the Duke's house in which his agent dwelt. Then in 1813–14 a large chapel was built, the predecessor of the present Gothic church in Norfolk Row; with six round-headed windows on each side its outward appearance was Protestant Nonconformist; a cross on its eastern gable was its sole demonstration of Catholicity.[5]

Some Catholic chapels of this Regency period were still, architectur-ally speaking, the adjuncts or wings or country houses. Such, in 1810 was the "churchwarden" Gothic chapel at Crathorne in the North Riding.[6] At Stonor in the Chilterns the medieval manor chapel was delightfully redecorated, and plaster-vaulted, in Regency Gothic; its East window has a large figure of Christ by the Birmingham glazier Francis Eginton.[7] But some "country house" Catholics still shrank from the building of separate and permanent chapels. So when about 1811 Robert Berkeley of Spetchley near Worcester employed John Tasker to design him a new mansion a large elegant, rectangular chapel was provided in the main block of the dignified house, with its Ionic order and façade of crisp Bath stone. As at Thorndon, it is of the height of two storeys, with bedrooms above it. The sashed windows have glazing bars as do others in the mansion, while the chapel's Ionic detail, and the plaster rosette for its chandelier, could as well be in a drawing room. But below its private West gallery a public entrance for the villagers reminded them that "going to prayers" need no longer be furtive. In other country houses upstairs chapels gave way to the permanent furnishing of rooms. At Parndon House in Essex the Amhersts worshipped in what had been the library, while in Leicestershire at Bosworth Hall the erstwhile dining room served the same pious purpose. Ornaments were still sparse and simple. At Parndon it need have been no aesthetic loss that the candlesticks, designed as Ionic columns with gilt capitals, were of mahogany, while both at Parndon and Bosworth *antependia* of stamped Spanish leather served as altar frontals.[8]

More consciously seeking an "ecclesiastical" style was the large chapel which in 1809 replaced the attic in the Jerninghams' mansion at Costessey near Norwich. Its designer was a member of the family, the barrister and amateur architect Edward Jerningham[9] who also Gothicised the Catholic chapel of 1791 at Stafford* and designed the far-seen "Castle" on his family's land just west of that town. The chapel at Costessey was apsidal, vaulted, and like that at Winchester was "Perpendicular" in style. It was said "in some degree" to imitate King's chapel at Cambridge. So antiquarian a building must have pleased John Milner, since 1803 Vicar Apostolic of the Midland District and thus responsible for Norfolk.

This period of a more conscious pursuit of style also saw architectural moves forward in Catholic places of education. The school at Sedgley Park near Wolverhampton, in its Staffordshire quarters since 1763, by now had various additions to the Queen Anne fabric of its central block. Then in 1800–01 an outer wing was widened to make an ambitious upstairs chapel; the architect was Thomas Dadford of Wolverhampton, better known as the engineer of several canals. It rested on an open arcade, and its "churchwarden" Gothic windows on the Gospel side were thought daring when "a Catholic chapel could hardly be made conspicuous with safety". A drawing of its interior shows fair decorative elaboration. Fluted Doric pilasters had urns and winged cherubs' heads above them, and an Adamesque pattern of ox skulls and drapery swags was poised above the sacristy doors. The altar painting copied Benjamin West's "Last Supper", and as in other chapels a gilt and painted leather frontal hung down before the altar.[10]

At Old Hall Green two modest wings, holding a chapel and a

---

* Some seventeenth-century Gothic stalls, ejected from Lichfield Cathedral, were put round the sanctuary. Gillow, *op. cit.*

refectory were added in 1805 to the original block. Their main super-visor, for a little over £1,550, was a local contractor named Thomas Bangs.[11] With new and larger windows they run flush with the façade wall of James Taylor's central block, and though they served useful purposes they were a disappointing substitute for the fine balancing wings of Taylor's earlier design. Then in 1804 Taylor himself was the designer of the college started at Ushaw, and opened in 1808.[12] The scheme was more spacious than at St. Edmund's. The buildings, of stone quarried on the estate, were arranged round a quadrangle though the Western wing was built later than the others. With their wide *ambulacra* downstairs the buildings are of the same type as at Old Hall Green. But Ushaw the College's larger dimensions made it possible for the first chapel, plain and roomy with a trio of eastern altars, to be in the back wing which also held the refectory. The southern block, at first of three storeys and with an "open" pediment, most clearly recalls Taylor's work at St. Edmund's; only its lower windows, with their rustication of a "Gibbsian" type, look back to earlier Georgian taste.

Less spectacular, but eventually important, was the "secular" seminary established in the Midlands. A Catholic congregation had long existed, with a secluded priest's house, at Oscott near Sutton Coldfield. A roomlike chapel had been built out in 1778. Then in 1794 a combined educational establishment for lay boys and "church students" was quietly started in the house. Bishop Milner later improved the chapel, installing a glass painting by Eginton whose work he had known since his Winchester days. He then sponsored greater changes. An upstairs chapel of 1814 was the first in England set aside for the aesthetically unfortunate devotion to the Sacred Heart. Romantic Gothic was here the style. But when in the next two years the Bishop spent over £600 on further improvements his taste had changed.[13] By 1817, so we gather from another source, he had "given up architecture and antiquities entirely".[14] The new colonnaded vestibule at Oscott led to an "Exhibition Room" whose façade was pilastered Grecian, while on each side of the new courtyard a Doric loggia led to a graceful curved pavilion end. From a print of this delightful composition one gathers that its architect was Joseph Ireland, a man of great importance for England's Catholic architecture before 1830.

The building of parish chapels continued apace in the last years before political Emancipation in 1829. Some were put up under the auspices of the four Vicars Apostolic. For others, much of the burden fell on the religious orders who manned the churches concerned. Many buildings, in both categories, were largely paid for by the "old Catholic families" who still displayed great and vital generosity. Many English Catholic churches are on their present sites because those plots were owned, or specially bought, by members of those families; their outstanding services to the Church of their allegiance by no means ended when Roman Catholicism was no longer illegal. The geographical distribution of Catholic chapels was also wider than before, so that down in Cornwall a private room in Falmouth was replaced, in 1819–21, by a one served by a French *Abbé* who had stayed in England, and who got much of the money from the French Royal Family.[15]

Two Regency chapels in the present Diocese of Nottingham can illustrate the two currents of taste which prevailed, both for Catholics and Protestants, in these Regency years. At Leicester a converted warehouse had served the few local Catholics since 1798. Then in 1817–19 Fr. Benedict Caestryck, a Flemish Dominican who had come over with his English brethren from their priory at Bornhem near Antwerp, got Ireland to design another, much larger chapel. This was in what a London Vicar Apostolic delightedly called "the good old style". In other words, it was in simple lancet Gothic, originally with a shallow apse and covered by a plaster vault whose ribs rose from shafts in the thirteenth-century manner; later in the century it gained a deeper, "ecclesiological" chancel, and a south aisle.[16]

But at Hassop in Derbyshire a conspicuous new chapel of 1816–18 displayed a totally different style. Money for its building had been left, in a will made before 1791, by Thomas Eyre who died in 1792.[17] Later members of the family mistakenly assumed the title of the Earls of Newburgh; it was another Thomas Eyre, who later styled himself the seventh Earl and who died in 1833, who employed Ireland on the delightful classical church. Very full accounts for its building operations survive; the total cost slightly exceeded £2,400.[18] The stone was local, but a special cart and horse had to be bought to bring timber from Chapel en le Frith, and other materials from elsewhere. Ireland forewent his fees, but the accounts show that he spent no less than 152 days away from London, on ten journeys to Hassop itself and another to Liverpool. Ireland also refers to even longer supervisory periods put in by his "pupil clerk", a young relative named J. J. Scoles, eventually one of the most important Catholic architects of the century. No less important are the actual details of the church. Its interior is rectangular, and over the sacristy is a library room for the original donor's valuable religious books. Plain Doric pilasters adorn the walls, the ceiling is coffered, and at the East end is the lower part of an important Baroque altarpiece. Four Doric pilasters adorn the exterior wall behind the altar. But the four-columned Roman Doric portice is more exciting. For here, and in the church's far-projecting eaves, is a clear adaptation of Inigo Jones's famous "Tuscan barn"—St. Paul's, Covent Garden as lately rebuilt by Thomas Hardwick.

In a few more years the Ionic-pilastered façade of a new chapel at Taunton* made a stylish addition to the long crescent, in simple Regency brickwork, which had lately adorned the town's western end. Yet Lancashire, very typically, was the chief English scene of Catholic building activity.

Some chapels were still unassuming enough. At Burnley, the centre of a large East Lancashire district where Catholic adherents were fewer than they were near Preston and behind Liverpool, a chapel of 1817 replaced a private one in Towneley Hall. It stood near the Towneley family's park, and Mr. Peregrine Towneley gave half of the needed £2,000. The chapel seems, however, to have been more notable for its singing than as a piece of architecture.[19] So too, in 1819, the church built at Clayton le Moors to replace the Walmsleys' chapel in Dukenhalgh House was said to be a "plain rectangular structure of no architectural pretensions".[20] But elsewhere in Lancashire new Catholic chapels were (and sometimes are) of more importance in their county's historic architecture. As in other regions the stylistic tension was neo-classic versus early Revival Gothic. It is best seen in Wigan—England's vintage town for Regency Catholic churches.

It was due to a sharp controversy between the secular clergy and the Jesuits that Wigan obtained, within two hundred yards of each other, the contrasting fabrics of St. Mary's and St. John's.

The building of these Wigan churches recalls the competitive efforts sometimes staged, on neighbouring sites, by Wesleyan and Primitive Methodists. Operations were simultaneous, but one recalls that the Jesuits had long served a large flock in Wigan.† Because their chapel of 1785 faced directly onto Standishgate their new church was built well back from the street, to allow the continued use of the older building.

* Now the local Masonic Hall.

† In the 1740s, when people attended a house chapel, they had been known as "customers".

The Jesuits, in January, 1818, got in first with their foundation stone.[21] Two were then laid for the Vicar Apostolic's "secular" church of St. Mary, one on St. Patrick's day, the other on that of St. George.[22] But St. Mary's was built quicker, being finished that year. The new church of St. John the Baptist was opened on June 24th (its patronal day) in 1819.[23]

St. Mary's whose architect is unknown to me, is a delightful gem of the early Revival Gothic associated with many "Commissioners'" churches built by the Church of England. The style is Perpendicular, most notably in the pinnacled and battlemented, yet quite un-medieval, façade onto Standishgate. The main West window is transomed and ambitious. The interior arcades, with the verticality of their pillars interrupted by side galleries, are in the manner of about 1440, while the ribbed and bossed plaster ceiling is typical of many put up in Regency Gothic churches. The church is essentially as it was first designed. In the sanctuary the East window of five lights is partly obscured by the pinnacled Victorian canopy of the throne set up for Benediction—a rite uncommon in the Catholic England of 1818 and difficult (as Newman later explained) to reconcile with the eastward fenestration of pseudo-medieval chancels.

St. John's is an utter contrast to St. Mary's. It is of local stone, bulky and spacious, built to hold a thousand people. It cost a little over £6,000—much more than most Catholic parish chapels of those days; money came in from many local Catholics and from collections made in the Jesuits' churches at Worcester and Norwich.[24] The main fabric is gauntly boxlike, "Methodist" in character but relieved by the low, graceful Ionic colonnade of eight columns across its West wall. The inside, with a western gallery on Corinthian columns and with its bench space wide and unimpeded, was also austerely built, for the fine pilasters at the sides were only installed in 1849. For splendour, one looked to the altar end, where a small apse is richly ceiled with ornamental plaster, and lined and flanked with noble Corinthian half-columns. We shall see how here, and at Claughton on Brock, the next generation still further glorified the actual altar. The designer of St. John's, who could also have been the architect of contemporary Baptist and Methodist chapels, was probably the local mason Robert Haulbrook whose bill accounted for nearly half the cost.[25]

A simple classical church was built in 1814–15 at Chorley, on land originally presented from their Lancashire property, by the Welds.[26]

There were also developments, at this time, in the two towns which the Industrial Revolution had made the largest in the country.

Another Catholic church was opened in Liverpool in the year of Waterloo. St. Nicholas', behind the Adelphi Hotel, has suffered in estimation from its long duty as a "pro" Cathedral; people reckoned that it fell too far behind the grandeur associated with an episcopal church. Yet viewed in its original "parish" rating it deserved far more consideration. For its broad fabric, "churchwarden" or early Revival Gothic with a rarely spacious and spectacular composition of western galleries, is of real importance. Its shallow apse, plaster-vaulted like many others of that time, is a nice Regency Gothic period piece.

Manchester's earlier chapels got a major reinforcement between 1818 and 1820. The large church of St. Augustine, Granby Row, cost about £10,000. Building conditions were typically late Georgian. No railways existed, so timber and other materials came up from Liverpool by the famous Bridgewater Canal and the Mersey-Irwell Navigation. Brick and stone were prime materials for this broad, flat-roofed "Early English" church, but a founder named Richard Ormrod was paid for sixteen cast iron pillars for the three-sided gallery; he deducted £5 as his personal donation.[27] Photographs from before the church's demolition show richly shaftly and moulded eastern lancets of an antiquarianism that would have pleased the lately deceased Carter or the prospering Thomas Rickman.[28] The architect, who as the contracting mason signed or countersigned the invoices, was one of Rickman's pupils, a local man named John Palmer;[29] he also designed what is now the Anglican cathedral at Blackburn. Near Blackburn we can also see his most stylish Catholic church. For Pleasington "Priory" is a remarkable work of the early Gothic Revival. It dates from 1818–19 impressively combining two tall western pinnacles, a rose window, a mainly Perpendicular fabric and also (rather oddly by medieval precedents) a clerestory in impeccable "Early English".

Meanwhile, Catholic churchbuilding was progressing in London. The well-known churches in Hampstead and Somers Town are of this "Regency" period, though Sir John Summerson has said that the latter's Grecian façade was added in 1830.[30] More ambitious, though no larger than the best Lancashire churches, was the new Moorfields church which replaced an earlier, more humble chapel. When new, this church of 1817–20 by John Newman was the capital's leading advertisement of a slowly reviving Catholicism. It had a classical façade and behind plain square piers it boasted the rare feature of shallow aisles. Behind the high altar a top-lit panorama of the Crucifixion dramatically appeared past a row of marble columns which are happily preserved in George Sherrin's modern, smaller church. Here at last was a spacious setting for the ritual of High Mass, with its three vested clergy simultaneously in the sanctuary.

This future pro-Cathedral of the Westminster Archdiocese suggested that although "triumphalism" was premature the time was ripe for England's Catholic buildings and services to show greater display. The routine in the chapels, like many of the chapels themselves, had so far been timidly unassertive. Some did, indeed, have ambitious music, with Haydn or Mozart masses and, in London at all events, the appreciated presence in their choirs of foreign opera singers. But in many churches Sung Mass was uncommon and High Mass unthinkable. Benediction, with the monstrance set high in a picturesque blaze of candles, was rare. The older members of these staid congregations had been conditioned to furtive concealment, and to such expressions as "prayers" and "customers". They found it hard to realise that in law at all events the days of catacomb concealment were over. What they needed, and what they now began to get from one of the outstanding men in our story, was a psychological shot in the arm.

Dom Augustine Baines had been born, in 1786, at Kirkby in the strongly Catholic hinterland of Liverpool. He became a Benedictine, and early next century played a leading part in the community, long resident at Dieulouard in Lorraine, which had lately revived at Ampleforth. He held many monastic offices, and is said to have designed the simple wings now added to an older Georgian house.[31] He was most able and energetic, conditioned to the Lancashire situation where Catholics were often a large part of the population, and could hold their heads higher than in most parts of England. Though Baines, like most "penal" Catholics had no later illusions about his country's speedy mass conversion, he saw that greater assurance and display were needed in the Catholic congregations of the less favoured southern areas. He got his chance to prove his point when in 1817 he took charge of his Order's important station at Bath.

Trafalgar year had seen the building in Bath of a stylish new Theatre. A little later, the Catholics took over the spacious, outwardly un-ornamental theatre building in Orchard Street.* But Baines felt that

* It is now a Masonic Hall.

this was a makeshift. His Journal of 1817–18 shows that he soon thought of a new chapel on a separate site. To gather ideas he visited Wood the Elder's Palladian chapel, with its cupola poised over a handsome portico, near one corner of Queen Square. But for the time a completely new church was impossible. So Baines turned with enthusiasm, and not without the element of controversy so common in his later activities, to the alteration of the one-time theatre. With the assistance of a Bath architect named John Lowder he enlarged his sanctuary. A finely detailed span of classical trabeation was supported on two free-standing Ionic columns and a pair of flanking piers, while Ionic pilasters backed the deep recess (originally the stage) and flanked the altar. In this classical setting, so congenial to his artistic tastes, Dom Augustine spent six highly successful years. He often had Benediction and High Mass and freely exploited his chance "to draw attention to the grandeur and solemnity of our services".[32]

Bath, at this time, was only one among many English spas and seaside resorts. The spa and bathing manias had set in, and the Catholic gentry were as keen as their Protestant social equals in their patronage of the growing resorts. Many chapels were built for their devotions, and in the Midlands and South many towns of this type got Catholic churches of more size and dignity than they could normally have expected. From the columns of the *Ordo* and the *Laity Directory*, and from other sources, many early details can be gleaned on this important aspect of England's Romanist architecture.

At Margate, so the *Laity Directory* of 1804 informs us, a "neat and convenient" chapel had by then been opened. This was the building which so offended Pugin's stylistic sensibility that he would kneel on the gallery stairs so as not to see its main worshipping space.

Cheltenham was now the rising inland spa, frequented by the exiled French royal family and aristocracy. The Abbé César, who had been Louis XVI's chaplain, said Mass in a hotel room.[33] Then in 1809 Dom Augustine Birdsall, a fellow Benedictine of Baines and eventually his antagonist, started a chapel of some importance. Lord Kenmare and the Spetchley Berkeleys were leading benefactors, and as the tramway from Gloucester had yet to be opened for carrying timber and other materials the cost (over £2,000) was much more than it would have been, a little later, during Cheltenham's spectacular building boom.[34] The classical chapel, which was widened in 1825 and which the Victorian Gothicists criticised as being "ill suited for Catholic worship" and "without a single exception the most unseemly religious structure in Cheltenham"[35] was rectangular, 53 feet by 36, and was in the Regency idiom so typical of Cheltenham's period of plain surfaces and delicate ironwork. A Guide of 1818 called it "neat and commodious", mentioning its roomy gallery and a capacity of 300.[36] Baines, who was there in 1817, thought it "neat and very chaste".[37]

In Hampshire, according to the *Laity Directory* of 1812, the builders of the chapels at Sopley and Burton appealed to Catholics coming to the "commodious bathing place" of Christchurch, while those at Harrogate found places in a special tribune in the Benedictines' chapel at Knaresborough. At North Shields the church of 1817-21 was a building of some ambition, by Robert Giles a local designer. It had side lancets, and a set of "Decorated" windows below its unusual feature of a western tower. Much money came from the Dunns, a well-known, prosperous family of Tyneside Catholics.[38] But when more was needed the appeal went to those who came for seabathing, one assumes to the budding resort of Whitley Bay.[39] At Darlington, a few years later, the Catholic chapel's enlargement was partly aimed at those who attended the spa at Middleton,[40] while at Carlisle both holidaymakers and residents might attend Catholic services. For when in 1823 plans were afoot to build the "plain new chapel", whose broad, high-pedimented frontage survives as that of a Church of Scotland church, its sponsors explained that this was the nearest Catholic church to the increasingly visited Lake District.[41] Lastly, we hear of a "neat, respectable" new chapel built at Leamington in 1827-8, with its good Ionic, pedimented façade sympathetic to the Grecian *genius loci*. That stylish spa must have been popular with upper-class Catholics, for the chapel held 500 people, and its benefaction list reads like a goodly roll-call of England's most devoted "penal" families.[42]

These families also helped, by the late 1820s, in a modest restoration of monastic life; here again one sees how great and lasting a debt is owed to them for the sites, and initiation, of much current Roman Catholic activity in England.

The English Benedictines of St. Gregory's, Douai first settled in the Smythes' Shropshire mansion of Acton Burnell, while at Ampleforth the house occupied by the community in 1802 had been built in 1793 as a home for the monk who had been chaplain, two miles away, to the Fairfaxes at Gilling Castle.[43] We have seen how Dom Augustine Baines is said to have designed the wings which had soon to be added.

The refectory block, the ceiling of whose dining hall is adorned with Grecian plasterwork and held up by two rows of Greek Doric columns, was run out at the back between 1818 and 1820. By now, moreover, a scheme for some much more ambitious buildings was afoot at Downside.

The Benedictines at Acton Burnell had migrated to Downside, high up in the Mendip country, in 1814. The first chapel for the small community and their school had been a downstairs room in the square, mullioned country house of the late seventeenth century. Then in 1820 they decided to spend not more than £3,000 *ad aedificandum Collegium et Sacellum;* their actual outlay, by 1822, was £6,628 7s. 3d. Three designs were considered, and Catholic architecture now comes into the fascinating sphere of architectural might have beens. One design was for a Grecian church and attendant buildings. Another allowed for a repetition of the mullioned house, the intervening space containing a lofty Tudor Gothic chapel. The chosen plan, by the young Bath architect H. E. Goodridge, was favoured because it was in "our national style".[44] This building was the most ambitious so far erected for the uses of England's reborn monasticism. An L-shaped block, quite unlike a medieval monastic quadrangle, contained classrooms, a public study room, and bedrooms in one wing; the other had a vaulted, apsidal chapel above a library and refectory. The style is early English; the main frontage and the chapel interior are convincingly so. Augustus Pugin admired the detail, and though some touches of Wells appear in these buildings, with their facing of Doulting stone, it was from Salisbury Cathedral that the architect is said to have culled many elements in his design.

The Friars also created new settings for the religious life. The Dominicans had long worked near Hinckley in Leicestershire, and there in 1822–4 they built a large late Georgian house as a priory and the headquarters of their small, slowly growing English province. The adjoining chapel was simply classical; a turret with a cupola and a more ornately Renaissance sanctuary followed later in the century.[45]

Parochial chapels, sometimes replacing older and cruder buildings, were now widely built. Gothic and Classical were the competing styles, and in both types of churches Grecian mural monuments were now more in evidence. Ignatius Bonomi, Joseph's son and pupil, moved north to Durham where he worked for the county authorities and also, in 1827, built his pleasing little Gothic church in the Elvet part of the city. Gothic was also chosen, the same year, for the charming little apsidal chapel at Chepstow. Its pointed tunnel vault has a criss-cross of thin ribs and rosettes, while the façade, with its curious pinnacles, is a naïvely ungrammatical blend of "Decorated" and early Tudor.

Among classical Catholic churches of these immediately pre-Emancipation years few were more imposing than Willow Lane Chapel started in Norwich in 1827. Its designer was John Thomas Patience, and its building arose from secular and Jesuit tensions not unlike those at Wigan.[46] This was the Jesuit stronghold, most handsome with its fine Corinthian altar end. Outside, the façade is in two tiers, blind arches and Corinthian pilasters appearing above a low Ionic colonnade which recalls the longer one at St. John's in Wigan. In Nottingham the George Street chapel replaced a tiny late penal one in 1828; it is now a wholesale book store. It is brick-built in a plain "Methodist" manner, but with a stone façade of some pretension and traces of a cross in the triangle of its pediment. Edward Willson of Lincoln, an antiquary and a collaborator of John Britton and of the elder Pugin, was this chapel's designer, a new name in our list of Catholic architects.[47]

In Liverpool, Irish immigration had now become a strong tide and new churches were much needed. St. Patrick's was built to serve the southern portion of the expanding town. It was opened in 1827, but had been started six years before, and a rainwater head is dated 1822. John Slater's design was said to combine elegance, economy (at about £9,000), convenience, and large size. The church's bulky dimensions, and its spacious galleries on simple Doric columns, provided for the vast congregations who from an early period had weekly High Mass and Benediction, while the particularly splendid "flowers" for the chandeliers, the outward curving Communion rails, and the large altarpiece with its bold trabeation and two great Corinthian columns displays touches of elegance.[48] What makes St. Patrick's outstanding is its western composition. The central part, quite striking with its bold cross in the pediment and a large statue of St. Patrick, is what one might expect. But two flanking porches, which also contain the gallery stairways, are cleverly made into western transepts, each one as high as the main façade and with its own four-columned Greek Doric portico.

Our last thoughts in this chapter must be on some buildings by

Joseph Ireland, on the final activities of Bishop Milner, and on his successor in the Midlands, the energetic, sanguine Bishop Thomas Walsh.

Joseph Ireland achieved considerable standing in the architectural profession. He was Ignatius Bonomi's pupil, and in 1808 started exhibiting at the Royal Academy.[49] When a project was afoot for a national monument to Waterloo he made plans for an elaborate building modelled on the Pantheon in Rome.[50] Like most contemporary architects (particularly over churches) he had to be "bilingual" in Grecian and Gothic.

In 1823 he travelled to Walsall, where the Catholics contemplated a new church. For twenty guineas he made a set of Gothic drawings, but the scheme was postponed.[51] In 1825 he was there again. A new site had been chosen and Ireland there made "on spot sketches", for the large, gaunt, unporticoed church completed in 1827.[52] The Grecian excellence of its interior belies the baldness outside, and a shallow-arched, coffered ceiling leads up to an East wall made splendid by four correctly Ionic half-columns.

Ireland's next Midland journey brought him directly into contact with the ageing Milner. For in January, 1826, he was at Wolverhampton to discuss the enlargement of the existing chapel. On "mature consideration" the decision was for a wholly new building. Despite what Baines had said about Milner's abandonment of "antiquities" the antiquarian spirit was strong in Ireland's first set of drawings. For they were, to quote him, "in the Gothic style of Henry VII,[53] and by 1826 a far more correct version of such buildings could be produced than in the 1790s when Carter had worked for Milner at Winchester. But Milner died that April, and no Gothic chapel was ever built behind the early Georgian house at Wolverhampton. Yet it seems that when in another two years Ireland built a chapel at Tixall the new work was from drawings like those unused Wolverhampton plans. For the Tixall Chapel is that which was later re-erected across the Trent valley at Great Haywood. That remarkable unaisled church, with its tall traceried and embattled turret, its excellent porch, its rich interior panelling, and its transomed, square-headed side windows, is convincingly "early Tudor" or "Henry VII".

What happened at Wolverhampton, under Bishop Walsh the new Vicar Apostolic, was the building of the present St. Peter's as a memorial to Milner, whose tomb is in the crypt. Gothic was jettisoned, and the

7 *Galleries in Birmingham*
   (a) *St. Peter's, 1786*
   (b) *St. Michael's, 1802*

church by Ireland is an attractive T-shaped Greek Revival building. Its nave is lit by lunettes, and has coffered cross-arches and delicately detailed pilasters. Light pours down on the sanctuary from the hidden lantern of a dome; another dome lights the South transept which may have been an older chapel's sanctuary. The church was opened in 1828, with High Mass and an eloquent sermon by Dr. Weedall, soon the enthusiastic patron of Augustus Pugin. [53]

Bishop Walsh, pushing on regardless of finance, soon started a vehement campaign of church extension. He had no particular views on style; he was, however, a stickler for scale. He had appreciated Lancashire's large Catholic flocks and churches, and resolved that "Staffordshire must be a second Lancashire".[54] In 1828 and 1829 he corresponded with Dr. Kirk of Lichfield, where in 1803 a chapel had replaced a stifling room above a bakery. Dr. Kirk was planning a new chapel at Farnworth. His bishop urged him to be sure of a sufficiently spacious building. He urged that he must not, when building look to *actual* numbers, and declared himself "an enemy to small chapels in these days".[55] He wanted all new churches to be capable of inexpensive enlargement and lofty enough to admit later galleries. For Thomas Walsh the prospects were fair and the atmosphere electric. By 1830 Dr. Kirk finished the roomy, brick-built and stuccoed late Regency chapel whose southern wall, and whose flat ceiling, remain as parts of a building sympathetically enlarged in 1956. His architect was the man who soon enlarged the Lichfield chapel in a strange blend of neo-Norman and "Transitional" pointed Gothic. He was Robert Potter, of Lichfield itself. Very shortly he worked as the main designer of what one may call the architectural *alma mater* of the "Second Spring".

8 *Liverpool, St. Patrick's, 1827*
 (a) *From the Street*
 (b) *Sacrarium and altarpiece*

Chapter IV

THE GOTHIC TIDE

In 1793 the Silvertop family, well-known Catholics in the Newcastle district, built a new chapel on their land at Stella in the Tyne valley. Within forty years another had to be erected. For the earlier building lay in the track of the railway projected, and soon laid out, between Newcastle and Carlisle.[1] This was not the first time that railway engineering caused the resiting of an English Catholic church. But this early occasion symbolised another, socially deeper change in English Catholicism. For the growth of transport and manufactures, and of a great industrial population, caused the steady urbanisation of the Catholic body. The townward flow of Catholics who once dwelt in villages or country towns, and then in the 1840s the vast influx of hungry, destitute Irish, swung the balance of Catholic strength from manorial estates to the streets, and often to the slums, of teeming railway centres, busy ports, and smoky factory towns. The amount of churchbuilding increased, while the two decades after political Emancipation also saw vigorous tensions between devotees of the available building styles.

Despite the Gothic advance some work of the 1830s and 1840s suggested that the classical disciplines were by no means played out. Some admirable work was by way of additions, improvements, and renovations to churches built in the plain, barnlike manner which many Catholics felt safe in the first years of their freedom.

Between 1826 and 1829 a large, plain, brick-built chapel had been erected in Hull from designs by an architect named John Earle.[2] Many were displeased with the barnlike baldness of this building. It was pointed out that the chapel was "susceptible of ornament" when money came to hand.[3] So in 1834–5 J. J. Scoles,[4] now busy both on classical and Gothic commissions, added plentiful ornament. The façade of St. Charles's received a Corinthian porch, side doorways, and other Italian Renaissance adornment, much of it imitating stone in Roman cement. At the sanctuary end four Ionic half-columns carried a rich entablature and a tempestuous sculptured group of the Trinity whose feeling is all Austrian Baroque. Well over £1,300 went on a new priest's house, and on these concessions to a growing urge for unshamed display.

More conventional, but also striking, were some changes at Claughton, and at St. John's Wigan, giving those churches what must then have been Lancashire's most splendid altar groupings.

At Wigan the Sanctuary was refurnished in 1834–5. J. J. Scoles, already working for the Jesuits elsewhere in Lancashire, carried out the work and made sketches for the High Altar.[5] So his, presumably, is the splendid Renaissance grouping above and behind the actual altar table. A stately, circular Corinthian *tempietto* (whose dome was later refaced with scagliola) covers the Exposition Throne and a Calvary rising conspicuously behind it. Scoles could also have designed the fine altar erection at Claughton on Brock. For in 1837–8 the Rev. Henry Gradwell spent over £1,300 on extending, and more splendidly furnishing, his chapel.[6] His altar erection is less graceful than that at Wigan. But with its tabernacle enclosed by a low Corinthian colonnade, and with a domed canopy above an angel-flanked Calvary, it is clearly of the same artistic family.

The church at Weld Bank, Chorley got a new façade, and a tower with a cupola, in 1845,[7] while at Lowe House, St. Helens successive alterations commenced in 1836 added a longer nave, transepts, and a tower with an ornate cupola to the simple chapel of 1793. Threefold "Venetian" windows were freely used, and the changes gave the church an opulent, assertive Renaissance air.[8] Complete replacements and wholly new buildings also proved the lasting devotion of many English Catholics to the Renaissance tradition.

At Worcester the Jesuits had already finished a handsome new church in 1829—Emancipation year. In the 1880s it received many high-Renaissance alterations, but its central section remains in a fairly unaltered Grecian state. An engraving and a photograph show that Henry Rowe its architect first gave it a dignified, pedimented Greek Doric façade, with two fluted columns *in antis*, and between them a sarcophagus above a pedimented doorway. Inside, as at Bath after Baines's changes, two Ionic columns flanked the sanctuary approach.[9]

Across the Midlands, at Grantham, the year 1832 saw Wilson of Lincoln completing a delightful little classical chapel, built at his own cost by Canon Tempest, of a wealthy Yorkshire family.[10] Unlike most Catholic churches of those days it proudly boasted a western tower capped by a graceful cupola. A cupola, not unlike that at Grantham, also adorned one end of the finely masoned, rectangular Catholic chapel built, in 1836, at Chipping Norton. Two well-to-do ladies provided money for what was, in the reign of William IV, an exceptionally good building for a new mission in a South Midland country town.[11] Its sculptured porches are of an unusual excellence, and one hopes that the cupola will rise again after the drastic repairs and liturgical rearrangements which are now (1966) in progress. Another church in the spa or resort tradition was that at Brighton, replacing Mrs. Fitzherbert's private oratories and an earlier, more central chapel. Mrs. Fitzherbert herself persuaded Lord Bristol to donate the site, and gave £1,000 towards the building work.[12] With its pediment and Corinthian pilasters it is still an adornment to Bristol Road in Kemp Town. Started in 1835, it was opened in 1837, just in time for the last rites of its chief benefactress. It contains her famous monument, with three wedding rings on her left hand. The carver was John Edward Carew, the Irish-born sculptor; he also carved the tablets at Old Hall Green whose portrait reliefs, with their flanking mitres and missals, commemorate Bishops Poynter (d. 1827) and Robert Gradwell who died in 1833.

Far from Brighton, in the little tongue of Derbyshire which spills over the Pennines into the cotton country, All Saints' at Glossop was opened in 1836, a building of interest for its obvious derivation from another Derbyshire church. The place had strong Catholic links, and its church was a larger version of Ireland's "Tuscan barn" at Hassop, though devoid of a portico and with a row of Doric pilasters instead. John Gray Weightman, who had been in the offices of Charles Barry and C. R. Cockerell, is given as the architect. But his young partner Matthew Ellison Hadfield, born at Glossop itself and with a maternal uncle who worked as the local agent for the Duke of Norfolk,[13] may also have had a hand in a building which links us to later architects whose work was anything but classical.

Here and there an important public chapel was still built as an annexe to some country mansion. Among the best is at Everingham in Yorkshire, completed in 1839 as the proud successor of chapels which long existed in the mansion of the Constable family. The church built by William Constable-Maxwell is said to have been modelled on a hospital chapel at Nîmes,[14] but the basic design was more probably worked out by a Rome architect, Agostino Giorgioli. In their turn, these plans seem likely to have been rendered on the spot by John Harper,[15] a young architect from Catholic Lancashire whose classical training had been under Benjamin and Philip Wyatt, and who had helped to design the memorial column to the Duke of York. By 1838 he was in practice in York, being a friend of Etty the artist.[16] The Everingham chapel is of truly Roman magnificence, an early Victorian equivalent to Wardour. A marble altar from the Papal capital was set in an apse, backed by fluted Corinthian pilasters, and roofed by a vault whose coffering is set diamondwise. Corinthian three-quarter columns adorn the walls of the nave, while between them the chapel's sculptured decoration (by Leopoldo Bozzoni from Carrara) displays a wealth of large statues and narrative reliefs.

In the Catholic strong-point of Lancashire, another Liverpool church was remarkable for its eventual style and for the dimensions needed by its large congregation.

The wide highway of Scotland Road, described in 1832 as "one of the finest and best frequented avenues in the town",[17] also intersected a populous Irish district. For some years from 1804 the Abbé Girardot served a chapel which was his private missionary venture.[18] When he returned to France the area came under the Northern Vicar Apostolic. Another church was needed, so in 1829 the local architect John Broadbent, another of Rickman's pupils, made some finely detailed plans for a galleried Ionic church which would have had an excellent West tower with a cupola.[19] But no Grecian church was ever erected in Scotland Road, and when in 1832-3 the present St. Anthony's was built Broadbent's designs were in Rickmanesque Early English.* The building Committee pointed out that the church was to hold 1,700 people *without galleries*.[20] Its length was 158 feet 6 inches, and its width

* About this time, Rickman himself designed the "Perpendicular" Catholic church at Redditch.

nearly half as much; such dimensions made it outstanding among the Catholic churches of its time, and fully on a par with the most commodious products of the Anglican "Commissioners". A crypt lay below it, and to control the "effluvia" a grouted arch was carefully built over every grave.[21] The opening in July, 1833, was a major event, with a band and a special choir at High Mass, and a sermon by Baines who thus revisited his native district.[22] The total expense, by August, 1834, was just over £12,470.[23]

The church itself, bar a few furnishings and despite much adjacent bombing, is essentially as it was when new. The façade onto Scotland Road has lancets and a projecting central section; all the lancets, the buttresses, and the fine arched recesses for the three altars, are in a grammatical thirteenth-century idiom. What most impresses is the church's vast, unpillared internal width; from the original pews in their four blocks all worshippers can readily see the altar. Like others of its date, this "pre-ecclesiological" church is better suited to modern liturgical needs than the more ambitious efforts of Pugin and his followers.

Further north in Lancashire three churches commenced in the 1830s threw light on a still lively stylistic controversy.

Church expansion now got under way in the largely Catholic town of Preston, the Jesuits having charge of most parishes. In 1832 they bought some empty ground north of the town, and there between 1833 and 1836 they built St. Ignatius', whose correct Perpendicular contrasts with the demure late Georgian St. Ignatius' Square which soon enveloped the church.[24] The tower and spire, disproportionately low, comprised the first steeple in a skyline now well punctuated in this respect. Scoles was the architect, and his clerestoried nave, transepts, and short sanctuary (later lengthened by Joseph Hansom into a stately clerestoried chancel) are a good essay in the English Gothic of about 1500. Scoles was simultaneously at work at Stonyhurst, in a very similar vein. The new church for the Jesuit College, replacing a converted stable, was said to be based on King's chapel at Cambridge. Its western pinnacles certainly convey a collegiate impression, but as this clerestoried church is aisled, with arcades of an early Tudor type, the building has more in common with Scoles's church at Preston.

In the south of Preston the bulky new church of St. Austin was built, in 1838–40, by the secular clergy. It was classical, and its designer was Tuach, a local builder who had been Scoles's clerk of works at St.

Ignatius'.[25] Its vast, unencumbered nave has a splendidly coffered, segmental ceiling, and many embellishments in a coarse late Victorian Baroque. At first the exterior was gaunt and barnlike, but a noble Ionic portico made a start for later splendours. Flanking vestibules provided bases for the two lofty Renaissance *campanili* which now give St. Austin's its markedly Mediterranean silhouette.

St. Austin's was opened in 1840, an important epoch for Catholic progress in England. Natural increase, conversions, the appearance of many "lost" adherents, and Irish immigration had caused great growth in the past fifty years. About 1840 the bishops reckoned that their flock in England and Wales now numbered around 452,000. The *Catholic Directory* of the same year announced the number of churches as 457, eighty-eight being in Lancashire. Ecclesiastical organisation was changed to meet new facts, and in this same year, 1840, the four districts became eight. Wales, Lancashire, and Yorkshire became separate districts, while the vast Midland District became the two territories known as Central and Eastern. The bishops still ranked as Vicars, Apostolic, with no officially fixed residences and no cathedrals. But this new subdivision of the country closely foreshadowed the fully constituted dioceses erected in ten years' time. Churchbuilding continued apace, with classicism hard-pressed in a defensive battle against a Gothic upsurge now reinforced by the driving fanaticism of a newly flushed "ecclesiology". Among the few who stood firm for the Greco-Roman tradition was Peter Augustine Baines.

The energetic Benedictine missioner at Bath had in 1823 been made assistant bishop in the Western District. His health soon gave trouble, so he repaired to the greater warmth of Rome, a place to which he took like a duck to water. The Eternal City, with its Baroque splendours unimpaired, and with the area just inside the Flaminian Gate made newly splendid by the neo-classic replanning of Valadier, stood gloriously complete. Not only did Bishop Baines revel in Rome's artistic beauties, but he made himself agreeable in the highest circles. He became so good a friend of Leo XII that the Pope planned to keep him in Rome as a Curial Cardinal; life in the Western District would have been far more peaceful had he done so. But in 1829 Leo XII died. So too did the ailing Franciscan, Bishop Collingridge who was Baines's superior in the Western district. Baines never received his red hat, but returned to Bath to inject a further dosage of *Romanità* into that beautiful Palladian city.

Dazzled as he was with his years amid the un-Gothic splendours of his Church's headquarters Baines was more than ever an advocate of classical churches in England. He took a poor view of much Gothic work which various denominations had lately erected. In a letter of November, 1830 which is largely a vivid tirade on church music, he said that he had noticed, in England, "an aversion to anything in the church being like anything out of it". This, he felt, was why English churches were in "what is called Gothic architecture, and are, unfortunately, unlike anything else in creation, whether among the works of God or man".[26] By now, moreover, he had taken dramatic local steps along the anti-Gothic path.

The Western District, with few Catholics and little money, had no seminary of its own. Despite obvious difficulties Baines determined to repair its deficiency. For this purpose, he first tried to control Downside. A sharp, unedifying, and from the bishop's point of view an unsuccessful dispute followed with his Benedictine brethren. Instead, Baines bought the great Palladian mansion of Prior Park, whose proud Corinthian portico looks down on Bath; it seems, from two explorations of the property he made in 1817, that he had long envisaged some dramatic Catholic use for the house and its flanking wings.[27] He thought that the estate could contain a junior school and a senior training college, also providing a *residenz* where the Vicar Apostolic could live in a dignity befitting his episcopal state. Prior Park, above all, was the place where Baines could express his ideas for the exaltation, within the limits of its English position, of the newly liberated Catholic church. The trouble was that the bishop aimed at strutting on too small a pastoral stage, and that what was credible at Ushaw, and soon at Oscott, was a chimera in Somerset. Bishop Baines, handsome, eloquent, imperious, and remote in his new-found dignity, should really have been a Baroque prince-bishop with Haydn as his *kapellmeister*. As things stood, he could achieve little of his aspirations. Yet he left his mark on Prior Park, and within limits elsewhere in his District. He was also, as Pugin ruefully found when he called, the last, most doughty champion of the "pagan" idioms so loathed by the angry young fanatics for new fashions in churchbuilding. Nor was the contest confined to structures; it touched ecclesiastical millinery. When Pugin would rush tearfully from services with vestments of the "Roman" or "fiddleback" pattern Baines got wrathful in the presence of medievally styled chasubles with pointed bases. There was much

9 *Liverpool, St. Anthony's, 1834*
  (a) *From Scotland Road*
  (b) *a broad interior*

10 *Wigan, St. John's, 1818–19*
  (a) *Classic interior*
  (b) *approach from Standishgate*

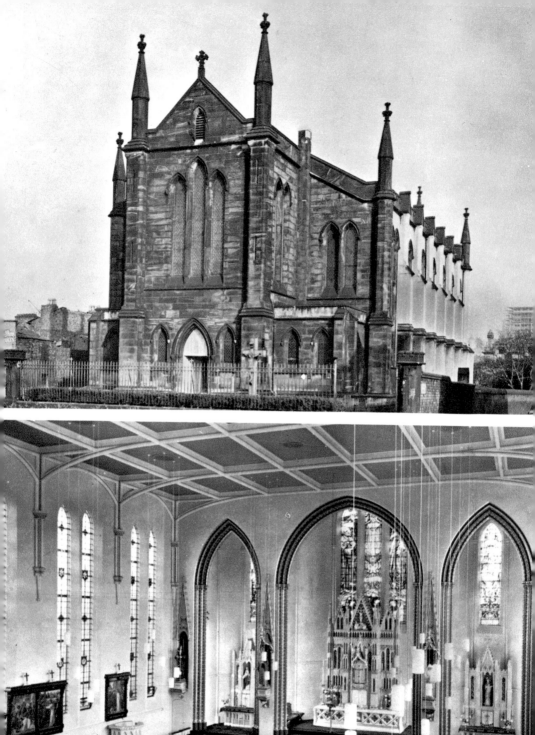

childishness in these honestly vented disagreements over the details of worship.

Baines's main work at Prior Park was the conversion of the service wings into the Colleges of St. Peter and St. Paul, and the laying out, in 1834, of Goodridge's noble stairway down the slope before the front portico. Baroque in conception, inspired by the Spanish Steps in Rome, and planned for Corpus Christi processions, it blends perfectly with its setting, so that I have often found visitors surprised to hear that it is not part of Wood the elder's design. The bishop's other idea was to build a splendid church, cruciform, domed, and with Corinthian porticoes, His site was behind and above the mansion which it would have overtopped, announcing to all Bath that here at least the Roman Church could flourish in glory. But many embarrassments frustrated the scheme. The idea, however, remained in Baines's mind. So when in 1840 the bishop heard that the President of Ushaw proposed to break new stylistic ground and build a Gothic chapel he swiftly wrote, from Frascati, with a version of his unattempted Somerset scheme.[28] He told Dr. Newsham that it was "quite impossible that this (a Gothic chapel) can ever look well", and that he would gladly send designs of a church which "would at once give a character in your College". He rightly judged that a domed church would look splendid beside Taylor's earlier buildings at Ushaw. A rough sketch in his letter shows that he envisaged a version of his scheme for Prior Park, with a dome on a tall drum, and a tetrastyle portico looking south over the deep valley below. But Dr. Newsham was unmoved, went Gothic, and employed Augustus Pugin.

Bishop Baines found some classical compensations elsewhere in this District than on the slopes above Bath. Not everything erected in his episcopate was classical, for when in 1835–6 the Catholics of Lyme Regis built their charming little vaulted church they got Goodridge to work in the Early English Gothic he had used at Downside.[29] At Weymouth Dr. Hartley the priest had long hoped for something better than the "private room in an inferior situation" which served his resident and visiting congregation; he reckoned that a "decent public chapel" would improve attendance. In 1830 he told Baines of his scheme for a chapel in the centrally situated Thomas Street. He thought of a rectangular building with a shallow sanctuary and a "moderately deep" west gallery. He drew comparisons, in matters of size and accommodation, with the local Methodist chapel.[30] When in

11 *Wigan, St. Mary's, 1818–19*
   (a) *Gothic scene*
   (b) *street facade*

12 (a) *Newport, Monmouthshire, Scoles's interior, 1840*
   (b) *London: Redemptorist church, Clapham*

1835 St. Augustine's was built elsewhere in Weymouth it had Corinthian pilasters across the upper tier of a good classical façade. In the same year the Visitation nuns who moved from Shepton Mallet to Westbury on Trym, over the Downs from Clifton, completed their L-shaped chapel (one wing for themselves, the other for the local laity) in a simple classical idiom, a later marble altar lies below an excellent dome which lights the intersection of the arms. Altars of this type seem to have been specially favoured by Baines. So when in 1837 the Benedictine priest at Swansea planned a chapel to replace one to which Mrs. Fitzherbert, who used Swansea as a seaside resort, had contributed he asked the bishop himself to make drawings for the altar, a Protestant gentleman having kindly offered some high-quality marble*.[31]

A new church in his district which must specially have pleased Bishop Baines was St. Francis Xavier's at Hereford. The Jesuits built it in 1837–9, on the site of one opened, in 1792, in a position unusually central for the Catholic chapel in an English cathedral city; the ground came from the Hereford property of the Duke of Norfolk. The designer of the new church was Charles Day of Worcester, the architect of Worcestershire's Shire Hall and of a classical Catholic church at Bury St. Edmund's.[32] Behind a portico with two Greek Doric columns *in antis* a broad, rectangular worshipping space has a gracefully coved ceiling. Nearly all the natural light comes down before the sanctuary from an unseen dome; one assumes that only those whose pews were near the front were expected to follow the service from missals. The altar grouping, between two Ionic columns, would not disgrace Wigan; a Jesuit who knew Rome is said to have designed it. The tabernacle, with its pillared drum and surmounting dome, is fairly closely derived from that by Bernini in the Blessed Sacrament chapel in St. Peter's. The opening, so the Herefordshire paper tells us, was attended by an "extraordinary degree of solemnity and splendour", with a "most effective sermon" by Baines. So strong an assertion of classicism soon drew fire from Pugin, who with typically discourteous fanaticism called this Hereford church a "pagan temple" and a "Catholic concert hall". Baines counter-attacked, and in the *Catholic Directory* of 1840 took "this opportunity of publicly acknowledging the obligation which the Western District owes to the illustrious body

* No church was actually built till Charles Hansom's Gothic St. David's of 1847, much earlier money having gone in the failure of a local bank.

who erected this noble monument"; he went out of his way to regret
the Gothic maniac's "unauthorised and virulent attack".

Far the largest Catholic congregation in Baines's District was in
Bristol. The Trenchard Street chapel was inadequate, so another was
planned, for the more stylish surroundings of Clifton, by a Franciscan
who must have had his bishop's active encouragement. As it is now a
cathedral, I mainly deal elsewhere (see pages 102–4) with this church of
the Apostles. It was started in 1834, the year when Goodridge its
architect laid out the great stairway at Prior Park; in the whole project
one senses an episcopal urge, not least in the scheme's size and ambition.
For had this great classical building been quickly finished it would have
stood out as the largest, most splendid Catholic church in England. But
this half-built shell was temporarily abandoned. In a few years Bishop
Baines, declining in health but not in spiritual vigour, gained unexpected compensation in Bristol. For in 1840 the Catholic Apostolic
Church (or Irvingites) had started a fine classical church in the middle
of the city; Richard Shackleton Pope, a local man, was their architect.
Financially, the Bristol Irvingites overreached themselves, and had to
sell their church cheap, at a loss of some £8,000.[33] The Catholics
bought the building, thus acquiring a splendid church with shallow
transepts, a proud Corinthian sanctuary, and a six-columned Corinthian portico overlooking what was still the open water of one limb of
Bristol's river harbour. On July 5th, 1843 Baines presided, and preached
a somewhat uneirenical sermon, at his final triumph, the opening of
St. Mary's on the Quay. He returned to Prior Park. Next morning his
valet found that the bishop had died in his sleep.

By the year of Baines's death the new school of Gothicists was pro-
lifically at work. Yet all denominations, particularly in the North,
still built Gothic churches of the "pre-ecclesiological" type. Details,
almost always "Early English" or "Perpendicular", were increasingly
scholarly and "correct", but planning was often boxlike and basically
Georgian with short sanctuaries, galleries, and a church's whole
atmosphere but slightly influenced by the neo-medieval fantasies which
gained impetus from some of the Waverley novels, and found expression in the inanities of the Eglinton Tournament of 1839. Before we
plunge into the Puginian upsurge we have still to notice a few Gothic
churches put up for the Catholics just before and soon after Victoria
became Queen.

The designers of these churches were not necessarily Catholics, for the time had not yet come when the Roman Communion in England could provide enough architects from within its own ranks. So in 1836 the Newcastle architect John Green designed the church at Alnwick whose attractive, fairly complex façade in the thirteenth-century manner is part of a grouped urban frontage.[34] The famous John Dobson of Newcastle, an architect whose Gothic was not that favoured by the Cambridge Camden Society, designed the group of church, school, and house which the Benedictines put up, between 1842 and 1844, for their old Durham mission at Birtley.[35] Coming South, we find good pre-Tractarian Perpendicular in the large church of 1835–8 at Banbury, chief centre of a staunch pocket of "penal" Catholicism. With its wide plaster-vaulted nave, an apsidal sanctuary, and a pinnacled tower, very tall for what was nominally an illegal structure, it followed the designs of a Mr. Derick of whose religion I am unaware.[36] The Perpendicular style, again with a dignified tower, was also used for the granite-built church commenced at Penzance in 1840, and contrived with pillars for eventual aisles embedded in its walls. A little later this fine church was said to be the "best ecclesiastical fabric in the diocese of Plymouth".[37] I doubt, knowing the Cornwall of the 1840s, that its architect's faith was that practised inside it.

Back in the North, Ignatius Bonomi's largest church for his coreligionists was St. Mary's, Sunderland, completed in 1835. Like St. Anthony's at Liverpool it is a fine "broad church", with a flat ceiling over its roomy nave, a short sanctuary, and the whole building in the "Early English" best displayed in the street frontage.[38] At Worksop, where Howard influences had always maintained a large Catholic body, the young M. E. Hadfield designed an excellent, commonsensical church of 1838–9.[39] The Duke of Norfolk paid, and this no doubt, accounts for the church's quality. "Perpendicular" was chosen for a fine five-bayed nave, unaisled so that all see the altar and the pulpit, and broad but nobly covered by a hammerbeam roof.

Two of Scoles's churches were worth noticing before he too conformed to ecclesiology. The St. John's Wood area was growing as a genteel London suburb, and there in 1833–6 the church of Our Lady, Lisson Grove was built by two benefactresses, the Misses Gallini. Some controversy, as between Jesuits and seculars, had arisen over its staffing[*]; the actual building is also of note. Its eastern part has been much altered

---

[*] For the details, see Bernard Ward, *The Sequel to Catholic Emancipation*, Vol. I pp. 57–64 and Appendix D.

since Scoles's time. The church is in London stock brick, with stone dressings, in the style of about 1230. Its "dog-tooth" decoration, its lancets, the wheel window, and the pinnacled buttresses of the western façade, are all of some merit. More so is the nave, with its five bays, and with the pillars supporting the plaster vaults having wooden cores and iron shafts to make them thin and unobstructive. The aisles being as high as the nave the effect is that of a "hall church"; the architect may well have been mindful of the famous choir in the Temple.

This idea of an "open", visually united church also appeared in Scoles's church of St. Mary whose towered, arcaded façade is prominent in Spring Hill at Newport. The dates were 1838 to 1840, and most of the style is correct Early English. As chapels lead off the eastern part of both aisles, the sanctuary end, with a shallow recess for the main altar, is five compartments across. All the church's arches rest on the thinnest of pillars, circular, of cast iron, and even more spindly than those in the Lady Chapel at Salisbury. This same effect had appeared in the Anglican Holy Trinity, Trowbridge, and Scoles used it again, with slightly thicker Irish limestone pillars, in St. Francis Xavier's at Liverpool which he started in 1842 for the pulpit-conscious Jesuits.[40]

Another church in Lancashire suggests that John Harper's early death was a real loss to English Catholic architecture. St. Marie's, Bury was built in 1841-2, in Perpendicular with an admirable six-light East window and a spacious, aisleless nave. The church faced the busy Manchester road, so Harper took his chance of a dramatic western composition. An early Tudor porch lies below a large, transomed West window. Surmounting the gable (itself overtopping the nave) a great lantern tower, ornate with its pinnacled buttresses and openwork battlements, is a grander version of that which crowns the West end of St. Helen's at York, where Harper worked.

By 1840 a vital Catholic building had been finished, closely linked to Augustus Pugin's name yet not much of it designed by him.

The Midland school and seminary soon outgrew Old Oscott. Dr. Weedall the President boldly arranged to build another college, two miles away on the hilltop site of New Oscott which looked down across open fields towards the smoky, still distant spread of Birmingham. Between 1835 and 1838 the three-sided court, with its chapel and service buildings balancing each other on both sides, was built at the daunting cost of £23,859 18s. 4½d.[41] The surviving accounts throw much light on the process of building. Though red brick was the main material stone also came from such sources as Tixall, Yorkshire, and Painswick. As railways had yet to reach that district materials arrived in canal barges. Ten pounds were paid to the Oxford Canal Company for a special crane at the nearby Tyburn Wharf, and the payments include many to "boatmen" who ferried the goods. Potter of Lichfield, for a commission of £1,000, was the supervising architect. When Pugin came along he only suggested the oriel above the main doorway and added a vaulted apse to the rectangular, perpendicular chapel with its timber roof. Potter's work is restrained and workmanlike, with wide *ambulacra*, like those at St. Edmund's and Ushaw, set within the blocks like the cloister alleys of some medieval friaries. His style, however, is not medieval but the simply-windowed, multi-gabled educational late Tudor of the Elizabethan court in St. John's at Cambridge. For medievalism of a more Plantagenet type one turns to the outer gateway. Here Pugin worked in the more flowing idiom of the fourteenth century now favoured among Victorian Gothicists. His building recalls the gateway of Stoneleigh Abbey elsewhere in Warwickshire. More significantly, it is somewhat like the lower gateway which Pugin built, in the romantic Staffordshire gorge of the Churnet, for the owner of Alton Towers and the patron of his heart, John Talbot the sixteenth Earl of Shrewsbury.

Chapter V

THE PUGINITES

At Burnley, Sheffield, and elsewhere in the North, and in the Mayfair district of London, there are "Puginesque" buildings whose architectural authorship reminds us that Augustus Pugin was not the only designer of the 1840s who built Roman Catholic churches with a layout and style displaying the new influences which had now become dominant, and which long maintained their hold.

The personality, and the Gothic preferences, of Augustus Pugin were much conditioned by his family background. His father, Charles Auguste Pugin, was a Frenchman of good family who fled to England from the Revolutionary Terror. Unlike the fugitive *abbés* he abandoned his religion. He obtained employment, at Carmarthen in West Wales where Catholicism was anyhow hard to practise, as a draughtsman with the rising architect John Nash. Though Nash was a classicist as well as a practitioner in "romantic" Gothic this Welsh period was one when the local scenery, and Nash's contacts with some gentry in Wales and its Marches, made him specially prone to Gothic influences, and to growing ideas on "the picturesque". Thomas Johnes of Hafod, Payne Knight in his mock-medieval "castle" at Downton, and Uvedale Price the apostle of the picturesque may all be reckoned among the formative influences on the two Pugins.[1] More important, for Charles Auguste and also for the precocious young son who followed his father as a designer draughtsman, was the elder Pugin's later employment, in London, on drawing and sketching for the firm of Ackermann and as a close collaborator with the antiquarian John Britton who had already formed the strong opinion that "Gothic" and "Christian" architecture could be exactly equated. Such was the aesthetic atmosphere in which the young Pugin received his arduous grounding. He did not invent the notion that Christian architecture must only be Gothic; he it was, however, who worked the idea within an ace of death.

Auguste Pugin married an English lady named Miss Welby.* His son Augustus Welby Northmore was brought up outside the Church which he entered, aged twenty-two, in 1834. From his father's family the architect must have inherited his foreign appearance. From the same source he seemingly got his quick, inventive strain. His speed of working, his fiery enthusiasms, the tearful, mercurial emotionalism which greeted his new discoveries, his successes, and his many disappointments, all these one may attribute to these Gallic strains which parted him from the more plodding empiricism of his patrons and fellow designers. Pugin's origins, so much reflected in his career, were also those of a great creative contemporary whose background also included an *émigré* father, abandoned Catholicism, and an English mother, whose inventiveness and nervous energy were those of Pugin, but whose character was unmarred by the architect's personal faults. Resemblances are many between the formative antecedents of Augustus Pugin and of Isambard Kingdom Brunel.

Augustus Pugin's entry into the Roman Church was by conversion. From his close study of England's (mostly Gothic) old churches he deduced that they had been built for worship very different from the services conducted in them about 1830. Historical enquiries suggested that the events whereby the Established Church had gained its position were a less happy process than one read in the history books. He hoped, after 1834, that his conversion would "not . . . be attributed solely to my admiration of architectural excellence"; it is just possible that had he been familiar with Catholic rites in Renaissance churches he would less ardently have accepted the antiquarians' idea that "Gothic" and "Christian" were interchangeable architectural adjectives. But this was, in fact, the proposition for which he lived, and in whose assertion he worked himself to madness and death.

Augustus Pugin's earliest designing experience had been on Gothic furniture commissioned from his father for Windsor Castle as

---

* It was important for Augustus Pugin that thanks to a legacy from his aunt, Miss Selina Welby, he had a reasonable private income.

13 (a) *Old Oscott: the College complete, c. 1815*
   (b) *New Oscott: a bird's eye view*

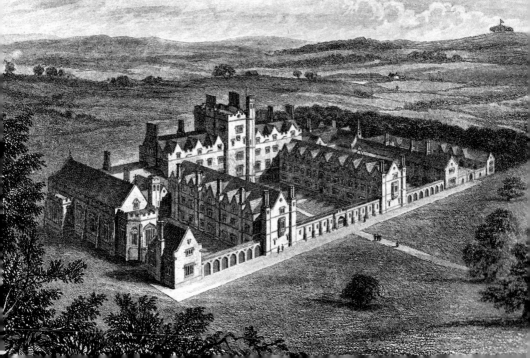

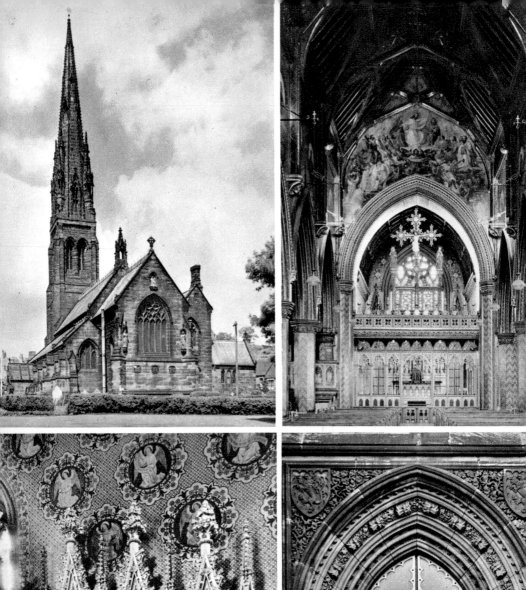

refurbished by Wyattville for George IV. Facility as a draughtsman was always his strong point; it was as a learned, inventive, and sensitive decorative artist that he most truly excelled. His vast decorative schemes for the Houses of Parliament, small details like his seal for the Cambridge Camden Society, some of his altar plate at Oscott, and the illuminated signature on many of his drawings are more convincing than all but the best of his actual buildings. One must, however, recall, that shortage of money caused the watering down of many of Augustus Pugin's most splendid architectural suggestions. Where he went wrong was in the unrealistic supposition that some of his schemes, for Southwark for instance or for a vast church and monastery at Downside, could ever have been built with the funds available to England's Catholics in the 1840s. Romantic visions of a Catholic Merrie England just round the corner did not make for hard-headed dialogue, or realistic *rapport*, between the architect, his patrons, and their bankers.

The architectural work of Augustus Pugin had its distinct phases and periods, less interesting and varied than those of J. J. Scoles, but showing a clear evolution from one set of neo-medieval ideas to another, more romantic, less compromising phase.

The first of Pugin's churches was not, however, Gothic but neo-Norman,* his contribution to the short-lived, somewhat unsuccessful first effort to revive the late Romanesque aspect of England's architecture. J. J. Scoles, with his church at Colchester, and in his large Islington basilica (whose Western towers are later than 1843) also contributed to this curious movement. Pugin's church of 1837–40 at Reading, unaisled, with an apsidal sanctuary, and with its style chosen to accord with the neighbouring abbey ruins, was an interesting expression of the same idea.

Pugin's earliest work was done before the Cambridge Camden Society and the "ecclesiologists" discovered, about 1840, that Perpendicular was "debased" and thus to be shunned. So he sometimes worked in the latest of the English Gothic styles. But his small church at Uttoxeter, commenced for Lord Shrewsbury in 1838 and said, by its architect, to be England's first post-Reformation Catholic church built "in strict accordance with the rules of ancient ecclesiastical architecture", was in an earlier Gothic idiom; a wheel window and

---

* From now onwards in this book my references to "Pugin" are to Augustus Welby Northmore; he must, however be clearly distinguished both from his father and from Edward Welby and Peter Paul his architect sons.

14 *Cheadle, Staffordshire by A. W. N. Pugin*
   (a) *From the south-east*   (b) *General interior*
   (c) *Piscina and Sedilia*   (d) *The "Shrewsbury" doors*

F

other thirteenth-century features appear in the little now left of the church as completed by Pugin. Yet his apse at Oscott, sympathetically to Potter's earlier work, was Perpendicular. More important were three other Perpendicular churches, for two of which the money came from Lord Shrewsbury, now keen on "ecclesiastical antiquities" and from the later 1830s the architect's close friend and enthusiastic patron.

St. Marie's, Derby succeeded earlier Catholic chapels in the town, and was built in 1838–9. As with many Pugin buildings the original scheme exceeded the reality. For the pinnacled West tower was to have had a tall, crocketted spire, while the western approach was to be up a double stairway, and so up a forecourt past flanking houses. The clerestoried nave and short vaulted and apsidal sanctuary alike show the goodness and defects of Pugin as a Gothicist. The five-arch arcades are somewhat weak and spindly, with no capitals to the pillars. The clerestory, in an East Anglian manner, has two windows for each bay; there and elsewhere the windows would have been up to date about 1500. The church's best features are decorative, not architectural. The chancel windows have closely patterned, richly coloured glass by John Hardman of Birmingham; they are, perhaps, the best of many he did for Pugin. The canopied sedilia are in the idiom of about 1340, while the Rood is supported, not by a visually obstructive screen such as Pugin installed in some smaller churches, but by the apex of a gracefully rising, lightly crocketted arch.

St. Alban's, Macclesfield, with the Talbot arms outside to signify its benefactor, was built in 1839–41, the follower of three successive chapels used since penal times. As at Derby, a light, lofty Perpendicular nave of five bays has two clerestory windows above each arch, and the whole building is in late Perpendicular. The short chancel is a fine Puginian dream, with a tall, uncapitalled entrance arch and a late Gothic Rood screen. The magnificent East window is of seven lights; its glass contains Lord Shrewsbury's arms. The altar rails are traceried, Pugin's stencilled decoration survives on the walls, and the richly canopied sedilia are marked *Sacerdos*, *Diaconus*, and *Sub-Diaconus*. These churches at Derby and Macclesfield are indeed a revealing pair.

Another of Pugin's works for Lord Shrewsbury combined fourteenth and late fifteenth century motifs. The Hospital of St. John the Baptist[2] (the Earl's patron saint) was built on the fringe of Alton village, near the ruins of the ancient castle which Pugin incorporated into the romantic *schloss* which he brilliantly poised above the Churnet gorge. A community of retired priests lived there and sang their plainsong offices in the adjacent chapel. The College windows of this grouping are many of them square-headed, and have "Decorated" tracery; their idiom suits a completion date of 1844, for "Perpendicular" was then discredited. But the chapel, dated 1840 in its nave windows whose inscriptions call for prayers for Lord Shrewsbury, is a small, congested little building in early Tudor Perpendicular. It manages to include a four-bay nave, a crowded chancel, and a small northern chantry. The West window has its central light blocked by a canopied statue, but the reredos stays below the bottom of the East window, without lessening the somewhat scanty light allowed by a copious display of coloured glass. Pugin's talent as a designer of furnishings comes out in the Perpendicular screen, and in the chancel pews with their ends topped by "poppy" heads.

The year 1839 had been that in which the Cambridge Camden Society started its devastatingly successful "ecclesiological" campaign.

The Camdenians or Ecclesiologists as they later called themselves, were Anglicans, and also High-Church Tractarians. It was from them that a few Anglican commissions came Pugin's way, among them the design of the Camden Society's ornately fourteenth-century seal. Pugin enthusiastically accepted the Camdenian tenets, expressing these newly fashionable beliefs with a passionate, single-minded, fanaticism all his own.

The ecclesiological movement automatically assumed that "Christian" and "pointed" architecture were one and the same. Norman Romanesque they tolerated. Renaissance and Baroque—the styles of thousands of churches in Europe and the Americas, they loathed and rejected. Their medievalism involved the building of long chancels, of naves with the aisles which Pugin thought essential for really "church-like" effects, and of many towers with actual or projected spires. Into the planning and detail of churches they read much symbolism unlikely to have occurred to hard-headed medieval builders. By the screens which some of them so frantically venerated they parted naves and chancels and obtained the "mystical separation" between those up in the chancel and those down in the nave. There is, indeed, much to be said for the mystical aspects of the Mass, and reaction may perhaps set in against the latest tendency to put altars where all gather round and none are far away. But Mass, as celebrated by the Roman Communion, was not what at first happened in ecclesiological Anglican chancels. Tractarianism and ecclesiology preceded ritualism, and it was long before holy water, incense, and candles invaded such "high" churches as All Saints', Margaret Street. One recalls that although J. M. Neale, the co-founder of the Camden Society, was the first Victorian Anglican clergyman to wear a chasuble that garment never fell from the shoulders of Newman or Manning in their Anglican days. The ecclesiologists largely failed to get back to the Middle Ages. Pugin was not correctly medieval in his altars and altar fittings; one waited till about 1900, and the diligent enquiries of the Alcuin Club, to find, and in "Sarum" Anglican action to see, what had really happened in medieval chancels. Meanwhile, the Camden-Pugin enthusiasts longed to start again where the mid-Tudor Reformers had forced the medieval church in England to leave off. What they failed to realise was that much had happened since about 1552. Their new and renovated buildings paid little regard to the Book of Common Prayer, the Jesuits and other Counter-Reformation stalwarts, or to the Sacred Congregation of Rites.

Even more disastrous was the misunderstanding, by some at all events of these Victorian churchbuilders, of the proper purpose of aisles. In the Middle Ages these had mostly been used for processions, and for the accommodation needed by Guild chapels and chantries. They were not, at Sunday Masses, the laity's sitting or kneeling places. But in many Anglican and Roman churches they were now fitted with pews, being used by people who thus had little visual contact with the service. This was, and is, most unhappy in Catholic churches, where even if chancels are short and unscreened in the post-Tridentine manner only some of those present can see the altar.

The other great ecclesiological innovation was an overwhelming preference for the English Gothic first used between 1230 and 1350. Lancet Gothic was admitted, and as Pugin found in such churches as St. Wilfred's, Manchester, built in 1839–42, it was usefully cheaper than the richly traceried window patterns.* But the ecclesiologists' ideal was the large-windowed Gothic of the Geometrical and Decorated type, with clerestories where they could afford them, but often without them so that some Pugin churches, as at Fulham and Salisbury, are dark inside. The eastern Midlands, and fine Lincolnshire churches like that at Heckington, yielded many patterns for copying. Perpendicular, as

---

* At St. Wilfred's the chief embellishments of a simple "Early English" church are a wheel window, and some trefoiled arcading, behind the high altar.

we have seen, was pushed brusquely aside; the whole movement got shot through with moral fervour and historico-artistic zeal.

It was their fanaticism, overdoing to the borders of heresy the views they had inherited on "Christian" architecture, which exposed its prophets to some sharp critical fire. Pugin's views were never fully accepted by the higher clergy of the Roman church. Baines's death in 1843 removed one opponent, and Bishop Walsh of the Central District seems not to have worried over the style of new churches provided they were large. But Bishop Wiseman, the rising Catholic prelate in England, was never Pugin's complete supporter. Pointed arches he could accept, but his long Roman residence kept him firm for short, unscreened chancels, and for "Roman" rather than "Gothic" chasubles. Lord Shrewsbury was Pugin's more important patron, so too was that keen convert, the Leicestershire Squire Ambrose March Phillipps, later romanticised as Ambrose Phillipps de Lisle. He soon commissioned Pugin to design an outstandingly important monastic group (see page 118). At his own Tudor Gothic home of Grace Dieu Manor, designed and built with a private chapel by William Railton the architect of Nelson's Column in London, he employed Pugin to design some alterations, also new furnishings for the choir services which he carefully revived.[3]

The Gothic dogmatism of the Puginites brought some replies from critics whose Christianity could hardly be challenged, but who could not admit that the Christian religion was somehow lacking in the worshipping places, or in the faith, of the early Saints and martyrs, of the first Popes and the Fathers of the Church, of the great monastic pioneers, and of most saints and devout men and women who had worked at, or since, the time of the Counter Reformation.

John Henry Newman, always an apt and piercing thinker, and by his own admission never a member of the Camden Society,[4] had some classic things to say on the Puginian crusade. In June, 1848, he thrice wrote on these matters to Ambrose Phillipps.[5] He reminded his correspondent that he had called down God's wrath on the Oratorians who had lately started work in the Midlands, and that Pugin had reviled the admirers of the Italian Renaissance. Yet he supposed, for the edification of this zealous convert, that "the Popes had given a greater sanction to Italian than to Gothic". Three days later he told Phillipps that it was "somewhat exclusive" to call Grecian or Italian architecture pagan, and that in classing as doctrinal error the opinions on ritual which varied from his own Pugin was "heretical and a little more". He later reminded the Leicestershire enthusiast that with Pugin the canons of Gothic were "points of faith", and that despite his genius he was intolerant and a bigot. With "only half Christendom on his side" he had excluded the other half (including the Vatican basilica) as pagan; his attitude implied that though Rome possessed doctrinal infallibility all architectural authority was enthroned in Gothic England. In 1850 Lord Arundel and Surrey wrote in a similar vein to an impenitent Phillipps. He felt it strange that the Puginites could forget that "so many Saints have received their inspirations" in the much abused classical churches, and that there were "men of piety on both sides of the question". He had, in all honesty, considered that "much of the enthusiasm on either side was in joke".[6]

Newman's objections to Puginism was not, moreover, confined to theory and doctrine; he reinforced his case with some sound practical arguments. What he needed, in 1848, was not an ecclesiologically authentic church but an Oratory. He was not opposed to Gothic. As a matter of general artistic taste this true son of Oxford preferred it to the Renaissance styles. In 1850 he firmly stated that Gothic, "on the whole", was a far more beautiful architectural idea than Grecian.[7] But he considered that Gothic could be adapted to the needs of an Oratory, and to conform with the liturgical rubrics in force under Pius IX.[8] Pugin vehemently disagreed. He would, so Newman told Phillipps, "as soon build a Mechanics' Institute as an Oratory; when in Rome he had refused to lay eyes on the domed Renaissance *Chiesa Nuova* of St. Philip Neri's Oratorians. "Is it wonderful", the future Cardinal wrote, "that I prefer St. Philip to Pugin?"[9]

Newman's general criticism soon found itself engaged with the liturgical inadequacies, for Catholic requirements in the 1840s, of a particular Pugin church.

In June, 1848 Newman preached at the opening of the church St. Thomas of Canterbury in Fulham. It had been built by his friend Mrs. Bowden. Its churchyard was long the one specifically Roman Catholic burial ground for the more fashionable parts of West London, and many notable Catholics (among them Joseph Hansom the architect and cab inventor) are buried there. Mrs. Bowden had met trouble with her architect. She had said she would have no screen. But Pugin insisted on installing one. The outraged benefactress had it taken out, so Pugin was not at the consecration.[10] Few Catholics then lived in the district. The church, unclerestoried and with three parallel aisles and a pleasant South-western tower and spire, is thus of modest size. Its arcades are simple, its windows are in good "Decorated", and though it has no transverse screen the narrow chancel is parted by side screens from the two chapels. The confined dimensions of the chancel, and the glare from the East window of five lights, were what troubled Newman.

In another letter Newman agreed that this church at Fulham was "very pretty"; but that it had "the faults of Pugin". He agreed that the architect was perfect in his details, but here at least he had found that a Pugin altar was too small for a Pontifical High Mass, and that his East windows were apt to be so large that everything else was hidden by the glare.[11] The trouble was that neo-medieval ecclesiology took no account of the post-Reformation devotions now increasingly common among the Roman Catholics of England. Such rites as Exposition and Benediction demanded that one's view of the monstrance, containing the tiny white Host and flanked by the glowing points of candles, should be backed by a solid altarpiece, not by the translucence of white or coloured glass. But the Puginites, as Newman explained to a later correspondent, would have none of this; to them, as he put it, the Sacred Congregation of Rites was a stumbling block. They exalted architectural style over "higher things". Whereas architecture should be modified as changes came in rites Pugin declared that it should stay as in the thirteenth century, and that though the living spirit should expand the "outward material case" should be static. He would, so Newman felt, "adore mullions and tracery more than the Blessed Sacrament". To his penetrating mind an architectural movement had become "a sort of antiquarianism, or dilettante, unpractical affair for Puseyites, poets, and dreamers".[12]

Yet despite his faults and misapprehensions, and despite the unrealism with which he and his friends rejected much of industrialism and hoped to recapture the splendours of a monolithically Catholic medieval England, Pugin did much for the Church to which he belonged for the last eighteen years of his short, fantastically busy life. One has also to remember that many of his buildings would have been more convincing, and less "thin" in architectural feeling, had there been more to spend. Pugin often did wonders with very small sums, his private income sometimes enabling him to decline his fees. His buildings, and his publicising zeal, gave his coreligionists new visions of glory and ambition, particularly in the building (or starting) of churches with vaunting towers and spires. I shall deal elsewhere with his cathedral, college, and monastic churches; we may glance here at a few which have always been parochial.

Some of Pugin's churches were small because of modest congregations and scarce funds. Such, despite the "raptures" to which it reduced its architect, was the little brick and stone chapel at Kenilworth. So too was that opened, in 1843, in Union Road at Cambridge, not far from the site of the later, and larger, church. Engravings show that St. Mary's on the Sands at Southport was a pleasant little unaisled building when finished in 1841; it was markedly ecclesiological, having a bellcote, many single-light windows, a "Decorated" East window and a screen complete with its Rood. St. Mary's at Liverpool, completed in 1844, was more ambitious; it had a clerestory but never got its projected steeple. It lasted forty years, being exactly rebuilt, not far away, when its site was bought for Exchange Station by the Lancashire and Yorkshire Railway.[13]* The large church at Woolwich, unclerestoried and also in the fourteenth-century idiom, also lacked the tower and spire of Pugin's drawings when it was opened in 1843. It never received them and now, like many Roman or Anglican churches of this time, it is being redecorated in light colours to offset its original interior dimness.[14]

But two of Pugin's churches were free from cramping financial restrictions, and could be built and furnished exactly as he wished. One of them, now the church of a Benedictine abbey, was the early Decorated cruciform building which he built at Ramsgate on a site adjoining his home. The other, only lately in part redecorated and a literally glowing memorial to the aspirations of Shrewsbury and Pugin, was the Catholic church in the small North Staffordshire town of Cheadle, built in six years and opened in 1846.

St. Giles's at Cheadle was built at Lord Shrewsbury's sole expense. He secured a most favourable site where the great steeple rises up over the very middle of the town; few English country towns have so imposing a church for the local Catholics. Though the body of the church, with an unclerestoried, five-bay nave, is moderate in size no money was stinted. Pugin was free to decorate and furnish to his

---

* This church of 1884–5 was bombed in the late war; the Downside Benedictines who serve the parish have replaced it with a modernised Romanesque church by Mr. A. G. Bullen.

heart's content. The pillars, the moulded arches, and the timber roof have more "body" and fullness than much of his other architectural work. The two porches and the south chapel are massively vaulted, and the building's whole style is that of about 1300. Inside, amid a wealth of sculpture, and amid heraldic and religious patterns in bright Wedgwood or Minton tiles, every inch is covered with painted decoration; the recent cleaning of some surfaces does not quite dispel a somewhat overwhelming, gloomy effect. There is, of course, a richly carved and panelled chancel screen. The altars and their fittings are not wholly convincing, and the building has more brasswork than an English medieval church could have contained. One would not, nowadays, wish for many such interiors, yet in this Cheadle church, as in the new Palace of Westminster, a rich period piece reflects the fullness of Pugin's fertile mind. Here at all events he could forget the humiliations of Derby and Fulham, and do as he liked.

More successful than the body of this Catholic church at Cheadle are its truly splendid tower and spire; only the darkness of the local sandstone makes it a little hard to appreciate the full wealth of Pugin's windows, niches, pinnacles, and delicate crockets. The entire composition is some 200 feet in height; from the West one enters the tower by the church's most splendidly ambitious feature. For the oaken doors swing on hinges exactly fashioned as the lions rampant *or* of the Talbot arms; the background is the *gules* of the field, and both are girt by the bordure engrailed *or* which completes the heraldic achievements of Pugin's noble patron.

By the time that Newman wrote to Phillipps on the "heresy" of Puginism the work of other Catholic designers showed how deeply ecclesiological and Puginian ideas had affected them. The Sheffield partnership of J. G. Weightman and M. E. Hadfield, the brothers Hansom, and even Scoles all worked in the newly fashionable vein. They were often more copyist than Pugin. For whereas Pugin's repertoire of detail was wholly medieval he never directly *reproduced* medieval features or buildings of any size. But his immediate disciples made precise borrowings from such places as Selby, Howden, Hecking-ton, and Carlisle.

The Weightman and Hadfield partners (especially M. E. Hadfield) designed two large, important, basically similar churches at Burnley and in Norfolk Row, Sheffield. Both are "Decorated", both have aisled and clerestoried naves, low transepts, and fairly deep chancels with elaborate East windows. Heckington references are specially strong in the Burnley church of 1846-9, but here the western tower is truncated and the spire unbuilt. At Sheffield, with many local Catholics and the Norfolks behind the replacement of the older chapel, a spire duly arose over the business centre of the town. With its many East Yorkshire and Lincolnshire borrowings, and adorned by a Pugin high altar and reredos, St. Marie's was opened in 1850.

Weightman and Hadfield were particularly busy in the North. A rural church of theirs is at Little Crosby, of 1845-7, the only place of worship in an almost wholly Catholic village. Yet again the style is early Decorated. The church is unclerestoried and has a simple, four-arch nave arcade with octagonal pillars; the roof was finely painted and stencilled by some of the Blundell builders of the church. The western tower, and a convincing broach spire beckon across the fields as one strolls over from Blundellsands—one might be nearing any medieval village church in the Midlands or some parts of the North. A more southerly work was Hadfield's small, strongly "ecclesiological" church at Kemerton under Bredon Hill. No steeple was possible here, so as in Pugin's small Southport and Keighley churches a bellcote was put up. Ferdinand Eyston, of the famous East Hendred family, built the church for tenants on an outlying estate; he it was who in 1844 signed the Certificate required by the Act of 1791.[15]

In the brothers Joseph and Charles Hansom two more leading figures appeared in England's Victorian Catholic architecture. Joseph was born in 1803 and Charles in 1817. Their father, a member of one of the many staunch Catholic families in York, was a joiner; the brothers' lives were rooted in that city's Georgian construction trade.[16] Joseph was apprenticed to his father, but branched off to more specifically architectural activity. It was some time before he settled down to the designing of churches. His earlier years were filled with his work as a builder in Birmingham, with the design of the imitation Roman temple which is that city's Town Hall, and with the invention of the even more famous (but to him unprofitable) Hansom cab. In 1842 he founded *The Builder*, the professional journal which still flourishes. Though his Catholic church at Ryde, completed in 1846, is "Early English", another of his early ecclesiastical works is in another style. For the Yorkshire church at Clifford, commenced in 1845 to serve the workers at a flax mill and replacing a disused Wesleyan chapel, is a

striking example of the neo-Norman style briefly fashionable in the
1840s; one pillar has the spiral patterning seen in Durham Cathedral.[17]

As Charles Hansom started later than his brother he could plunge
straight into the Gothic favoured by the Ecclesiologists. An early
patron was Dom William Bernard Ullathorne, the Benedictine who
duly became a bishop but who in 1843 was the parish priest at Coventry.
From then onwards, as one soon saw in Liverpool and Swansea, and
in the charmingly placed little church at Usk in Monmouthshire,
Charles Hansom was the favoured architect of the English Benedictines. St. Osburga's at Coventry replaced the ricketty chapel which was
less than forty years old when Hansom's new church was opened in
1845. He designed a fine clerestoried nave, and a south-western tower
(built later) allowing for an octagonal top stage and a slender spire.
The initial cost, apart from accounts by Hardman for various decorations and from Wailes of Newcastle for windows, was about £5,700.[18]
The style, as often in those days, was the "Geometrical" of about
1290.*

Another Benedictine parish church by Charles Hansom, initially
costing about twice the Coventry building, was St. Anne's in the
Edgehill area of Liverpool. Its nave was built between 1843 and 1846;
the rest is later Victorian. Here the style is early Decorated, and St.
Anne's proved Charles Hansom's talent by being an excellent essay in
the purest ecclesiological Gothic. Many details, including the spandrels
of the West doorway, two ornately canopied stoups, and the whole
conception of the tall clerestoried nave, are fully in the spirit of Pugin
himself. Here again Wailes and Hardman worked on embellishments,
while £371 19s. 6d. went in fees to Charles Hansom. The sum of £50
was also paid to J. J. Scoles, who must have been somehow concerned.[19]

Scoles himself went ecclesiological as the 1840s progressed. The
Corinthian basilican church at Prior Park, commenced in 1844 and
left unfinished during a long period of chequered fortune for the great
property with which Bishop Baines had saddled the Catholics of the
West Country, was sympathetic to its surroundings and was one of
Scoles's best classical works. But by now his most faithful patrons the
Jesuits had capitulated to the new fashion. So ecclesiological Gothic
appears among the many styles in which Scoles designed. His stylistic
progression, from classical through neo-Norman and pre-ecclesio-

* This church was bombed in 1940; it has been restored by Messrs. Harrison and
Cox of Birmingham.

logical Gothic to the Gothic of the Camdenians, makes him a more interesting architect than Pugin and his single-minded followers.

The best known of Scoles's churches is the English Jesuits' head-quarters at Farm Street in Mayfair. Started in 1844, it took five years to build in its original form; the outer aisles and opulent chapels are later Victorian work. Most of it is "Decorated" and of much splendour —a preacher's church with no screen and a short sanctuary, but equipped with a fine altar erection by Pugin. The church was to have been vaulted, and seems at first to have had an almost flat roof of the early Tudor type.[20] Its ecclesiology is somewhat eclectic, for while the great window above the High Altar copies the Cathedral's East window at Carlisle the Farm Street frontage derives from Beauvais.

By 1850 Scoles had worked, more restrainedly, in the Eastern counties. His moderate-sized Chelmsford church of 1847 was said by *The Builder* to be "Early English, or rather transition from Early English to Decorated."[21] But at Yarmouth, another Jesuit commission, he replaced a converted warehouse by an excellent church of 1848–50 whose style is Perpendicular, whose pinnacled tower (without its projected spire) arises proudly at the north-western corner, and whose flint, ashlar, and flushwork exterior deliberately honours East Anglian building traditions.

In 1851, the year before he died, Pugin finished the main structure of St. Joseph's, the church for English-speaking Catholics at St. Peter Port in Guernsey. Its unclerestoried nave, with its aisles extending as far as the end of the chancel, recalled his church at Newcastle which now contained the bishop's throne of the new Catholic diocese of Hexham. The Guernsey consecration was by Cardinal Wiseman, the new Archbishop of Westminster who was also responsible for the unfilled Southwark bishopric whose territory included the Channel Islands. Amid the building of convents and of many parish churches, and amid vast problems caused by their recent, overwhelming numerical reinforcement from famine-racked Ireland, England's Roman Catholics had now to reckon with the matter of Cathedrals.

Chapter VI

SOME CATHEDRALS

===

The visitor to an English cathedral of the Roman obedience has to lay aside nearly all his visions of the cathedralesque. To him an English cathedral is a large church, cruciform and not less than 300 feet long. It mostly dates from the Middle Ages, and though its services are conducted by far fewer resident clergy than those who once dwelt within its precincts the whole atmosphere of quiet dignity, of Mattins and Evensong regularly and beautifully sung, is still that enshrined in "Barchester". The great building's towers or spires arise above the neat lawns and mellow canonries of a Close where cars move only to parking places, and where preference goes to the leisured strolling of sightseers.

For reasons which were unavoidable for England's Catholics of the 1850s not one of their newly constituted cathedrals could match up to these ideal conditions. Few of them had been built as such. Most bishops appointed to these first thirteen sees had to place their thrones in churches built, and mainly used, for parish purposes. The same generally applied to the churches which became the cathedrals of the later Victorian Catholic bishoprics. There were, indeed, some interesting schemes for cathedrals of more architectural ambition. Yet only after 1892 did Westminster, the metropolitan see, start a cathedral whose scale, and whose liturgical routine, would genuinely rival those boasted by the ancient cathedrals of the Established Church.

The setting up of a new hierarchy in England had been discussed for some years before it actually occurred. The northern clergy had petitioned to this effect in 1837, but no more was done than the doubling, in 1840, of the Vicars Apostolic. In 1847, with a new Pope in office, the English bishops returned to the attack. Wiseman and another bishop went to plead the case in Rome. Pius IX soon made the basic decision that England and Wales were to have a normal Catholic hierarchy; this implied that the new bishops would take their titles from towns in their own country, and that their residences and *cathedrae* would be in clearly defined localities. A scheme allowing for twelve dioceses, under an Archbishop of Westminster, was soon sanctioned. Though some delays, and differences over details, now followed it seemed that 1848 would witness the new changes. But late that year the Revolution in Rome, and the Pope's flight to Neapolitan territory, plunged all into chaos and caused further delay. Yet a new hierarchy could now be reckoned as certain. Existing churches could reasonably be earmarked as cathedrals, and new ones could be built on the assumption that their sanctuaries could soon contain the thrones of territorial bishops.

With Garibaldi again in exile, and with Pio Nono back from Gaeta the scheme for English bishoprics was at last carried through. Approval came in the early autumn of 1850, Cardinal Wiseman was now free to issue his bombastic, tactlessly worded Pastoral, and to sally forth from the Flaminian Gate on the long journey to his archdiocese. In the final allocation two dioceses were created in Lancashire, instead of one as originally proposed. In London the Thames divided Westminster from Southwark as in medieval times it had parted London and Winchester. The Archbishop presided over a dozen suffragans. All thirteen, one assumed, would duly need cathedrals. As it happened, the metropolitan see was among the last to achieve that goal.

When a renewed hierarchy was first discussed it was assumed that the London District would remain essentially as it was, and that the Catholics of all London would come under one bishop. In such a case, so it seemed by 1848, the large, ambitious new church in Southwark could be that prelate's cathedral. Its actual planning and building had in any case been a notable episode.

The initiative had come from Thomas Doyle, the energetic priest of the Southwark chapel opened in 1790. As this building was too small for his congregation he wished to build a large church to hold all its parish's worshippers.[1] In a desperately poor locality he slowly raised enough money to make a start. He asked Pugin to design his new building. But Pugin's ideas, though allowing for a spacious nave, far transcended those of Fr. Doyle. What the rector wanted was ample room for his teeming flock. Pugin envisaged a minster-like church which would give London its first sight, since the days of Westminster and St. Paul's in all their medieval glory, of a superb setting for the splendours of revived (and course Revival Gothic) Catholic worship.

Pugin's drawings of 1838[2] could have given us one of the greatest achievements of the Gothic Revival, a transpontine answer to Barry's Parliamentary towers. His cruciform church would have had a six-bay nave, shallow transepts, a vast central tower like that of Lincoln Cathedral, and a short apsidal chancel with a High Altar up many steps. This stupendous church's internal height would have exceeded that of Westminster Abbey. The whole concept, allowing for much "Decorated" detail and including some rather spindly nave arcades, was like an immensely elaborated version of Pugin's church then being built at Derby; its Rood was to be at the apex of a delicately rising arch such as one sees in that Midland building. Pugin supposed that the great church in South London could follow medieval practice by being built in stages as money came in.

One therefore sees that no reasoned dialogue occurred between the client and his architect. The climax came in 1840 when Pugin presented his plans to the Committee. He was asked obvious questions about costs, accommodation, completion dates, and modifications to fit the sum actually in hand. With peremptory rudeness he rolled up his drawings and left the room. He was eventually persuaded to make other designs and these, without the clerestory which they indicated for the nave, were used for the actual St. George's.[3] This was slowly built, and finished without the upper stages of its western tower, and without the crocketted spire designed by Pugin to be 320 feet in height, in 1848. The actual building, with its aisled, unclerestoried nave, and with a fairly deep chancel having two chapels, was more "parochial", and in its "ecclesiological" idiom more of the fourteenth century, than the church designed in 1838.[4] The arcades with their clustered columns and foliate capitals, and the splendid East window of nine lights, improved on the earlier version. Some neo-medieval excitements appeared in the chapels leading off the South aisle, and in the rich chantry of the Petres. That of the Knills, who were Pugin's relatives by his third marriage, was inserted later by Edward Welby

Pugin; among its rich details are some like those of a chapel he designed at Ushaw.

The new church at Southwark was opened in July, 1848. The occasion was splendid, with a massive concentration of bishops and clergy; among the altar servers was a future Archbishop of Westminster, the young Herbert Vaughan.[5] By now the hierarchy was assured, and St. George's was earmarked as the Roman Catholic cathedral of an undivided capital. But when in 1850 Bishop Wiseman (who opened St. George's) came to London as Archbishop of Westminster he found his own diocese without any imposing cathedral. For the rest of Victoria's reign the see made do, at first with the Moorfields chapel and then with George Goldie's large, hideous mid-Victorian Gothic church of Our Lady of Victories in Kensington. It was left to Vaughan to build an even more ambitious Catholic cathedral than that in Southwark.

Frustrated inadequacy also long beset the diocese of Liverpool. The official throne was erected in the Regency Gothic St. Nicholas', a church which was conveniently central and controlled by the secular clergy. But South-west Lancashire's large Catholic population suggested that something more cathedralesque was what Catholic Liverpool really deserved. So in 1853 a decision was made to build a substantial cathedral in the Everton district. The chosen architect was the young Edward Welby Pugin, only nineteen years old and in the earliest, aesthetically most satisfactory phase of his career. His design, which might have been built and which was actually started, was as imposing as his father's first scheme for Southwark; here, moreover, one had a projected cathedral designed from the start as such. It was planned in the early "Decorated" of about 1300.[6] A five-bay choir would have had a gable over each clerestory window. An ornate polygonal chapel, or Chapter House, would have jutted out from its South aisle. Above the crossing a great tower and spire would have been the tallest building on Victorian Merseyside, and the nave was to have had at least seven bays. The easternmost projection was to have been a Lady Chapel, three-aisled in the manner of Salisbury. This was actually built, surviving now as the church of Our Lady Immaculate, Everton; I am told that it is soon to be replaced by a more capacious building. But churchbuilding and educational needs frustrated the rest of the cathedral, and St. Nicholas' long enjoyed its "pro" Cathedral status.

15 (a) *Woodchester, Gloucestershire: church by Charles Hansom*
    (b) *Nottingham Cathedral: reordered choir*

Things were better in the other Lancashire diocese of Salford. When the large church of St. John was started in 1844 it was not on the cards that it would serve as a cathedral. Nor did this status seem likely at the time of its spectacular opening in August, 1848, the ceremonies coming as a northern riposte to the previous month's ecclesiastical junkettings at Southwark. But when in 1850 the county of Lancashire was found to contain two bishoprics of the Roman obedience the new church at Salford was the obvious cathedral for the more easterly diocese. It was cruciform, 200 feet in length with a central steeple and a vaulted, four-bay chancel which looked convincing as a Chapter choir. The church is by Weightman and Hadfield; despite the late Gothic character of its nave arcades its general style is "Decorated". The late Mr. Cecil Stewart pointed out that its designer had copied wholesale, in a way that Pugin never countenanced, from Selby, Howden, and other actual works of the fourteenth century.* Yet despite a certain stiffness, and a mordant coat of South Lancashire grime, their cathedral is not without dignity; in the 1840s it was Catholic Lancashire's most important statement of ecclesiology.

Over the Pennines the Catholics of Yorkshire long lacked a Cathedral. The whole county made a diocese whose title came from the old minster town of Beverley. But the bishops lived at York, and the puny Catholic church at Beverley itself never ranked as a cathedral. When in 1878 England's largest county was split, for Roman Catholic purposes, into Leeds and Middlesbrough the interesting church of St. Anne received the first named throne. It had replaced the Dominicans' chapel in 1837–8. Its architect, a local man named John Child, had built a fair-sized church in late Perpendicular Gothic, with a short sanctuary and a tower and spire.[7] Pugin, who was still in the "Perpendicular" phase of his career, admitted that it was "good, for an early attempt", at the revival of England's medieval glories.

At Middlesbrough, a steelworking town of recent growth and much Irish immigration, the lofty church of St. Mary, by George Goldie who did much Catholic work in his native county of Yorkshire, became the cathedral. It had been started in 1876; in the coming years it was well equipped with painted altarpieces and other furnishings to mark its new dignity.

When in 1842 the energetic Fr. Worswick started St. Mary's church in Newcastle his purpose was to give more worshipping space for a

* See Cecil Stewart, *The Stones of Manchester*, 1956, pp. 49–51.

16 (a) *Monastic Choir: Mount St. Bernard*
  (b) *Cathedral interior: Plymouth*

G

growing Catholic community.[8] Though roomy and fairly ambitious, the church which Pugin designed was not notably cathedralesque. But as the largest Catholic church in the chief town of the North-East it was the obvious cathedral for the new diocese of Hexham (later Hexham and Newcastle). Like the noble classical buildings of the adjacent Grainger-Dobson developments it is marred by Tyneside grime, and the tower and spire (built later by Hansom and Dunn) are unduly massive and high for its unclerestoried bulk. Yet Pugin's "Decorated" church has its good Gothic Revival points. A western window has some "ballflower" ornament, the stone pillars and arches of the seven-arched, continuous arcades are respectably fourteenth-century, and in the well-screened choir the capitals are foliate to denote that area's greater dignity. No clerestory was built, so the resulting gloom has been relieved by some ugly dormers cut in through the roof. Pugin was good at East windows; here at Newcastle his admirable composition of seven lights has the Tree of Jesse by Wailes the local glazier.

The Cathedrals of Cardinal Wiseman's Midland suffragans were more interesting than those in the North; at Birmingham, St. Chad's is on any account a church of historic interest and reasonable merit.

By the 1830s the late Georgian chapel which lay along Shadwell Street was too small; it also seemed to fall behind the dignity of a town which was busily increasing its stock of churches and public buildings. In 1834 a subscription was opened for a more ambitious church. Not enough came in, and the project was shelved. But designs were actually made by the well known Thomas Rickman who then lived in Birmingham. This, I imagine, was the scheme pictured on the first page of a Catholic weekly.[9] The western façade is that featured in the engraving; the building would not have resembled Pugin's St. Chad's. The pinnacled towers, the gabled main doorway, and the façade's general impression would have recalled that of York Minster, still more the version of it lately built in London by William Tite as the Presbyterian church in Regent Square. The main window would, however, have been a "rose", not mullioned. Within the limits of its site this St. Chad's would certainly have been impressive, its dimensions being "truly cathedral" and almost equalling those of Joseph Hansom's Corinthian Town Hall.

When the idea of a new St. Chad's was again pursued Pugin was all powerful in the Midlands as "Professor of Ecclesiastical Antiquities" at Oscott. From a drawing of 1838 preserved in the College it is clear that he made an initial design, for a large church but more modest than the reality and with only one tower. What he actually saw built, between 1839 and 1841, was a building of bulky, massive splendour, but restricted in its length by the fifty-four yards (see page 52) of the Shadwell Street site. By the time that it was opened, and housed the fortunately discovered relics of its patron Saint, St. Chad's was probably envisaged as an eventual cathedral.

St. Chad's is now poised on the very edge of Birmingham's Inner Ring Road; one also sees that its design was much conditioned by the steep slope of the ground. For the site falls away below the transepts and the short chancel. Below this section of the new church Pugin followed medieval precedents like those of Worcester and Canterbury Cathedrals. He built a crypt, and side chapels, in a pseudo-Norman style, which make one imagine that they are older than the rest of the cathedral. In one of these chapels is the grave of Pugin's second wife. Here too, to honour cathedral clergy and others, are some reasonably convincing Victorian brasses of the type also seen at Alton, Oscott, and St. Mary's at Wigan.

Pugin explained that his Birmingham church was in "a foreign style of pointed architecture"; there is, indeed a Germanic or Flemish feeling in the gaunt brick exterior, with its pair of spire-capped towers, and in the steep, continuously falling sweep of the roof over the nave and its aisles. The building's main merit lies inside. An aisled nave leads up to transepts, and then to an apsidal sanctuary with tall windows. This is so short that when St. Chad's became a cathedral the screen was moved West, closing the crossing to make a choir which still seems congested, with its medieval stalls from Cologne and some genuinely medieval Rhineland woodwork included in its high-canopied throne. The Rood screen, well traceried and cusped in the early fourteenth-century manner, is one of which Pugin was justly proud. The most Germanic effect comes in the design of the nave. For the slender, enormously tall pillars and arches support no clerestory and are those of a "hall church"; the full impression of such an interior is lessened by the downward fall of the roof timbers in the aisles. Yet this part of St. Chad's is an inspiring work; it must certainly have seemed so on the grand occasion of its opening (with Gothic vestments tartly criticised by Bishop Baines), in June of 1841.

By the time that St. Chad's was finished work was about to start on a church both larger and more "cathedralesque" than the future Catholic cathedral of Birmingham; it seems to have been more consciously intended for the status which came to it in 1850.*

The church of St. Barnabas at Nottingham replaced the chapel opened in 1828. It stood on a good site in a more westerly, more spacious part of the town, Pugin was the architect, and the ever generous Lord Shrewsbury met about half the cost.[10] As often happened with Pugin churches the original plans were for a building more ambitious than the one actually built. Yet this cruciform church, with its central tower and a spire whose broaches are adorned with canopied statues, was a notable effort. It has an eastern Lady Chapel which is, on its minor scale, in the manner of Salisbury. When the building was opened in 1844 it was the largest English church of which the Roman Communion could boast; its consecration, like the ceremony at Birmingham, was a major occasion. The clerestoried nave has five bays and the choir has three. A modest internal height precluded tall lancets above the two eastern arches looking through to the Lady Chapel, so a wheel window makes an attractive alternative. At first the church had a choir screen, being dim with interior stencilling and painting of the type which soon amazed the Catholic parishioners of Cheadle. Amid the present renovated scene of lighter, more cheerful colouring, with the High Altar now below the tower (and thus seen by those kneeling in the transepts), and with the throne on the original site of the High Altar, the large southern chapel glows brightly with the restored colours of Pugin's mural painting and rich Hardman glass.

What troubled Pugin about this Nottingham church was its lack of large traceried windows. For financial reasons Early English, not Decorated, had to be the style, so that nearly all the windows are narrow lancets. Bar the actual shapes of its pillars the cathedral's idiom is extremely close to that which Pugin used for the first part of the Cistercian Abbey church of Mount St. Bernard in the adjacent county of Leicestershire. What he felt was that the lancet style was "well suited to a Cistercian abbey . . . but very unsuitable to the centre of a crowded town". He said that if five traceried windows had been introduced this Nottingham church would have been a "grand and

* Bishop Walsh of the Central District went to live in Nottingham in the 1840s, and he seems to have thought that there, and not in Birmingham, the headquarters of a Midland diocese might actually be sited. His house, now used by the cathedral clergy, is much decorated with his episcopal monogram.

satisfactory building".[11] He rightly pointed out that its interior was too dark. In the nave aisles, in particular, each lancet is only just wide enough to hold the width of a little shield of Lord Shrewsbury's arms.*

The Talbot family soon found themselves involved in cathedral building in the beautiful town whence they took the title of their earldom. The diocese of Shrewsbury was given Shropshire and Cheshire as its territory. The Catholic congregation in Shrewsbury had used a chapel since 1774 and were enlarging it in 1825. The sixteenth Earl very naturally felt that this was a suitable town for his churchbuilding beneficence, so he obtained plans for a cathedral from Augustus Pugin. Both he and his architect died in 1852; it was left to Edward Welby Pugin to collaborate in the new venture with the young seventeenth Earl.[12]

The fledgling architect designed a large, cathedralesque church for Shrewsbury. But his projected dimensions would not fit the available site. They were altered, and the building started in 1853 was on a modest scale and without its projected steeple. Meanwhile the Earl formed schemes for Edward Pugin to build a large "pro-cathedral", elsewhere in the diocese, in the growing town of Birkenhead. But his death in 1856 frustrated the idea, and though Edward Pugin later made drawings for a large apsidal church, with a stately tower and spire, in the new port,[13] he was lastingly denied the satisfaction of building a Catholic cathedral on each side of the tidal Mersey. The Shrewsbury church was finished in 1856. It was, and is, unlike most people's notions of a cathedral. But like many of Edward Pugin's earlier churches it is a creditable piece of Victorian Gothic. Its plan is that of a parish church as understood by England's Catholics under the Roman influence of Cardinal Wiseman. The chancel is short, with a sumptuous, vaulted chapel leading off it to the South. Each nave arcade has five main arches, plus an eastern one of much less width; their capitals are attractively foliate, and the whole church imitates the style of about 1290. The clerestory windows, like those in the nave at Lichfield Cathedral, are convex-sided triangles. The East and West windows, one of seven lights, the other of six, may survive from Augustus Pugin's earlier design; they well display the family talent for large windows in broad walls.

Edward Pugin's prolific career reached a peak in the 1860s. This was

* Judging by photographs, Pugin's Cathedral at Killarney is clearly out of the same architectural stable as the one at Nottingham.

the decade which saw him working on a new cathedral for the diocese of Northampton, which stretched from Western Northamptonshire to the East Anglian coast. Unlike the western Midlands' it contained no concentrations of Catholic strength. Yet Bishop Amherst, the second holder of the see, decided to replace the small "pro-cathedral", which then remained as an annexe to the one he started in 1863-4. A lofty, clerestoried Gothic nave was built. Edward Pugin's sketches for the complete, early "Decorated" building show a tall north-western tower and spire.[14] Beyond the nave there would have been no transepts, but a long choir, with side chapels and its upper windows crowned by the somewhat fussy little gables which Pugin and other architects were now apt to include in their designs, would have given the finished building the dignity and dimensions of a cathedral. However, the nave at Northampton remained on its own, till in 1954-60 the cathedral was enlarged, and made cruciform, by transepts, a squat central tower, and a short chancel, all "Early English" by Mr. Alfred Herbert.[15]

Our final thoughts must be on the Catholic cathedrals of the two dioceses created out of the Western district.

The city of Bristol was the only provincial town which had an Anglican bishopric as well as its new see of the Roman obedience. To avoid confusion of titles the new bishopric was named after the Clifton district of the city. It was there that the church of the Apostles could serve as a "pro-cathedral". The building itself is one of England's architectural tragedies. It could have been outstanding in the whole country's religious architecture. It is actually the wreck of earlier, ambitious hopes; its main fabric makes it the oldest building among the Roman Catholic cathedrals of England.

I have said (see page 75) that this church was started in 1834, that Baines probably encouraged the scale of its design, and that Goodridge of Bath (then busy on the ceremonial stairway at Prior Park) was the chosen architect. The priest immediately responsible was Fr. Edgeworth, a Franciscan friar. His scheme was doubly hampered. It would always have been hard to raise the money for so challenging a project. The site, though scenically striking, sloped steeply and contained loose, shifting lias rock which made it unable to support the bulk envisaged; many Bristol builders have ruefully found how awkward for their purposes are the view-commanding slopes of their beautiful city. It was here that Fr. Edgeworth and Goodridge proposed to build a great classical church, with a crypt below it to allow for the slope. Corinthian three-quarter columns were to adorn the walls of its nave, whose western end was to be dignified by a noble six-columned Corinthian portico and a sculptured pediment. The pedimented transepts were each to have two Corinthian columns *in antis*, while between them the crossing and sanctuary were to be lit by a tall Corinthian lantern freely based on that favoured model, the choragic monument of Lysicrates.[16] The nave would have been uncomfortably dark, but one imagines that the sanctuary would have been not less splendid than that of St. John's at Wigan. The project, for the largest, most impressive Catholic church in Emancipation England, was a clear challenge to the Gothicists.

The unfortunate Fr. Edgeworth was left to accomplish this Bainesian scheme. He had great trouble with his foundations. Money ran out when the portico was half raised, and when the nave and transept walls had only reached the tops of the column shafts. The gaunt hulk, with its magnificent Bath stone masonry, was abandoned as a roofless shell. So it stood when in 1846 William Bernard Ullathorne came from Coventry as the Western Vicar Apostolic. He resided in Clifton, deciding to make the church usable for immediate worship, and as an eventual cathedral.

Though a local architect named Fripp had "settled" the foundations[17] Scoles had already sent in a gloomy report. But Ullathorne called in Charles Hansom, much applauded for the church he had lately built for him at Coventry. The Bishop told his architect to pocket his reputation and follow instructions.[18] The sturdy Vicar Apostolic had once been a sailor, and he felt that some principles of wooden ship construction might usefully serve his aim of providing a roofed church within Goodridge's masonry shell.

The church started in 1834 was probably meant to be unaisled, with an unimpeded interior. But Ullathorne and Hansom felt that on such a sloping, friable site the outer walls could never carry a broad and heavy roof. So a lighter covering was to be carried by two vertical rows of thin timber balks, cased to make them "stouter to the eye" and leading up to round-headed timber arches a little like those of the Norman period still surviving in the Bishop's Palace at Hereford. Above those main arches a complex of lengthwise beams, of smaller arches, and of crosswise timber ingeniously distributes the weight of the roof. More remarkable was the method whereby this timber roof structure was upheld from below. Beneath the floor the substructure of the church was laid out in two long, parallel compartments, each one being roofed by a shallow, segmental masonry vault. It was near the *crowns* of these vaults, and not on the stouter side walls of the crypt that the timber pillars were made to descend. To cushion the vaults against the full pressure of their burden, and to distribute the weight along the length of the building, the Bishop proposed, below the bases of his pillars, to run a series of beams in a lengthwise pattern. These continuous beams, to his nautical eye, recalled two keels whence the pillars arose like the masts and other central uprights of a pair of ships. The whole contrivance was ingenious, somewhat risky, and aesthetically unhappy. But once Charles Hansom had perfected this ecclesiastical version of "ship shape and Bristol fashion" Clifton's church of the Apostles could be opened in September, 1848.[19] The pinnacled altarpiece installed by Hansom was in the ecclesiological Gothic which he normally favoured; it set the fashion for later Gothic furnishings in what had been planned as a great classical church. Then in the 1870s Charles Hansom was commissioned by Bishop Clifford to start, but fortunately not to finish, a new façade and a complete recasing and obliteration of Goodridge's imposing Bath stone masonry. All the work was to be in Lombard Romanesque, with a tall campanile on one side. An incongruous, arcaded façade, and a covered atrium and a large hall on the site of the never completed entrance portico, were the only portions built.[20]

During penal times Catholicism seems to have become virtually extinct in the area of Plymouth. Late in the eighteenth century, with Irishmen increasing among the sailors of the Navy and the dockyard workers, and with Irish publicans established at Plymouth Dock (as Devonport was then called), a Catholic congregation grew up in the naval town. The first chapel, in 1792, was over an inn stable in Plymouth Dock. Then in 1806–07 a French *abbé* built a chapel, near the Naval Hospital, in the Stonehouse district between Plymouth Dock and original Plymouth. Irish soldiers in the garrison helped to swell the congregation, so in 1828 the sum of £120 15s. od. was spent on a "commodious gallery" in the late Georgian St. Mary's Chapel.[21] Such was the building which served, in 1850, as a makeshift cathedral. It seemed patently inadequate to the well connected priest who became the second Bishop of Plymouth.

William Vaughan belonged to the famous "penal" family of Court-field in the Wye valley. He was related to the future Cardinal Arch-bishop of Westminster, and Cardinal Weld was his uncle. The nine-

17 *Preston, St. Walburge's, by Joseph
    Hansom (a) Apse (by Nicholl) and
    steeple (b) Interior, with roof*

18 *Mixed Victoriana (a) Maidstone, by
    C. G. Wray (b) Ipswich, by G.
    Goldie (c) Dover, altarpiece by E.W.
    Pugin (d) Stanbrook Abbey, altar-
    piece by E. W. Pugin*

teenth century was the time of the Vaughans' greatest ecclesiastical glory, for it was then that they produced an amazing galaxy of priests, nuns, bishops, and archbishops. The future bishop of Plymouth was born in 1814. Educated at Stonyhurst and Oscott as well as in France and Rome, he became a priest in the Western District and held the post of President at Prior Park. While at Clifton he was much involved with the fitting out for worship of the unfinished church of the Apostles. Then in 1855 he became a bishop, remaining for forty-seven years in his far western see.

The bishop soon started a church whose design and dimensions made it worthy of its dignity and large for so sparsely Catholic a diocese. It seems, as it did at Westminster in the last years of the century, that here was a Vaughan "thinking big"; it is said that the bishop gave much of his personal fortune for the furthering of the work. Though some accidents occurred during building operations this church at Plymouth was opened in 1858, the most imposing of England's new Catholic cathedrals to be built as such. Its tall, graceful, incredibly slender spire was added later to the north-western tower.

Despite the placing of its steeple this cathedral is a Devon version of that in Nottingham. Joseph Hansom, then in partnership with his brother Charles, was the architect. As at Nottingham the building is cruciform and in a simple thirteenth-century style, but its paired or tripled lancets keep company with choir or transept windows having "plate" or "Geometrical" tracery. Both the nave and the choir limb have five bays, but the Plymouth building ends in an apse and its Lady Chapel does not project at a lower level than the roof of the choir. Octagonal granite pillars give a westcountry flavour to the nave, but in the choir more pretension was obtained by making the pillars of marble, and by giving them foliate, not moulded capitals. Like many of England's Victorian Catholic cathedrals and churches this Plymouth building has lately been lightened and redecorated. What it has never lacked, with its cruciform plan and long choir, is a genuine feeling of the cathedralesque.

No cathedral was at first established in the Welsh part of the diocese of Newport and Menevia. Outside the border country of Monmouthshire Welsh Catholicism had met with almost total extinction; the Anglican dioceses of Bangor, St. Asaph, and St. David's were said, in 1781, to contain but 309 Catholics between them.[22] In 1784 those in Glamorgan were down to seven or eight; in another nine years they

19 *Manchester, St. Francis, Gorton, by E. W. Pugin*   20 (a) *Manchester: Holy Name, by Joseph Hansom*
(b) *Gorton: altar composition*

numbered three.[23] By 1850 the more numerous Catholics of South Wales were most of them poor Irish immigrants, at work in the mines, in the docks, and in the iron works. Their humble churches were unthinkable as cathedrals. That at Cardiff, which had succeeded the ground floor room of a cottage opened out into a shed, was a modest neo-Norman building by Scoles; it had been paid for by a lady of the Eyre family who lived at Bath.[24] At Merthyr Tydfil, in 1842, the Catholics had made do with a stinking loft above a slaughterhouse.[25] Despite its greater size and dignity Scoles's church at Newport never attained cathedral status. The diocese's cathedral was long near Hereford, in the English county which had, along with Wales, been in the old Western District. Unlike the others it was a monastic cathedral, served by Benedictine monks in the manner of medieval Norwich or Worcester. This admirable church is best treated in our next chapter.

Chapter VII

SOME CONVENTS AND COLLEGES

The French Revolution had been the unexpected impetus which caused a restarting in England of monastic life. When things were quieter in France a few English communities returned to that country. This happened to the Cistercian monks of Lulworth. Another returning community was that of the Benedictine monks who had formed St. Edmund's Priory in Paris, and whose church had been the burial place of James II and other Stuart notables. As their Paris buildings had been secularised these monks could not reinstate themselves in the French capital. Instead, they took over the school buildings at Douai once used by the community of St. Gregory's which had, since 1814, been established at Downside. There, in the 1840s, they built a church which may be reckoned a part of our subject. For the architect of this college-like, apsidal chapel in the thirteenth-century manner was Augustus Pugin.* It first stood on an open undercroft. But this later was fitted out, as a refectory, by Charles Hansom who thus fulfilled yet another of his Benedictine commissions; some shrines and stalls were also made to his designs.[1]

But most of the refugee communities stayed in England; they were duly joined by others who helped them to give England its second taste of specifically monastic architecture. There were, of course, many differences between their position and that of the monks, nuns and friars of medieval England. The numerical relationship between the

* The French Government has lately rated it as a *monument historique*.

modern monasteries and nunneries was, for instance, very far from that which prevailed before the reign of Henry VIII. In modern times the Orders for women have been more numerous than they were before the Counter-Reformation. Convents of women have far out-numbered the monasteries and friaries occupied by men. In the Middle Ages England's conventual establishment had been a leading part of the spiritual and artistic achievement of a monopolist religion. In the nineteenth century the English convents of the Roman obedience were only some of the religious buildings put up by a small minority; they eventually shared the field with convents built by the Anglo-Catholic wing of the Established Church. Yet they were, in many cases, a significant part of the vast amount of religious architecture put up in Victorian England.

Many of England's Catholic convents were accommodated in buildings never designed or specially laid out for their religious purpose. Lack of money, and the changed conditions of modern conventual life, have often meant that monks and nuns (particularly the latter) live and work in what were originally large houses. These have been specially bought, or presented by Catholic donors. They have then been adapted. Classrooms and other apartments have often been added, so too have chapels. These chapels have often served both the nuns of a convent and the laity of a parish. The L-shaped plan, with a nuns' choir in what was once a private room, and a nave running off at right angles from the sanctuary, has been a favoured plan. But we must chiefly be concerned with the buildings which take their place as modern ex-amples of specifically conventual architecture.

We must first glance at a few convents where building work of some note was done in the decades between their migration and the year 1840.

Few of these nuns from the Continent were at once settled in lasting new homes. Not many were as lucky as the English Carmelites of Antwerp, who settled down, as early as 1794, at Lanherne in North Cornwall. They took over an old manor house of the Arundells; for them as for other communities it was immensely fortunate that the "penal" families had kept many outlying, seldom used, properties. This house is still, with the addition of a later chapel for the laity, these Carmelites' place of residence. For their own devotions they soon used an enclosed gallery at one end of what had been the "great saloon" of the Arundells' house.[2]

More important, as *new* Catholic architecture, were the buildings put up in the 1830s by three convents of Benedictine nuns.

The community settled at Montargis in France had three successive residences before in 1835 they finally reached Princethorpe near Rugby. Their new priory was planned by a non-professional designer named Craven who had also built some religious houses in Spain. The domestic buildings recalled the new convent which the nuns had been forced to abandon at Montargis. But the chapel* was in tune with what was normally popular in the England of the early Gothicists; one thus saw a curious blend of "somewhat Churchwarden" Gothic and reminiscent *Louis Seize*.[3] More remarkable, as a demonstration of classicism, was a fine chapel discreetly built by some nuns in Somerset.

The community of English Benedictine nuns in Paris made their way to England in 1795. For some years they pursued the religious life in a property of the Hussey family at Marnhull in North Dorset. From there, in 1807, they moved to a house of the Cliffords, the rambling, doubly quadrangular complex of Cannington Court near Bridgwater. The present buildings are mainly Elizabethan or early Stuart. But they stand on the site, and reproduce the basic ground plan, of a small medieval priory. They probably include some pre-Reformation masonry; if so, those stones have twice over been those of a Benedictine nunnery. For their chapel these latter-day Benedictines used an upstairs room which may well, from its position on a contemporary plan of the buildings,[4] cover the site of the old refectory. They settled down in their new home, and the Franciscan Bishop Collingridge, Vicar Apostolic of the Western District, long lived in the convent and died there in 1829. Soon before his death there came the new privilege which urged the nuns towards a striking architectural development.

What the nuns obtained was permission to have the perpetual adoration of the Blessed Sacrament. They felt that their existing chapel was too small, so they decided on a new one. A benefactor in Bath expressed the hope that the new building would in every respect be suited to its purpose, and "commensurate with the grandeur and dignity" of the new state of affairs.[5] What the nuns erected was both splendid and ingenious. For they planned to fill the complete area of

* It was replaced, about 1900, by a neo-Perpendicular church whose architect was Peter Paul Pugin. The tall tower has one turret which is higher than the other, with a slim spirelet in the manner of some old churches in and near Bristol.

their inner courtyard with a polygonal, domed chapel, having a shallow sanctuary and room both for themselves and for the local laity.

Their first plan, according to unsigned drawings now at Colwich,★ was for an elongated octagon, with plain interior walls, a rectangular sanctuary, a private western gallery, and a richly cofferred dome running up to a skylight. But an equal-sided octagon better fitted the available space. Such a chapel, with its dome just peeping above the ancient ranges of the Court, was what they actually built, adorning it inside with the excellent Corinthian pilasters which well adorn the building now used as the hall of an Agricultural Institute. By the autumn of 1830 the nuns' new chapel was roofed, and its cupola was half plastered.[6] It was opened in July, 1831. But the nuns did not long enjoy the new setting for their cherished devotion. They soon had a sharp dispute with Bishop Baines; so insoluble was the problem that in 1836 they migrated to the Midland District, and took over their present quarters—the romantic Gothic, castellated mansion once called Mount Pavilion at Colwich near Stafford.

The nuns long established at Cambrai, and exiled thence after trying sufferings, had two moves before in 1808 they settled, at Abbot's Salford near Evesham, in a rambling, gabled manor owned by a Catholic lady.[7] They were there for thirty years, moving on to the Georgian mansion of Stanbrook near Worcester. By 1838 a bulky chapel, in the "Georgian-Nonconformist" manner with a shallow apsidal sanctuary, a coved ceiling, and several round-headed windows, had been built. The architect was Charles Day of Worcester,[8] soon busy on the "Catholic concert hall" already noticed at Hereford.

The Benedictine monks were now well settled at Ampleforth and Downside. Their communities were far smaller than today, so their first Victorian buildings were modest. The brothers Hansom collaborated on the church built at Ampleforth between 1855 and 1857. The actual building was Charles's responsibility, while Joseph designed altars, stalls, and other fittings.[9] The style was imitation Decorated, and the church was of moderate size. A three-bay chancel contained the monks' choir, there was a southern transept, and then a short, un-aisled nave to accommodate the school. No tower was attempted, but a graceful turret, capped by a spirelet, arose to hold a bell. A more

★ These are presumably by John Peniston, the Catholic civil engineer who was County Surveyor for Wiltshire, and is mentioned by George Oliver (*op. cit.*, p. 375) as the designer of the actual chapel.

ambitious, still surviving building was the new College, complete in 1861 and designed by Joseph Hansom with a turret ingeniously used as a fire escape. It is a workmanlike piece of Victorian educational Gothic, in the manner of the fourteenth century and with its spacious, hall-like Study Room covered by a flat ceiling whose main beams rest on richly traceried brackets.

At Downside it soon appeared that Goodridge's buildings of 1822-3 were too small for a growing community and school. In 1839 Pugin made plans which would have caused the demolition of the old house, and for some additions to buildings already on the site.[10] Then in 1842, while he was working on Mount St. Bernard and the Cathedral at Nottingham, he produced typically ambitious plans for a complete new monastery and school. The domestic and teaching buildings were to have been in four great quadrangles. All existing blocks were to be swept away; the completed buildings would have among Pugin's most spectacular achievements. The style was to be "early lancet", with a church about 300 feet long. Its eastern end, having a Lady Chapel and smaller chapels to flank it, would have resembled the equivalent portion of Nottingham Cathedral. The great nave would, however, have been far longer than that in the Midland town, and two towers with spires would have marked its western end.[11] But the architect's dreams remained on paper. Money for such a project was not to hand, and the monks reasonably shrank from the demolition of their serviceable existing buildings. So in the 1850s Charles Hansom was commissioned to make alternative plans. Here again what was built fell considerably short of the designer's intentions. But the modest, L-shaped Gothic block, which still forms the nucleus of Downside's sprawling complex of school buildings, was put up in 1853-4.[12]

The most attractive English Benedictine church of the 1850s was not first planned for monastic uses.

Francis Richard Wegg-Prosser, like Phillipps de Lisle, was an enthusiastic Catholic convert whose financial position enabled him to do much for his new Church. Originally named Haggitt, he changed his name when in 1839 he inherited the beautiful estate of Belmont near Hereford. His relative was Archdeacon Prosser, a cleric born in the year of Culloden and advantageously married to Sarah Wegg, the daughter of a rich north-country banker.[13] The archdeacon bought the Belmont estate as a setting for placid and dignified retirement. It enabled his young relative to take a natural place among the county gentry, and Wegg-Prosser soon sat as one of the county's Members of Parliament. He was keenly religious, a follower of the Tractarians, and a lifelong friend and correspondent of Newman. He was therefore deeply distressed when in 1848 the see of Hereford was controversially filled by Dr. Hampden, long known for the liberality, or even heresy, of his views and one of Newman's noted antagonists. It seems that the *cause célèbre* of this episcopal appointment was a leading reason for Wegg-Prosser's reception into the Roman church.* The new convert soon started, on his Belmont property, to erect a visible thank-offering.

Wegg-Prosser began, quite modestly, with the building in 1853 of an almshouse with its own chapel, and of a school chapel (now a library) whose chancel aped the fourteenth century and whose nave is late Perpendicular. The young Edward Pugin designed both of them, also the larger church commenced in 1854. This was of considerable splendour but of parish-church planning and dimensions, being meant for the district's laity. It had a short chancel, and its nave and crossing, along with the transepts which were originally of equal size, are excellent work of Edward Pugin's early period which was also his best. The three-bay nave has two clerestory windows to each bay. The varied tracery is all in the "Decorated" vein. The large West window, whose tracery fills an abnormally high proportion of the space and includes a cross within a circle, is notably good. The clustered piers and rich arches of the crossing are somewhat obtrusive but also very fine; above them there rises the tower whose top stage is of the 1880s. The church's eastern portion, fussier and less satisfactory than the truly excellent nave, was deeply affected by the later history of Wegg-Prosser's new ecclesiastical establishment.

The church had been built *in vacuo*. No arrangements had been made for its staffing. The Jesuits and others were asked to serve it, but declined. The Benedictines, with ambitious ideas of what they might do in Herefordshire, were the clergy who came to the rescue.

When the new hierarchy was organised the Benedictines obtained the care of the diocese of Newport and Menevia. Wales, which had no monastic cathedrals before the Reformation, was to have a monastic chapter, with its monks worshipping in a cathedral priory. It was proposed to build such a priory at Newport; other sites were con-

---

* For another possible by-product of the Hampden appointment, one may consult Anthony Trollope. For the bishop's wife, who vigorously redecorated the Palace at Hereford, is said to have been the original of Mrs. Proudie.

21 *Abbotskerswell; in the chapel,*
St. Augustine's Priory

sidered before the Benedictines resolved to make the church at Belmont their cathedral, and to build a monastery to house the monks, and the novices for the whole English province. Monastic buildings, Gothic but in general much plainer than the church, were built and used from 1859. The church itself had to be lengthened to house a proper monastic choir. So the eastern limb, of four bays with a sanctuary of two, is later than the nave and transepts; it was twice extended, and the High Altar had three moves before its final fixture in the ornate sanctuary of the mid-1860s. The building is of modest height, so that no continuous clerestory was built. But on each side two richly traceried windows, triangular with curved sides, form projecting dormers. The whole atmosphere of the cramped little cathedral was devotional; it gained added atmosphere from the enlargement of its northern transept to make a chantry for Bishop Brown who died in 1880. His tomb, and the altarpiece, have pillarets and canopies in a riot of prickly polychromy by Peter Paul Pugin. The church had been consecrated in 1860. Wegg-Prosser asked Newman to preach, but the Oratorian declined, pleading age and the awkwardness of the railway run from Birmingham. So the assembled company heard Ullathorne at High Mass, and Manning in the evening.

Another Abbey in England resembled Belmont in that it was not originally intended for Benedictine monks. Though the hilltop Abbey at Farnborough in Hampshire was built while Victoria reigned it is not typically Victorian. Its Gothic is wholly French, and its founder was the widowed Empress Eugénie.

After Napoleon III died in 1878 the Empress decided to plant a religious community whose church could be the burial place of the Bonapartists. The Emperor's body was duly interred there; so too was that of the Prince Imperial which had been brought back from Zululand. Some French Premonstratensian canons came to serve the newly built church.[14] They and the Empress eventually disagreed, so in 1895 the monastery was taken over by French Benedictines from Solesmes. The church is a fascinating exotic in the pine-clad Aldershot country.

Eugénie's architect was a Frenchman, Gabriel Destailleur. He was an adept in the styles common in Europe between 1500 and 1650. At Waddesdon in Buckinghamshire, and on sites in many Continental cities, he had been profitably employed on vast, ornate residences for the Rothschilds. What he built at Farnborough was an ornate little fantasy in the Flamboyant Gothic of late medieval France. The church

22 (a) *Portsmouth Cathedral: design by J. A. Crawley*
　　(b) *Kensington: design for University Chapel, by E. Goldie*

is cruciform, and has a short nave of three bays, stone-vaulted with transverse arches and a bold display of pendents. Behind the short apsidal sanctuary, with its fantastically traceried trio of round windows, there runs an ambulatory. The eastern vault is sustained by bold flying buttresses, while above the crossing this gem of reproduction Flamboyant is somewhat oddly crowned by a Renaissance-type dome.

By the time that the Farnborough church was finished in 1888 some domestic blocks in other Benedictine houses showed how much had changed, in the manner of monastic life, since the medieval days of cloisters as main living and working spaces. The building of the great church at Downside is best left till a later chapter, though the scheme dates from back in 1872. It was also at this time that Edward Hansom started extensions which included a large refectory, and a ponderously Gothic, many-storied monastery block whose effective, vaulted cloister is only a communication passage and whose accommodation is unmedievally laid out in "cells", or study bedrooms.

From 1879 onwards a Victorian Gothic block, not unlike that at Downside, was put up to house the German Benedictines from Beuron whom Bismarck's *Kulturkampf* had exiled to Erdington, not far from Oscott. The church—dark, ornate, and ecclesiological "Decorated" by Charles Hansom—had been built in 1848–50. Its vaulted tower and surmounting broach spire are its best feature. It had cost over £20,000, its builder being a rich convert priest who meant it to serve a parochial mission.[15] It was poorly suited for Benedictine worship; we shall see how ambitious plans were later made for its replacement. But domestic accommodation could hardly wait, so here in Birmingham's busy northern suburbia we see the imposing, many-storied façade of a block in the Decorated style, designed by a local architect named A. E. Dempster[16] and having a bulky, pinnacled tower to complete its southern end.

The Benedictine nuns at Stanbrook duly made some ambitious building efforts. Edward Pugin designed them a new church to give space for fuller choral and liturgical worship. Its main structure allowed for a chancel and an unaisled nave; the nuns' choir stalls were neatly fitted into the window recesses of the five-bayed structural nave. Beyond a delicate ironwork screen an ornate sanctuary has a rose window set clear above the elaborate altarpiece. The date of this reredos, 1878, makes it a posthumous work of its designer who had died in 1875; it was worked, from his drawings, by those much patronised church sculptors, Messrs. Boulton of Cheltenham.[17] Some toning down was later done to its profuse abundance of Caen stone tabernacle work and pink marble pillarets. The church itself had been finished in 1871. Though it is not from Edward Pugin's best period it is well planned for its purpose, and its somewhat lavish Geometrical Gothic is better than much else that was built in the very middle of Victoria's reign. Here at Stanbrook a Victorian Catholic church is more ambitious in reality than on paper. For the architect's drawings of 1869[18] show a tall western bellcote, and not the tall tower whose slim corner spirelet rises high above the lush Severn countryside. The first Gothic domestic block, by Pugin and Pugin, was started in 1878.[19] Its planning and idiom put it in the same class as the domestic quarters at Downside and Erdington. In the 1890s, while Ampleforth's monastery block was arising to the Perpendicular designs of Bernard Smith,[20] another wing was run back at right angles from this first nunnery block, with its noble view across the nearby river to the Evesham Vale.

Further thoughts on Stanbrook lead us on to the story of two important nunneries specially built as such amid the pleasant scenery of South Devon. The conventual buildings at Abbotskerswell near Newton Abbot, and up the hill on the Dawlish side of Teignmouth, were both the final resting places of English communities whose first homes had been abroad, and which were forced, by the onward rush of the French Revolution, to find temporary lodging elsewhere in England.

A house of English Austin canonesses had been founded, in 1609, at Louvain. Their career in Flanders was much distinguished by the close connexion of many of the nuns with some of the best known "penal" families. It was in 1795 that they left for England; having foreseen their uprooting they had, before the storm broke, sent many of their relics and treasures to safety. For a few months they were at Hammersmith, and then at Amesbury in Wiltshire.[21] For sixty years from 1800 they were in a mansion at Spettisbury, between Wimborne and Blandford in the placid valley of the Dorset Stour. There in the rural peace of Hardy's Wessex they built a new chapel, with a shallow plaster vault, which Bishop Baines opened in 1830.[22] But ecclesiology soon fired their imagination, for in another nine years Augustus Pugin designed them a new church, correctly Gothic and with two bays each for its nave and sanctuary. As in many of the Pugin family's churches, an extremely high pitched roof would have given this chapel a great feeling of internal height.[23] But no such church ever arose at Spettisbury, and in a few more years the canonesses left Dorset for reasons hardly foreseeable in the last year of the eighteenth century. For the projected building of the more southerly section of what eventually became the Somerset and Dorset Railway made the sisters feel that this would be a noisy and smoky intrusion into their Enclosure; had they then known of the "Slow and Dirty's" modest level of activity they might, perhaps, have stayed where they were. In 1860 they obtained the right to have perpetual adoration of the exposed Sacrament. In that same year their new convent in Devon was begun; the nuns' new privilege had a major effect on the design of its church.

An early Victorian house named Abbotsleigh had been bought as the nucleus of the new Priory. Joseph Hansom was the architect of the buildings which were finished by 1863. Bishop Vaughan of Plymouth took a close interest in the operations and he, so it seems, did all the correspondence with the architect.[24] The main convent block, of three storeys and with an octagonal tower, has that tower capped by a somewhat Rhenish spirelet. A more striking work is the conventual church; here indeed one has a rare, purpose-built period piece. The structural nave (as at Stanbrook housing the canonesses' choir) is a rectangular, ornate mid-Victorian work. The main timbers of its roof come down to double sets of polished marble shafts whose capitals, like all others in the church, are ornately carved in the manner of about 1280. A clerestory of convex triangles admits much of the light, while the back rows of the stalls are recessed, bay by bay, in the thickness of the walls. What makes this chapel in South Devon so great a rarity is the planning of its sanctuary. For this is laid out as an architectural *expositorium* for perpetual adoration, with the monstrance exposed, high above the cramped sanctuary with its narrow altar, in the upper Throne which dominates the whole ornate composition. What Joseph Hansom designed was an octagonal, high-capped tower of distinctly German appearance, and within that space he contrived an inner octagon as the immediate setting for the altar. Its arcaded wall, and the slim pillars and curved members of its open arches, make a rich casket for the special devotion of this convent. The Throne itself is a fantastic affair, with a slender canopy rising so high that the canonesses in their stalls, or adoring at their *pries dieu*, cannot see its tip which rises nearly to the top of the tower space. Letters reveal that when in 1863 this altar was set up it was not designed by Joseph Hansom himself. For that year found the architect much preoccupied, among other things, with the unhappy breaking up of his short partnership with Edward Pugin. So the work was entrusted to Benjamin Bucknall of Stroud, a pupil of Augustus Pugin whose other work falls into a later chapter.[25]

The community of Benedictine nuns which is now at Teignmouth was founded, in 1622, at Dunkirk.[26] The Stuarts were now restored to the English throne, and as this was the short period when Dunkirk was an English possession, the opportunity seemed favourable, and some important help came secretly from Charles II himself. A new convent, with an unaisled and apsidal chapel, was duly built. Here, until the time of the French Revolution, the nuns continued their conventual life. In 1793 they were driven from Dunkirk, but after two years' imprisonment they were allowed to leave for England. For over sixty years they were at Hammersmith, but in 1861 Cardinal Wiseman advised the community to move. Miss Isabella English, the sister of one of the nuns and eventually made a Papal Countess for many services to Catholicism, bought the Teignmouth property and was in other ways a major benefactress. Miss Tasker, later another Papal Countess whose young nephew, F. W. Tasker, became an architect whose church work we shall find to be of some note,* was also most generous.[27] As with St. Augustine's Priory, Bishop Vaughan took the closest interest in the new work; his concern extended to a change of architect. The designer first chosen was Gilbert Blount, mentioned by Abbess Selby as "a very upright man and moderate in expense". He made plans for a complete conventual complex.[28] But this, it appears, was too dear for Bishop Vaughan. George Goldie was appointed instead of Blount, who later got his compensation when in 1865 to 1867 he built the new Priory at Carisbrooke for the Dominican nuns. It was to Goldie's designs, between 1861 and 1863, that the imposing convent block and its chapel were built to serve as St. Scholastica's Abbey at Teignmouth.

Goldie's buildings are all of them in the early French Gothic style which he greatly favoured. In the tall, essentially unmedieval conventual blocks the silvery grey limestone of their main construction is brightly variegated by Bath stone dressings, and by bands of the red sandstone so well known to thousands who have made the famous coastal railway journey from Teignmouth to Dawlish. The chapel is

* His obituary, in the *Building News* of May 20th, 1904, mentions a house he had built, at Brentwood, for his aunt, the late Countess who had died in 1888.

less striking than the one at Abbotskerswell, and as the Teignmouth Benedictines had not, by 1863, obtained the right to perpetual adoration it was not designed with that devotion in mind. Goldie's drawings of 1862[29] show that his first version of the church was different from that which exists. For in the manner of some medieval nuns' churches it was to have been divided lengthways along its structural nave, with its single altar seen by the nuns in their choir on one side, and on the other by visitors and the girls of a small boarding school. But the actual church, with its slim, somewhat fantastic turret over the abbess' stall at one end, is narrower and more simple than that of the earlier design; one assumes that it was found to be less expensive. Between the sanctuary and the nuns' choir a space was allowed, as had been done in the community's Dunkirk church, for the girls of the school. The structural nave is plain, but the apsidal sanctuary, with its paired shafts of rich red marble and an abundance of stiff foliate carving, is typical of George Goldie in his more ornate mood. A fairly elaborate iron-work screen parts the sanctuary from the choir of the nuns, and the whole church has of late been much improved by its redecoration in colours of an un-Victorian lightness.

For monastic planning on the true medieval pattern we must go back in point of time to the Abbey of Mount St. Bernard. This was founded, for a colony of Cistercian Trappists from Mount Melleray in Ireland, by Ambrose March Phillipps who bought the site high up in the Charnwood Forest country of Leicestershire. The first monks came in 1835, installing themselves in a modest cottage. The church, and conventual buildings of a quadrangular and obviously monastic type, were soon started. Lord Shrewsbury was another benefactor, and with such patrons Pugin was the inevitable architect. The church's structural nave (now the choir of a much expanded community) and many domestic buildings were finished by 1844.

The style of the church is a simple lancet Gothic which Pugin considered "well suited to a Cistercian abbey", and which he also, less willingly, used for Nottingham Cathedral. Here at Mount St. Bernard it is wholly successful. The quiet, simple solemnity of the church, as now extended in a way unexpected by its original architect, makes it one of Pugin's best creations. The arcades, with plainly chamfered arches and round pillars, have no triforium stage between them and the lancets of the clerestory. Three tall lancets comprise the western fenestration of Pugin's nave. But the eastern portion, with its transepts and central tower of the 1930s, a central High Altar, and a five-bay laity nave in the idiom of the earlier work, is not as Pugin planned it. For his drawings of 1840[30] show a central tower crowned by the un-Cistercian appanage of a tall broach spire. East of the crossing they prove that what was first planned was a short sanctuary, of two bays and square-ended, of the type which the Cistercians first standardised by about 1150. Pugin's drawings for the claustral buildings, and for the simply constructed polygonal Chapter House, are for ranges very much as they actually stand.

Down in Dorset, while Mount St. Bernard was being built, developments were afoot in England's one house of Cistercian nuns.

The community had long been in Paris. After Post-Revolutionary migrations to Switzerland and Russian Poland the nuns reached England in 1801.[31] Here too they had some temporary homes, but in 1802 they settled in a property of the Arundells at Stapehill near Wimborne. They used the long, barnlike chapel of an existing mission. With help from the monks of their Order still at Lulworth they added to their buildings. Under an aristocratic, authoritarian abbess named Mde. de Chabannes their numbers increased. So severe were their austerities, and so many were their deaths, that Bishop Collingridge intervened. He shrewdly feared hostile agitation and legal intervention should the facts become known, so he tempered the régime of wha was described as a "hothouse for Heaven".[32] Then in the 1840s the time came for more clearly conventual buildings. The nuns had a visit from the Dowager Queen Adelaide and Queen Victoria's mother. They left a handsome donation, and money also came from Queen Marie Amélie of France.[33] Some domestic buildings came first and then, between 1847 and 1851, Charles Hansom built a long Early English church to serve the nuns and the parish. In the manner of medieval nuns' churches like that of St. Helen off Bishopsgate in London there were two parallel naves with sanctuaries, completely screened off from each other. A sharply capped belfry arose at the south-western corner.[34] More conventual buildings followed once the new church had been built.

French antecedents also lay behind the building of England's one modern house of Carthusian monks. In the 1860s the community at Grande Chartreuse was anxious to make a foundation which could be a place of refuge in the event of political difficulties in France. The fall of Napoleon III increased their fears, so in 1873 they bought the

property of Parknowle (now Parkminster) at Cowfold in central
Sussex. There between 1876 and 1883 a complete monastery was built.
It is planned on traditional Carthusian lines, and its cottage-cells are
disposed, as of old, round a spacious Great Cloister. The architect was
a Frenchman named Normand.[35] His buttressed, rectangular church is
in the earliest Gothic manner. Behind its altar end a tower and spire
rise high above the low countryside. *The Builder*, in a short note on
this "costly Roman Catholic monastery", whose expense it quoted as
£160,000, gives 160 feet as the steeple's total height.[36]

Oratorian and Jesuit churches, and some built by the Franciscan
Friars, can be considered along with "parochial" buildings. We can,
however, consider some of last century's achievements by the Dominicans.

In the 1820s they had done building work on their Leicestershire
priory at Hinkley. The domestic quarters, in appearance unconventual
by medieval standards, but in practice well suited to their needs, were
in a plain late Georgian house. The chapel was a simple classical
building of the type then built for such parishes as Thetford and
Leamington. In 1839 a turret, with a bell, was built with special Home
Office permission.[37] Not far away, at Atherstone in Warwickshire, the
same year saw the completion of a priory for Dominican nuns.
Ambrose March Phillipps was their benefactor for the first buildings in
a plain Tudor Gothic. But the L-shaped chapel of twenty years later
was built in well detailed Early English.[38]

More exciting, by now, was the building of the church and priory
at Woodchester. In most particulars they were medieval Gothic—a
Cotswold counterpart to Wegg-Prosser's later benefaction in the
Wye Valley.

Like Wegg-Prosser, William Leigh of Woodchester was a wealthy
convert who wished to make some striking thank-offering. He had
made his pile in South Australia, where he gave land, and much money,
to the new Catholic bishopric and cathedral at Adelaide.[39] In the
valley between Stroud and Nailsworth he bought a beautiful,
awkwardly sloping site for a fine church. He had some Puginian ideas
on recommencing Catholic activities where these had been rudely
interrupted under Henry VIII, and for the founding of an establishment where missionary activity would combine with such neo-
medieval glories as daily High Mass, chantries, and offices sung in
choir. Like Wegg-Prosser he planned his church with few clear ideas

on how, in the English Catholic conditions of the 1840s, it might be staffed. Nor was the building process entirely straightforward.

The Passionists, on Bishop Wiseman's advice, were the clergy actually chosen to serve the church built between 1846 and 1849. Leigh had naturally turned to Pugin as the architect for his monastic dream. Pugin obliged with drawings for a building which would be "very simple, but quite monastic—in all its details"; the single block would have been like the eastern range of what was actually built.[40] Where the trouble came was over the church. Leigh's first idea was for an ambitious cruciform building. Pugin wisely pointed out that so large a building, on such a site, was beyond the money available; he plaintively remarked that he was "the most unfortunate man in existence for scites [sic] of ground".[41]

Pugin then sent two fine sketches for a church not unlike that existing at Woodchester. He provided for an aisled nave, a long four-bayed choir, and an unattractive tower much taller than that actually built. As in some other Pugin projects the pillars were weak and spindly for their height. The cost would have been high, and Leigh's means were not unlimited. The donor suggested some scaling down. But Pugin wrote that a nave so altered would be "A miserable job" and begged to be excused his commission.[42] He asked that no other architect should use or adapt his sketches, declining to send detailed drawings lest another might actually render his scheme.[43] But architectural plagiarism, of a sort, was what happened at Woodchester. The church actually built is a modified version of Pugin's design, with a shorter chancel which is somewhat cramped as a friars' choir, and a nave two-dimensionally as proposed by Pugin but with shorter, sturdier pillars. The architect, suggested by Bishop Ullathorne, was Charles Hansom;[44] the builder was Taylor of Coventry who had erected Hansom's church in that town. The clerestoried nave is of six bays and the chancel, with its delicate stone screen and stepped sedilia, is of three. On the northern side an effective turret has a spirelike cap. The whole feeling, reinforced by the carved effigies of Leigh and of a Carmelite bishop, is strongly ecclesiological and the style is chaste early Decorated. The church ranks as one of Charles Hansom's best—but one must remember its debt to Pugin.

The Passionists were still at Woodchester as the church neared completion. Fr. Dominic Barberi, who had received Newman and is now a *Beatus*, was on his way to visit his Gloucestershire brethren when he died, dramatically, at Reading Station. But the Passionists found it hard to meet Leigh's requirements for the performance of the full choral offices. So in 1850 they left. The Dominicans came instead, establishing a noviciate for their growing English province. Priory buildings were therefore needed, Charles Hansom designed them, on the quadrangular medieval plan, with the cloister walks "built in" as in the remains of the Dominican friary at Bristol. The Chapter House has a doorway and some windows in the fourteenth-century style, the small refectory (now a library) was given a recessed reader's pulpit, and many Cotswold Tudor chimneystacks rise high above the buildings. The whole priory was convincing enough for the taste of the 1850s. It is not, one imagines, what the Order which has built La Tourette would now erect on such a site.

The nearness of the Woodchester Dominicans to act as chaplains and confessors attracted to the valley a colony of Franciscan nuns from their Order's convent at Taunton. They came in 1860; a stone-built house became the nucleus of some large, austere Gothic conventual buildings. The upstairs chapel, not untypical of the finer ones then built for communities of nuns, is an imposing building by Charles Hansom, completed in 1869.[45] It boasts an antechapel, four bays for the nuns' choir, a most spacious sanctuary, and a wooden vault, The style, as appears from the large side windows and from the wheel window set high above a sugary Gothic altarpiece, is a rich version of the early "Decorated" used for the church a mile away along the Cotswold hillside.

Two Dominican town churches can also be noticed here. The English province's headquarters was located in London, at Haverstock Hill. A church was started in 1863, the architect being Gilbert Blount who also worked for Dominican nuns at Carisbrooke and at Stone in Staffordshire.[46] But little progress was made, so that when in 1873-4 the present friary church was built it seems to have been to a new design. Charles Alban Buckler was the architect, a figure of interest among Victorian Catholic designers. For his father was John Chessell Buckler, the antiquarian artist whose numerous drawings of old churches are so valuable a record of their appearance before they endured the Victorian onslaught. Charles Buckler and his three brothers all became Catholics, and as all the brothers became Dominicans it was natural that the Order of Preachers should give Charles some commissions.[47] Back in 1857 he designed a dignified, clerestoried,

late Geometrical nave for the Woodchester Dominicans who needed a
church for the parish church they then served at Stroud.[48] Other
Buckler churches are apt to be straightforward, unassuming buildings.
But not so the vast aisled auditorium at Haverstock Hill, nearly three
hundred feet long and with a marked Flemish feeling in the great nave
whose gauntness is not improved by a hideously bracketted iron
catwalk running below its clerestory. Up in the apse the altarpiece is
a "wedding cake" confection very remote from the austere purity now
associated with the Dominicans.

Little better as a building, but with its apse at first more simply
garnished, was the bulky, transeptal Dominican church at Newcastle.
It was started in 1869 and opened, without its projected tower and
spirelike cap, in 1873.[49] Its architect was Archibald Dunn, trained in
Bristol under Charles Hansom[50] and joined at Newcastle, in 1871, by
Hansom's son Edward who came as a younger partner. His bulky
church is ponderously French Gothic of that style's early phase; wheel
windows and stiffly foliate capitals give the flavour of about 1200 to a
basically Victorian interior. This was lined, not with plaster but with
cream-coloured brick to withstand the sooty Tyneside air.[51] The apse
is strikingly lit by a continuous row of lancets; below their rear arches
one has what is now this church's great treasure. For the fine wooden
canopied work, convincingly fourteenth-century and with details like
those in the Lady Chapel at Ely, was first in the choir of Peterborough
Cathedral. It was installed, to the designs of the architect Blore, in
1832. John Britton[52] tells how a "mean" Gothic screen and organ case
had been put in about 1780. But when in 1828 he wrote on Peterborough "new and better taste" had come, and as the clergy were now
"genuinely qualified to appreciate the genuine styles of Christian
architecture" they completely refurnished the choir. Their architect
was a man "whose extensive knowledge of Christian architecture, and
industrious habits" well qualified him for this job. His work seemed
both excellent and adequately "Christian". But it was not good enough
for Sir George Gilbert Scott, who ejected Blore's woodwork and
replaced it with some of his own. For some years the stallwork lay
out in the Close. Then in 1895 some Newcastle Dominicans saw it,
bought it cheap, and placed some of it round their apse. There we may
still admire it; below the four largest canopies, four splendid Baroque
figures, in the richest woodwork of the Flemish school, represent
St. John the Baptist and three Evangelists.

To end this chapter, we may briefly turn to three collegiate works by the chief paladin of "Christian" architecture. Two of them once formed a very similar pair; the third is really "parochial" in design.

Pugin's chapel at St. Edmund's College and the one he built at Ushaw were closely alike. That at Ushaw came first. Once Mgr. Newsham had plumped for Gothic he engaged Pugin, who in 1840 designed a chapel on the site of the present library. Drawings show it as a T-shaped building, with five bays and an antechapel.[53] Along its southern side a row of sacristies and chapels would have ended in a tower capped by a graceful broach spire. The style, as in other contemporary Pugin designs, would have been lancet Early English, elaborated inside with some trefoil-headed arcading and covered by high-pitched roofs as at Mount St. Bernard. But this building would have been too small, so in another three years Pugin planned the chapel built between 1844 and 1848. Here again the shape was that of a T, with an antechapel which made the ground plan like those of the Oxford chapels of New College and All Souls'. But those chapels are Perpendicular, and as Perpendicular was now taboo the Ushaw chapel was Decorated. This design too provided for an unexecuted tower and spire. The chapel had a choir screen, Puginesque fittings on medieval patterns, and much glass and metalwork by his faithful collaborator John Hardman. The chapel was opened with enthusiasm; F. A. Paley's exaggerated verdict was that is surpassed all "Oxbridge" chapels bar that of King's at Cambridge.[54] Other buildings followed during Ushaw's great wave of constructional fervour. Between 1849 and 1851 the Hansom partners gave the College a two-storeyed library block which resembled Charles Hansom's projected hall for Downside and foreshadowed those he actually built for Clifton and Malvern Colleges. But the three-sided Junior College (with its own chapel), other academic buildings, and a collection of small chapels, were built in the 1850s to varied designs by Edward Pugin.[55] The chapels of St. Charles and of St. Michael and the Holy Souls, and the cloister whose richly panelled walls enshrine the Stations of the Cross, are minor gems of his richest work. The vault and the traceried screen of the former and the groined vaulting of that of St. Michael are specially exquisite. But the main chapel lasted less than forty years; its larger successor falls into a later part of our story.

Pugin's "Decorated" chapel at St. Edmund's, surviving with later extensions, was built between 1845 and 1853. Here again the drawings allow for an unachieved tower and spire; they also cater for a western cloister, enclosing a cemetery, as at New College, Oxford.[56] The antechapel has a pair of transomed West windows and noble two-arched arcades. The screened-in tomb of Bishop Griffiths is in the southern transept, while off that on the northern side the vaulted Lady Chapel was planned as the tower's base. The open-arched choir screen, in an early fourteenth-century idiom, most happily vindicates Pugin's passion for these furnishings, while his fine curvilinear East window of seven lights confirms one's opinion of his talent for fenestration.

Cotton Hall, in the beautiful hill country of northern Staffordshire, was built in the Georgian period. It still has a Roman Doric porch, and a two-storeyed bow window to command a fine view down the valley towards the Shrewsbury estate of Alton. The Gilberts were its late Georgian owners. But in 1843 they became extinct, and Lord Shrewsbury bought the place as a home for his nephew. But Bertram Talbot never lived there, so in 1846 the Earl offered this remote retreat to Frederick Faber and his budding Oratorians.[57] They added to the house, and their first plans for a Pugin church were modest in scope.[58] But as work progressed their conception was changed. What was finished in 1848 was a fair-sized building, combining a community choir and a nave for the laity. No Catholic church in England can be more exquisitely placed.

Though Pugin himself may have somewhat overrated it,* this church at Cotton is a polished essay in his ecclesiological early Decorated. It is long, unclerestoried, and has a southern aisle; its feeling of length was increased by the new sanctuary of the 1930s. The tower and its broach spire rise high at the south-western corner. Below a fine West window in the earliest Decorated idiom a richly shafted and moulded doorway is all 1300 till one notices the amusing incongruity of its label stops which show the biretta-capped heads of Renaissance Oratorians. The arcade of six arches has sturdy round pillars and capitals of carved foliage. One pillar alone has no capital, for this was the one which marked the break between the nave and the Oratorians' choir. The East window, of five lights with a couple of four-lobed designs in the tracery, is that for which Pugin said he could die. It is good, but some others from his drawing board seem to have a more lethal emotional content.

The Oratorians left Cotton for Birmingham in 1849. After various

* He said that it was the "only perfect church in England".

changes, and a period of closure, the property again served Church purposes, housing the school which had long been at Sedgeley Park. Several academic buildings, in various Gothic or neo-Georgian idioms, have since been built, and Faber's church serves school and parishioners alike. But in its plan it is essentially parochial, thus resembling the majority of those built by England's Roman Catholics in the central Victorian decades.

Chapter VIII

MID-VICTORIANA

The time between Pugin's death and Manning's last years was a period both prolific, and generally undistinguished, for Catholic church-building in England. We need not doubt the pastoral usefulness of the buildings put up in the central sector of Queen Victoria's reign, for many spiritual comforts were certainly obtained by those who built and used the churches. But in a book which views the Catholic contribution to this country's church architecture one must mainly consider the aesthetics, and the architects, of the churches built and furnished while Wiseman and Manning held sway at Westminster.

Between 1850 and 1880 many Catholic churches were built to join those which were new in the last years of the Vicars Apostolic. Like those of the 1840s they often replaced some previous, provisional buildings. In Liverpool, for instance, a wooden shed was the predecessor of Edward Pugin's church of St. Vincent de Paul. The change was all to the good, for the new building is a fine work, in the "Decorated" style of the architect's Belmont period. Magnificent East and West windows combine with others to flood the interior with light. There are reminiscences of Belmont itself in some smaller windows, and some of the altar compositions are rarely sensitive for work completed soon after 1860. When some hundreds of these new churches had been opened the standard pattern of England's Victorian churches of the Roman obedience was clear enough.

Outside Lancashire these Catholic churches were inevitably fewer than their Anglican and Nonconformist counterparts. A medium-sized town might get half a dozen new buildings for the Church of England as against a single worshipping centre for all elements of its Roman Catholic minority. The architectural periodicals (notably *The Builder*) contain a vast quarry of information on the dates, materials, and designers of these new places of worship. Under "Church-Building News", "Nonconformist Church-Building News", and "Roman Catholic Church-Building News" the relevant details are faithfully chronicled. The "Roman Catholic" sections are fewer, and as a rule less voluminous, than those which cover the achievements of Scott, Street, Teulon, Butterfield, and the great host of more local architects who designed for the Established Church. Yet the Catholic output was substantial. It was, however, geographically uneven, reflecting (as it still does) the mainly urban spread of England's emancipated Catholicism.

These churches were mostly put up in the towns of large or middling size. Some villages which had long had chapels in the mansions of Catholic landlords replaced them with small churches. Most of these were Gothic, though at Ince Blundell near Liverpool the new public church, adjacent to the house and built in 1859, to Scoles's designs, at the expense of the classically minded Blundells, is a rectangular, Italianate Renaissance building with a rounded apse. Among the Gothic buildings one may list one by Buckler in the Eystons' stronghold at East Hendred,[1] and another, in the Carylls' West Grinstead territory, by J. A. Crawley who got other commissions in the then undivided Southwark diocese.[2] Another, at Shefford in Bedfordshire where the mission dated from late Penal times, was a flamboyant Gothic church, in tune with the origins of its donor. For the benefactress of this church of the 1880s was Mrs. Lyne-Stephens, a rich and pious widow who had been an actress in Paris, and then the wife of an East Anglian landowner. Her architect was S. J. Nicholl, a pupil of Scoles and at one time a partner with Willson of Lincoln.[3]

Many Catholic churches in the towns are on sites marking them off from the more ambitious efforts of Victorian Anglicanism. Catholicism being weak among the rising business and professional class one did not, in most provincial towns, find its churches amid the neat avenues and aucuba-girt villas of prim Victorian suburbia. A few, as in Gloucester and Exeter and more strikingly (for obvious local reasons) at Arundel might be on sites not far from the town centre. But more

23 (a) *Arundel Cathedral; design by Joseph Hansom*
   (b) *Arundel: interior*   (c) *Spanish Place, by E. Goldie*
   (d) *Newcastle on Tyne: St. Michael's, by Dun and Hansom*

were built for the convenience of mainly artisan or labouring congregations, for people who needed, in those days before universal
bicycles, to be as near their churches as they were to shops and factories.
A Victorian Catholic church was often built in what was, and sometimes is, the town's Irish quarter of gasworks stokers, railway gangers,
or dock labourers. It is thus that Catholic churches teem in Liverpool's
dockland belt. Here and there, in towns where the Irish joined deeply
rooted "penal" congregations, second churches were deliberately built
to ease tensions between the indigenous and the immigrant faithful. So
at York Joseph Hansom designed a church for his native city when in
1847-9 he was the architect of the three-aisled, unclerestoried church
of St. George in the Walmgate district. St. Patrick would seem to have
been a better patron for a pleasing essay in Puginesque "early Decorated", and the building of St. George's postponed (most sadly in view
of what happened in another thirteen years) the building of a "really
fine" church in the Minster district. Elsewhere in Yorkshire, the Irish
among the Catholics of Sheffield were wisely given a church of their
own in 1856. The Duke of Norfolk gave some of the money and the
gaunt, utilitarian church of St. Vincent duly arose above the mean
streets of the Croft Lands.[4] The architects were Weightman, Hadfield,
and George Goldie, the last named being the young architect who
duly laid a heavy hand on the Catholic architecture of Yorkshire. Like
the Hansoms he was a Yorkshireman, being born at York in 1828. His
mother was a daughter of Joseph Bonomi, so that Ignatius Bonomi
was his uncle and he could also claim kinship, further back in time,
with Angelica Kauffmann. Catholic architecture was in his blood, but
dire mid-Victorian ponderosity tended to overlie the better aspects of
his aesthetic ancestry.

All too often these churches for growing Catholic congregations in
industrial towns were gaunt and bulky, unappealingly designed, and
cheaply built. The best one can say of them is that they are no worse,
aesthetically, than many churches simultaneously built by other
religious bodies. Where churches of better quality were put up the
devout pennies of the Anglo-Irish poor were less responsible for their
greater distinction than large benefactions by converts or Catholic
gentry of ancient lineage.

The larger, more important Catholic churches in England conformed more and more to a generally standard pattern. Their style
might be more or less faithfully medieval, but in their plans the ruling

24 *Ushaw: the redecorated chapel*

factors were those laid down by the Sacred Congregation of Rites. Deep chancels and screens, once Puginian enthusiasm had worn off, were virtually unknown. So too, under Roman influences and in accordance with the preferences of Wiseman and Manning, were Gothic vestments. It was inconceivable that these mid-Victorian churches would be used for such innovations as a largely vernacular liturgy or for Mass facing the people. As it happens, they are somewhat better suited for such ceremonies than the deep, screened chancels preferred by the Puginites.

The ruling idea in these mid-Victorian churches was that the High Altar, being used for most Masses on Sundays and festivals, should not be too remote from the nave. This was, in essence, the idea behind the "Jesuit" planning of the sixteenth century. So these churches in England are really Counter-Reformation structures in Gothic dress. For those in the eastern part of the nave the idea worked reasonably well; for those sitting or standing at the back of the long rectangle it was rather less useful. The eastern limbs of these churches are short, containing little but the High Altar and a reasonably roomy sanctuary. Transverse screens are rare, and no rows of choir stalls lie between the altar and the people. The choir and the organ are normally skied up above the nave in a western gallery. To avoid blocking the last arches in the nave arcade this final bay often allows for its musical furnishings by running west of the actual arcades, being divided by a solid wall from the last compartment in each of the aisles. Organ chambers are rare, and a small chapel often stands on each side of the sanctuary. One will be dedicated to the Virgin Mary, the other, as like as not, to St. Joseph or the Sacred Heart. More frequently than in their Anglican contemporaries these Catholic buildings end in apses, for French Gothic (of the late thirteenth century) was as strong a draw for their architects as the sequence of English, square-ended, medieval styles.

Whatever the shape of the East end, more care was now taken to design and furnish it so that exposition and Benediction did not clash with the letting in of some light from above the High Altar. For a time, however, there was some trouble over the reconciliation of large East windows and high-rising Gothic altar compositions. Two similar churches, by the same architect, show how an awkward problem eventually got handled in different ways.

The fine buildings for the Catholic congregations of Taunton and Abergavenny were started in 1858 and opened, within a single month, in 1860. Their architect was Benjamin Bucknall[5]. His two churches, with their clerestoried naves, stately chancel arches, chancels of moderate length, and "Decorated" windows are basically alike, though that at Taunton later received a fine western tower, pinnacled and buttressed in the local manner but with detail of a type one would see on Somerset's old church towers had that county's great wave of church-building occurred a century earlier. Both churches have admirably Puginesque East windows, large and in each case of six lights. But while the reredos at Taunton is reasonably unobtrusive, at Abergavenny the lower half of the East window is nullified by the unmannerly pinnacles and crinkly carving of a large, delicately carved altarpiece-cum-throne which was piously donated about 1883. But by then it was better realised (as Scoles had seen at Farm Street) that an East window must be set high if a monstrance is to be noticed below it. So architects duly catered for what had become a firm requirement. In some cases the East window was drastically diminished. We find it thus at Trowbridge, in the pleasant little "Decorated" church designed, in the 1870s, by Joseph Scoles's son Alexander (later Canon) Scoles. For a small, circular, and traceried East window is high up in the East wall and is only lightly crossed by the high pinnacle of the throne. But at Bootle, where the lofty, dignified church of St. James had to be built, in 1885–6, to replace one whose site was absorbed by the Southport line of the Lancashire and Yorkshire Railway, the solution was different. For Charles Hadfield of Sheffield, who on the death of his father Matthew Ellison Hadfield took over the commission, built a noble chancel, of two bays but vaulted as one, with the cill of its Geometrical East window so high above the floor that in a few more years the East wall gave ample space for his splendid reredos with its niches in two tiers.

Another, more intractable problem arose from the continued building of new churches with wide, pew-congested aisles. Many Catholic churches in country towns had no need for anything but plain rectangular naves. But when some of these naves had to be made more spacious they were often enlarged sideways. The aisles thus built created much dead ground wherein worshippers were (and are) cut off from the preacher and the celebrant. We have seen how this danger lay deep in Puginite and "ecclesiological" planning; it continued in most of the larger churches put up in the decades after Pugin's death. Not till late last century do we find wider efforts to avert this visual difficulty. But in one great church of the 1850s, a building which ranks among Joseph Hansom's best, and whose roof is perhaps the most masterly ever put over *any* Victorian church, a clear view of the altar and the pulpit was triumphantly achieved by Jesuit patrons.

St. Walburge's at Preston was built, between 1850 and 1854, to serve the town's westward extension; the apse of its sanctuary was added later by S. J. Nicholl.[6] What Joseph Hansom created was a vast, aisleless auditorium. The style, as one sees in the side windows and in the doorways, lancets, and round or triangular windows of a well composed West front, is that of the period soon after 1250. The interior recalls a great Palace hall, or even a vast refectory; this second impression is reinforced by the approach to the pulpit up an arcaded stairway in the northern wall. The internal breadth is nearly sixty feet. To cover such a space the architect constructed a stupendous, high-rising hammerbeam roof. Westminster Hall must certainly have inspired him, but the detail of his complex structure is that of a period a century earlier than Hugh Herland's monumental carpentry, and while at Westminster each hammerbeam is tipped by a horizontal angel those at Preston sustain the standing, canopied figures of saints. No less notable are the slightly later tower and spire of St. Walburge's southern side. Here too the style is late thirteenth century, and the silvery limestone of this exquisite steeple contrasts well with the dark local stone of the nave. Pinnacles and small flying buttresses support the spire from each corner of the tower, and the spire itself rises clean, uncumbered, and with breathtaking grace to the tip of its vane, over 300 feet high and only slightly lower than that of Norwich Cathedral.

Although in their architecture these Victorian Catholic churches had much in common with the buildings of the Church of England, or even with such Nonconformist ventures as Charles Hansom's cathedralesque Congregational church near his home in Clifton, when one came to furnishing and equipment the Catholics dwelt in a different world. Provided they conformed to the ruling liturgical directions they never bothered with faculties or with other processes of the law. They did not have to expect such excitements as ritual prosecutions or Kensitite riots. No questions arose over the basic doctrine one should teach, and one did not have to ask whether or not one should wear vestments, put crosses or candles on the altars, use incense, or have statues in one's church. Aesthetically speaking, the trouble was not one of too little but the problem of too much. However great may be the devotional comfort inspired by these fittings one now recoils from the taste and seemliness of many *objets de culte* with which churches by the Pugins, the Hansoms, and the Hadfields became growingly congested.

The general body of England's Catholic churches now declined in architectural quality; most Anglican churches of the period were little if any better. Here and there an Anglican architect of the Street or Butterfield grouping produced a building of powerful design and reasonable detail. These were often the central churches of important towns, or were placed in favoured, opulent suburbs. The explanation of their higher quality is largely the simple fact that the members of the Established church could raise far more money than the Catholics, who were mainly found in working class areas and whose low-income majority was only slightly leavened by a few richer benefactors.

Not only was the Gothic designing of the Catholic architects increasingly coarse and heavy, but Ruskinian influences brought in a riot of unhappy polychromy. Multi-coloured brickwork was allied to Gothic of a supposedly French or Italian stamp, while unsympathetic colours appeared not only in the pillarets of altarpieces but in the columns of main arcades. Pink granite and pink marble were used in many of these pillars, and the effect is seldom good. One sees the point in St. John's at Bath, a church by Charles Hansom which replaced the converted theatre and which was opened in 1863; its excellent tower and spire, built later to the architect's designs, produce a western frontage clearly inspired by that of the great medieval church at Grantham. The vaulted, apsidal chancel, with exterior gables and an inner adornment of trefoiled arcading, is an exquisite period piece, and the church's general design resembles that of Charles Hansom's slightly earlier church of St. Peter's, Cardiff. But between the chancel and the tower at Bath the nave and its transepts are a disappointment, and the cylindrical columns of pink marble make one think of rolls of galantine just out of their tins. By the 1860s there were, indeed, some sad aesthetic lapses even among the better Catholic architects.

The early 1860s saw the end of J. J. Scoles's varied career, and he died in 1863.[7] He left as pupils S. J. Nicholl, and his two sons who both combined the priesthood with architectural work. Joseph Scoles's last church was the large structure of Holy Cross, in the mining outskirts of St. Helens.[8] Its style is a gaunt version of the "ecclesiological Decorated" he had used at Farm Street. A curious wooden arch, with much tracery above it, parts the sanctuary and the nave, while the flat roof recalls that which first covered the church of the London Jesuits. Here at St. Helens the flat roof is of special interest, for its shape was chosen to minimise the church's pressure and thrust on the soil of a district much honeycombed with mining subsidence. The same factor operated when in 1869 Joseph Hansom designed a church at Hindley to replace the gaunt chapel of 1789. The roof, and the clerestory of small triangular windows, are supported by six structural bays. But each of these bays is split, as was done at Beauvais, into two compartments, so that the weight is spread through a dozen arches on each side, each arch being narrow, acute, and rising from two slim, rectangular piers.

Few Catholic architects of this time were of more promise than William Wilkinson Wardell; his early disappearance from the English scene was a real loss to our Victorian architecture. A close follower of Pugin, he was first a civil engineer and then started architectural work.[9] Most of his English churches are in London and the Home Counties. A few, like that at Greenwich with its graceful spire, and Holy Trinity, Hammersmith whose spire was placed by Joseph Hansom on Wardell's finely vaulted tower, are in the ecclesiological early "Decorated" favoured by Pugin and Charles Hansom. The Hammersmith church, with its well worked detail, and an angel-studded hammerbeam roof, is an excellent period piece, commenced in the year of the Great Exhibition. More important still were two others among Wardell's London churches.

The Redemptorists' church on Clapham Common was originally built in 1849–51. It had some later additions, including a deep, double-aisled North transept by Bentley,* and an outer north aisle which was an earlier work by the same architect. As Wardell built it the church had a straightforward plan, in the "Decorated" style and with a north-western tower and spire. The clerestoried nave has six bays, and a fine timber roof in a Gothic idiom later than that of the rest of the church. It leads up to a masterly two-bayed, vaulted chancel, well lit by its large six-light East window and quite worthy to rank beside Butterfield's gloomier, likewise vaulted chancel at All Saints', Margaret Street.

* Bentley, who lived at Clapham, was also the designer of the admirable brick built monastery block, an Arts and Crafts Gothic work as good as anything he ever did.

Wardell designed two neighbouring churches in the East End. His cruciform building in Poplar was eliminated by bombing; its successor, likewise cruciform but on the plan of a Greek cross, is by Adrian Gilbert Scott and an imposingly traditionalist reproach to the bright modernities of its "Lansbury" surroundings. The vast church of S.S. Mary and Michael in Commercial Road survived the bombing and was itself the pastoral successor of the Virginia Street Chapel. With its clerestoried nave of eight bays and a chancel of three its length is nearly 200 feet, and the church is decidedly long for its other dimensions. But it is highly impressive. The arch of the uncompleted tower has extremely rich mouldings and clustered shafts, and the windows display a fine range of Puginesque curvilinear design. The chancel, with clustered pillars, is richer than the somewhat gaunt nave, and its modest altar erection does not impede the great eastern window of seven lights.

The completion date of this great church was 1856. Next year its architect emigrated to Australia, remaining there till he died in 1899. It was a profitable move, for Wardell got much work as Inspector General of Public Buildings in Victoria. His two Australian Cathedrals, at Melbourne where his model was Lichfield, and in Sydney where the East end of the great building has reminiscences of the Angel Choir at Lincoln, were more ambitious than any Victorian Gothic cathedrals put up by the Catholics of England.

Edward Welby Pugin's prolific career continued at full pitch till his death, aged forty-one, in 1875. Like other Catholic architects of the Victorian era he also had Irish commissions, and he designed buildings for Belgium and Cuba. He was Augustus Pugin's son by his second wife, inheriting much of his father's passionate, stormy nature. Like Augustus Pugin he indulged in "severe labour and intense application". He was "lively in temperament", and prone to depression. He added to his troubles by lawsuits and speculation; he desired that the words "Here lies a man of many miseries" should go on his grave.[10]

We have seen how Edward Pugin's earliest buildings were apt to be excellent, in the spirit of his father's best achievement. He worked less well in the 1860s and 1870s. In his apsidal church at Dewsbury he did, indeed show much skill in exploiting a tapering and sloping site, and there is real grandeur in his large church of St. Gregory at Longton, deep in the Arnold Bennett country of the five towns and the successor to a humble, pre-ecclesiological Early English building. Of brick and stone, it has a lofty, clerestoried nave leading on to a dramatic, apsidal sanctuary whose tall, traceried windows are in a Franco-Flemish Gothic idiom. A colossal wheel window admits light through the western wall. A Mr. Radcliffe gave much of the £7,000 laid out on this church. It was opened in 1869; Bishop Ullathorne remarked that it would be a "great boon to the poor Catholics in this dreary town of sin and mud".

A Flemish feeling also pervades Edward Pugin's Franciscan church which rises high above the railway sidings and drab streets of the Gorton area of Manchester. This is no surprise in view of the Belgian origin of the friars who came to start the mission.[11] The church was built between 1866 and 1872; the nave and its vaulted apse may indeed have been Pugin's model for his contemporary church in the Potteries. But what matters about this great church in Manchester is the handling of its western end as one sees it from along Queen's Road—it is unexcelled, in its majestic originality, by the exterior of almost any mid-Victorian Gothic church. A nicely vaulted vestibule is contained within the projecting depth of three tremendous buttresses; between them a couple of two-light, Geometrical windows lie deeply shadowed. The middle buttress broadens out, at the top, into the backing of a cleverly hooded figure of Christ on the Cross, while above the gable a slim *flèche* rises ethereally into the wan Lancashire sky.

Nearly all of this period's more notable Catholic churches were designed by architects whose religion was that of their patrons. Some country or small-town churches, or those in larger towns where few Catholic architects existed, were by local men, not necessarily Catholic. But for the more important jobs it became nearly universal to employ England's numerous, reasonably talented Catholic architects. The clergy naturally employed men who were within the fold and easy to brief for their needs. In any case, some Anglican architects were too busy for anything but Church of England commissions, while a few (like Street and Butterfield) had scruples over working for denominations other than their own. In its architecture, as in other respects, England's Victorian Catholicism largely flowed as a separate, though growingly important, stream.

A leading exception to this trend was the noble church of St. Peter at Lancaster, built in 1857-9 and since 1924 the Cathedral of a Roman Catholic diocese.[12] Here the architect was the inevitable local choice—Edward Graham Paley the well entrenched Lancaster designer, who

25 (a) *Parkminster, Sussex: Carthusian Priory*   26 *Liverpool, St. Clare's by*
   (b) *Norwich, St. John's*   *Leonard Stokes, 1890*
                                     (a) *General interior* (b) *The font*

along with Austin his partner obtained a large slice of the good Anglican business available in Victorian Lancashire. His early "Decorated" church, having references to Beverley Minster and others in Yorkshire, is a striking success, cruciform with a clerestoried nave, a north-western tower most gracefully capped by a lightly crocketted spire, and with its more recent throne installed in an apsidal chancel which is delightfully covered by a timber lierne vault.

But for the most part the Catholic architects obtained the available work. Gilbert Blount was fairly prolific, and at Gloucester his moderate-sized, ornate, somewhat congested church of the 1860s was finished off with a graceful broach spire, high-pitched above the open arcading which makes an attractive topmost stage to the tower. But Blount never excelled his great work of 1853–5, the splendid clerestoried nave of St. Anne's, Spitalfields, not far east of Hawksmoor's masterpiece of Christ Church.[13] The full plan was for a great cruciform centrally towered church for the combined use of the Marist community and the parish laity. But the apsidal sanctuary is of the 1890s, and Blount's nave, of five bays with an aisleless half bay to hold the organ gallery, is of splendid quality. It is a fine essay in the "Geometrical" Gothic of about 1270. The clustered columns have varied foliate capitals and support sharply pointed, moulded arches, and above the clerestory the high-pitched roof has convincingly medieval arched braces. The West window is a splendid rose of a Geometrical pattern; it comes as the main element of an ambitious western façade which must, when new, have lent distinction to a district of drab slumdom.

Other architects of this period gained special patronage in particular areas. C. G. Wray, whose work included churches at Maidstone and Market Harborough,[14] was helped, in his employment on the "school-churches" favoured in the Nottingham diocese, by being related to Bishop Bagshawe, the close follower of Manning who held that see in late Victorian times. We have seen how the forceful ugliness associated with the name of George Goldie was much in evidence in the Beverley diocese which till 1878 included all his native Yorkshire. It was indeed unfortunate that a typically ponderous, incongruously French Gothic Goldie church was the new St. Wilfred's at York, started in 1862 and near enough to the Minster to excite unhappy comparisons. Another practitioner in early French Gothic, sometimes in grey stone but also, on some occasions, in nasty polychromy of

27 (a) *Folkestone: design by Leonard Stokes* 28 *Westminster Cathedral*
   (b) *Watford: Holy Rood, by Bentley*   *by Bentley*

stone or brick, was Henry Clutton. At Formby he built a decidedly ugly church which was opened in 1864.[15] The same year saw the opening of his new church at Leamington, with "paired" nave pillars in the manner of Sens and a tower placed boldly beyond its southern aisle.[16] Its style, and its harsh red brick, are most unmannerly in the Regency context of this beautiful spa town,* while Clutton's work of the 1870s in the church of the Sacred Heart at Bournemouth is little more encouraging. One can hardly believe, amid such insensitivity, that Bentley was Clutton's pupil.

Matthew Ellison Hadfield, a prominent Sheffield citizen and a Councillor of that town, was busy, alike on churches and on secular commissions for the Norfolks, till his death in 1885.[17] His son Charles, who for over twenty years had worked with his father, completed some of his commissions and then in his own name continued the practice.

We still have to notice the varied, faithfully Gothic, and still reasonably prolific Catholic buildings of the Hansom dynasty.[18] Charles, as it happened, did little church work after 1870. By then he was comfortably resident at Clifton, in a Catholic diocese where ecclesiastical opportunities were by now rather limited. Already, and for the rest of his career, he was busier on such non-Catholic work as three public schools (Clifton College, Malvern College, and Kelly College at Tavistock) and on buildings for the Bristol School Board.[19] But in 1877 he completed the nave of a small church at Wells, late Perpendicular in its side windows but in its ambitious West window copying flamboyant work in a church in Normandy.[20] In deference to the city's genuine medieval glories the church was deliberately built in a more accomplished, and more expensive, way than was normal for the Victorian Catholic church of a small country town. Charles Hansom died in 1888. By then his son Edward, along with Archibald Mathias Dunn, was busy in the Newcastle partnership which lasted till 1893.† Though the partners were responsible for a few churches in the Midlands, and for the ornately "Decorated", still unfinished church

---

* A considerably better Clutton church, in its style and in the placing of its tower resembling his contemporary job at Leamington is the one built by the Duke of Bedford at the Fitzford end of Tavistock. For various reasons this building never received Anglican consecration, and after a chequered career of full use, partial use and closure, it became the town's Catholic church in 1951.

† Dunn's son, Archibald Manuel, continued as Edward Hansom's partner.

opened in Julian Road, Bath in 1881, their main entrenchment was in the Hexham and Newcastle diocese. Their best north country buildings, and two striking commissions much further south, are best handled in later chapters.

Charles Hansom's Gothic was always faithfully "ecclesiological". Joseph his brother was wider in his range,[21] and as one sees in his small church at Falmouth could be more robustly unconventional in the grouping of his architectural masses. The year 1869 saw him start what is certainly one of his masterpieces—the Jesuits' great stronghold of the Holy Name near the University in Manchester. The lightly pinnacled, octagonal top stage of its tower is much later, by Adrian Gilbert Scott and with a resemblance to the central tower of Liverpool's Anglican Cathedral.[22] But the main body of Joseph Hansom's church was completed in 1871. The style is a lofty, vaulted French Gothic, and the great width of the nave gives it an ample preaching space. But past the transept area there is an eastern limb whose apsidal sanctuary, being narrower than the nave and girt by an arcaded ambulatory, has a flavour of the great Catalan cathedral of Gerona.

Another of Joseph Hansom's Jesuit commissions was St. Aloysius' at Oxford; it cannot stand comparison with his Manchester church. Newman's scheme of the 1860s for an Oratory at Oxford had fallen through. So too had the project for a great Tudor Gothic parish church which would have vied with King's Chapel at Cambridge, or with the one which Wolsey planned for Christ Church. The actual St. Aloysius', completed in 1877 and later furnished with its twin tier of canopied statues in the apse,[23] is in a heavy version of the early French Gothic in vogue when Oxford University first came into being; it is aesthetically closer to the nearest zone of North Oxford's villadom than to the English late Gothic of Waynflete or Wolsey. Its square piers, decked with black or pink marble shafts, divide a visually convenient nave from aisles whose narrowness confines them to a function as passageways.

By the time that St. Aloysius' was built Joseph Hansom had as his partner Joseph Stanislaus his architect son. The young designer completed or embellished some of his father's tasks (among them the large church of the Servite Friars in South Kensington), and after Joseph Hansom's death in 1882 worked on in his profession; the Servites were soon his patrons for their more or less Early English church at Bognor.[24] Away across the flatlands of the Sussex coastal plain he had already

helped his father on a particularly splendid church at Arundel. Here, in
the great vaulted building with its soaring apse and narrow ambulatory,
and with the base of its projected tower and spire, is the French Gothic
of about 1250, of a lighter, more delicate type than that used at St.
Aloysius'.[25] It gives a strongly Continental air to the charming little
hillside town. The one incongruity about this Gothic masterpiece of
1869–73 is its dedication. The fifteenth Duke of Norfolk had a strong
devotion to St. Philip Neri, so he put his church at Arundel under the
patronage of that saintly figure of Renaissance Rome. The founder of
the Oratorians must, I feel, be a little disconcerted as he looks down on
the un-Renaissance splendour of the Duke's offering.

The Oratorians, being faithful to the architectural example of the
builder of Sta Maria in Vallicella, were the staunchest classicists amid
the overwhelming Gothic vogue. Despite Manning's advocacy of the
Roman styles mid-Victorian Catholic churches in the classical tradition
are extremely rare. One such is in Wapping, where St. Patrick's was
built in 1879–80; its designer was F. W. Tasker, whose interesting
career ran on till the early years of the coming century. The church
was a private benefaction, and two more bays and a narthex were added
in 1892.[26] The well-lit interior is basilican, and two rows of round
columns, Ionic and of Bath stone, support its architraves. Outside, the
pediments at each end, and their far-projecting eaves, give the "Tuscan
barn" impression of Covent Garden, Hassop, and Glossop.

A more special London case of Catholic classicism had been in 1864
when George Goldie designed a church, in Great Ormond Street, for
the Hospital of St. John of Jerusalem. There was no question here of his
usual Gothic ponderosities, for his brief was to model the building on
a Renaissance church in Malta. So a two-tiered classical façade became
the frontage of a pilastered nave. A delightful domed space stood before
the sanctuary, the altar being covered by a Corinthian *baldachino*. This
charming exotic was rebuilt, as the centre of a larger composition, by
Goldie's son Edward, when in the 1890s the Knights of St. John moved
out to St. John's Wood, there building the famous Hospital of S.S.
John and Elizabeth.[27]

The most spectacular classical Catholic interior in the provinces was
not that of a new church but a transformation. St. Wilfred's, Preston
was at first a large, gaunt building, of brick and in the "Methodist"
manner. This "capacious house of worship" was opened, in 1793, on
the fourth of June which was George III's birthday, *Messiah* being

performed before the actual function.[28] Then in 1879–80 Fr. Ignatius Scoles, S. J., with S. J. Nicholl his father's pupil, reconstructed the building.[29] A little dark, mellow brickwork survives outside from the older church, but most of the exterior is of harsher brick, with pink and grey stone and lavish sculpture in terracotta. Inside, one is amazed at what was called "a gorgeous basilican interior". The aisles are faced with yellow marble and have pink Corinthian pilasters, while the nave's architrave is upheld, on each side, by five superb Corinthian pillars of polished grey granite. The sanctuary is apsidal, and though there and in the lavish chapels one finds a certain coarseness in the sculpture the whole effect of the sanctuary end, with its richly coloured marbles picked out by gilding and lit from above, is of a splendour only equalled by that of the London Oratory.

When in 1852 Newman moved the Birmingham Oratory from Alcester Street to Hagley Road he had to be content with an unimpressive, severely utilitarian church. He had, indeed, obtained plans from the French architect Viollet le Duc, but these were never used.[30] His ideas were still ambitious, for some unsigned drawings of 1853 are for a basilican church in Lombard Romanesque.[31] The nave was to have been 115 feet long, and unlike the present Oratory this church was to have had a façade running flush with Hagley Road. Then in that same year Newman built his simple, barnlike church, with its roof transferred from an abandoned factory.[32] So far as this building could boast of any style its idiom was classical. When in 1858 an aisle was added by John Hungerford Pollen, Newman's architect for the polychrome Byzantine chapel which he had put up for his Catholic University in Dublin, that aisle was given a round-arched arcade. Two years later an architect named Thomason made plans for another Lombard Romanesque church.[33] But they remained unbuilt, and when Pollen added an apse and two transepts these extensions were in a "Norman" style. This twice extended church remained till after Newman's death in 1890. The Oratory house had in the meantime been built in the idiom of a Roman *palazzo*; it is there that Newman's room is reverently preserved, as the Cardinal knew it, as a most convincing religious and literary shrine.

The London Oratory was first established near Charing Cross, in what had been a dance hall named the Lowther Rooms; Pugin's attack on this chapel was unusually virulent. Then in 1853 the Oratorians moved to their present site off the Brompton Road. It was there that J. J. Scoles built the long, rectangular church which lasted for nearly thirty years. The barnlike Birmingham Oratory may have been his model. But this London interior had more definitely classical touches than Newman's church, and when the sanctuary was lengthened it was lined with good Corinthian pilasters.[34] But by the 1870s Scoles's church was too small. So plans were made for the grandiose assertion of St. Philip Neri's *Romanità*.

An important competition was held for the new Oratory church which started in 1880. Roman classicism was required of all contestants, and it seems that although the Oratorians themselves made the final award they were helped in their assessment by the eminent non-Catholic designer Alfred Waterhouse. Thirty architects put in designs, their price range being from £40,000 to £140,000.[35] Few if any could have actually built a Renaissance-classical church, and some were clearly much at sea. Except for Herbert Gribble, who won, and for Clutton the runner-up,[36] the competitors' names were not at the time disclosed. They lurked under such pseudonyms as *Ut puto*, *Laetatus Sum*, *Non timete*, and *Domus Dei* whose idiom resembled that of Sansovino. *Con Amore* alone "betrayed Gothic sympathies" by dispensing with the classical orders. But the attributions of some of the designs are known. Clutton's drawings allowed for a somewhat ponderous church; its dome was to be on a heavily rusticated drum, and two square-topped *campanili* were to flank its façade.[37] George Goldie's design was surprisingly better than most of his Gothic work; one feels that this kinsman of the Bonomis and Angelica Kauffmann may have missed his stylistic vocation. His London Oratory would have had a façade with two excellent domed towers, and a Baroque central section recalling that built by Ferdinando Fuga onto the piazza end of Sta Maria Maggiore in Rome.[38] From other designs preserved at the Oratory one sees that one John Kelly would have given the dome an attractive tall drum, while some unpleasant, over-ornamented plans came from a mercifully obscure architect named George Nattress.[39]

The winner, Herbert Gribble, was quite an outsider. A Plymothian, and a draughtsman with Joseph Hansom, he had added an aisle to Hansom's unimportant little Gothic church down by Mutton Cove in Devonport. The London Oratory was his only important work, and he died, aged forty-seven, in 1894.[40] It is a most successful exotic, well conveying the atmosphere of the Counter Reformation. The nave, with squared piers, paired Ionic half-columns, and noble Corinthian pilasters, has a bold cornice below its vaults and leads easily to the dome space before a spacious sanctuary. There the decoration, in the manner of St. Philip's time, is relatively restrained. The best thing in the church, in the transept on the Epistle side, is the gorgeous, genuinely Baroque altarpiece of the 1690s from a secularised Dominican church in Brescia. The church's general plan gives it more in common with S. Andrea della Valle in Rome than with the *Chiesa Nuova* not far away. The colonnaded façade may seem tame, but its pediment should have been more dramatic, while Brompton Road, like Ludgate Hill, was to have been confronted with two noble *campanili* like those of S. Agnese which in downtown Rome overlook the Piazza Navona.[41]

When the Oratory was finished in 1883 it was England's largest, most spacious Catholic church. For this reason it was there, and not in Our Lady of Victories, that Herbert Vaughan was enthroned as Archbishop of Westminster. The dome was added later, in sympathy with Gribble's intentions, by George Sherrin who designed the new, and classical church to replace the Regency Moorfields Chapel. But soon after the Oratory was first used London's other big Catholic competition job proved that Gothic, of a purer, more satisfactory type than that which had been rampant in the 1860s and 1870s, still had a distinguished part to play.

Chapter IX

A LATER GOTHIC PHASE

In the middle 1880s, when a competition was held to replace Joseph Bonomi's Spanish Embassy Chapel, Victorian Gothic had entered a final, and more pleasing, stage of its chequered career. Alike among Anglican and Catholic churchbuilders, and to an increasing degree among the Nonconformists, ecclesiological traditions still flourished. But the worst horrors of mid-Victorian wilful inventiveness and colour riot were now over. A pupil of Ignatius Bonomi, John Loughborough Pearson, was now in the first flight of Anglican architects. His larger churches, with their high vaults and mystic ambulatories, are among England's best nineteenth-century buildings. It might, indeed, have seemed rather late by now for the correct, impressive Early English of the Pearson school. Yet these backward glances seem justified, in a few notable late Victorian Catholic churches as well as in those by Pearson himself, and not least in the great Gothic building at Spanish Place.[1] Here in the Baker Street zone of London, and in a few other places where large private benefactions made it possible for Catholic churches to soar above the general run of Victorian mediocrity, some fine contributions were made to the late ecclesiological achievement.

Joseph Bonomi's Spanish Embassy Chapel of 1791 (see page 39) was enlarged in the nineteenth century and obtained the addition of a campanile. By the 1880s it was too small for its worshippers. A somewhat awkwardly shaped site was bought, and a competition was held

29 (a) *Westminster Cathedral: Lady Chapel*
(b) *Birmingham: Oratory, by E. Doran Webb*

to choose the designer of an ambitious church to be dedicated to St. James the patron of Spain. The Spanish Embassy retained its interest in Spanish Place, and King Alfonso XII gave some money for the work.[2] A sharp departure was planned from Bonomi's neo-classicism. For the new building was to be Gothic, and none but Catholic architects might compete for what was sure, in such a location, to bring the winner much prestige.

Nine architects submitted designs; their efforts are reviewed, in a somewhat querulous tone, by *The Builder*.[3] Herbert Gribble competed, in a style more consistent than that of Brompton Oratory with what one might expect from an assistant of Joseph Hansom. Peter Paul Pugin and Messrs. Dunn and Edward Hansom were among the better known Catholic entrants. J. Kelly, W. H. Pownall, A. E. Purdie, and C. G. Wray were none of them of special note. But we shall find that Leonard Stokes, aged twenty-seven in 1885, became most talented in a Gothic idiom less ecclesiological than that he now seems to have used in a five-aisled design, with a hexagonal central space, which he entered for Spanish Place. Gribble's design was "purely English Gothic", but allowing for tracery more ornate than that submitted by some others, while Peter Paul Pugin loyally followed his family's propensity for a lofty interior and a highly pitched roof.

The winning design, entered under "Goldie, Child, and Goldie", was actually that of Edward Goldie, the son of George Goldie who died, in 1887, just before the church was actually started.[4] It was a nice coincidence that the architect of the new church in Spanish Place was the great grandson of Joseph Bonomi who had designed the building now replaced. Edward Goldie's work, like other churches he designed elsewhere, proved him a less ponderous, and more sensitive architect than his father.

Though the tower and the spire of Edward Goldie's design were never built, the body of St. James's is very much as one sees it in the sketches of his design. In the nave triforium, however, the arches are not single openings but are divided into two by paired shafts, while in the apsidal sanctuary the windows at the triforium level are single lancets, not two-light, plate-traceried openings. The whole church, particularly its noble vaulted interior, is in the vein of Pearson's better achievements, yet its thirteenth-century Gothic owes more to the French idiom of Westminster Abbey than it does to such "Early English" masterpieces as Salisbury Cathedral or the nave of Wells.

30 *Neo-Renaissance*
  (a) *Brompton Oratory*
  (b) *Preston, St. Wilfred's: refashioned interior*

At its liturgical western end a large rose window completes the French impression. The whole church is of stone, with double nave aisles, a predominance of lancet windows, and continuous arcades to mask the effect of the apologetically shallow transepts. The basic simplicity of Goldie's work gives way, in the tall sanctuary, to a display of foliate bosses in the vaulting, while in the spandrels of the middle tier of its lancets adoring angels recall the Angel Choir at Lincoln or the South transept at Westminster.

St. James's Spanish Place was opened, with its nave incomplete, in 1890. By then two major provincial achievements could be credited to one of the unsuccessful competitors.

By the time that a new church was mooted in Spanish Place a crisis of accommodation had overwhelmed the Roman Catholics of Cambridge. Pugin's chapel off Union Road was now inadequate, and a new building was essential. The new rector felt that any such church should, in its own century, be a rival to the medieval glories of Cambridge. What was built, after a choice from several designs sent in by Dunn and Hansom, is certainly better than the chapel of St. John's College and the general run of the town's Anglican churches of last century. The fifteenth Duke of Norfolk gave half the money for a commanding site near the existing church, while Mrs. Lyne-Stephens (see page 128) was the decisive benefactress for the great cruciform church of Our Lady and the English Martyrs which was built by 1890.[5]

The style, appropriate in view of the native country of the lady who paid for the building, is French rather than English Gothic. The unaisled, apsidal sanctuary is particularly French in feeling, while the tracery, the foliate carving, and some other details would have fitted a date about 1300. But the steeple, in its north-western position recalling that of St. Mary Redcliffe in Bristol, has more English touches. For that far-seen Cambridge landmark the spire, with a cluster of pinnacles at its base, is a simple version of the one at St. Mary's Oxford, while the doorway, by which one enters the transeptal narthex of the nave, is Tudor Gothic of a type that would not be out of place in King's College chapel. The nave, unlike the sanctuary, has no triforium, and a spacious choir space fills the crossing beneath the low lantern tower. The arches into the two transepts are not designed as single openings, for each is parted, by a slim octagonal pillar, into two smaller arches; the device is that employed, by Dunn and Hansom, in a fine church which they were building, at the same time as this masterpiece in Cambridge, in their own city of Newcastle.

As at Cambridge, large benefactions lay behind the building, between 1889 and 1891 and for nearly £20,000, of St. Michael's in the Elswick district of the Tyneside metropolis. Here again Dunn and Hansom worked in an ecclesiological vein, not in the "Arts and Crafts" Gothic now gaining a foothold. They were, however, in tune with the current fashion, as one sees it in much work by G. F. Bodley, in that the style of this beautiful church was that of the late fourteenth-century transition between "Decorated" and "Perpendicular". St. Michael's is far more pleasing than Pugin's church which had become the Catholic cathedral in Newcastle; it was probably the best of many Dunn and Hansom churches in Roman Catholic Northumbria.[6] With a length of 134 feet it is of moderate size; its design and execution are what make it so sensitive a building.

St. Michael's, like its designers' work at Cambridge, is a transeptal church, but here in Elswick the shallow transepts project no distance past the walls of the aisles. The church's best, most picturesque point is its lantern tower, octagonal and with its due array of pinnacles and panelled battlements, which soars high above the crossing. But the whole building, with its short chancel and a clerestoried nave of six bays, is a finely varied essay in curvilinear Gothic; its high quality appears in the wide range of its tracery designs. Transoms occur in most of the larger windows, while below that in the East wall an imposing reredos, in two tiers of niches and with a special concentration on the figures of North country saints, runs all the way across the dignified chancel.

More cathedralesque than any of these late Victorian churches, and indeed having the dimensions one associates with a small medieval cathedral in England, is the great church of St. John the Baptist which rises high on the western outskirts of Norwich. Like our Lady and the English Martyrs at Cambridge it tends to be known, by such local *ciceroni* as bus conductors, as "the Catholic Cathedral". It was the gift, to his coreligionists in the chief city of the county whence he took his title, of the fifteenth Duke of Norfolk. It is, perhaps, the grandest of the Roman Catholic parish churches commenced in England in the nineteenth century. It replaced two older chapels, one in the middle of Norwich and one, not far from its own site, at Willow Lane.[7]

The designer chosen for this important building was George Gilbert, the eldest son of that leading Victorian architect Sir George Gilbert Scott. The nave was opened in 1894. George Gilbert Scott died soon afterwards, and it was his brother, John Oldrid Scott, who carried on the work. It was finished, with no deviations from its original style and with no hint of "Arts and Crafts" Gothic, in 1910. Here in this great cruciform centrally towered church, with proportions not unlike those of Winchester and St. Alban's Cathedrals, we have ecclesiological Early English of the most unflinchingly native type. Only in the apsidal Lady Chapel, said to resemble some work at Laon, do French Gothic touches break in. The short chancel, with its two tiers of lancets and a tieceron vault, is more ornate than the long, austere nave. The whole church, with what Professor Pevsner has called "self-effacing historicism",[8] shows a kinship with Pearson's work which was reasonable enough in 1882 but which, by the time of its completion in the year when the young Giles Gilbert Scott finished his excellent Arts and Crafts Gothic church at Sheringham not far away,[9] made it something of a period piece.

The last quarter of the nineteenth century, and the first few years after 1900, made a period of peak activity for many Catholic architects in the second flight. By now the rate of Catholic church building was falling off, and many of the buildings put up came not as new foundations but as the replacements of earlier, and often makeshift places of worship. Not all the Catholic architects then in practice, Charles Hadfield for instance or Edward Goldie, could wholly employ themselves on their church work. But some did manage, in these late Victorian years, to achieve a fair ecclesiastical output. They mainly, and unambitiously, kept within the imitative confines of a fairly close historicism. Yet in one respect they sometimes differed from the Gothic Revival architects, whether Anglican or otherwise, who had held the mid-Victorian field. They were more likely to produce versions of Perpendicular than those earlier designers whose canon had been "Early English" or "Decorated". So we find, at Aylesbury in 1893, that Edward Goldie completed a small aisleless church whose architectural idiom was attractively neo-Perpendicular and whose nave roof was of the hammerbeam type most favoured in the fifteenth century.[10] But only a few of those architects who worked into the present century joined in the newer, more poetic expressions of revived Gothic which fall to be noticed later in this chapter.

The last quarter of the nineteenth century covered the main activity of Peter Paul Pugin, Augustus' son by the third and last of his wives. His career seems to have been less tempestuous and controversial than those of his father and half brother. But like them he died (in 1904) comparatively young. His output, as befitted a member of so energetic a family, was extremely large, being much increased by his virtual monopoly of new commissions in the Scottish diocese of Glasgow.[11]

The counties on each side of the Mersey still provided good business for Catholic church architects. Three at least were based on Liverpool. One was a Gothicist, named James O'Byrne. He also designed the new sanctuary, of Renaissance design like the rest of the church, at St. Austin's, Preston;[12] his churchbuilding career had stretched back into the 1870's. J. F. Sinnott, whose business later had the name of Sinnott, Sinnott and Powell, was another. The Sinnott, Sinnott, and Powell church of S.S. Peter and Paul, Great Crosby was built in 1892–94.[13] It has a West front whose character is English late Decorated, but the interior of the spacious nave is of a more Gallic type. The tall arcades, with foliate capitals copied from early French Gothic, lead into aisles whose height is so nearly that of the nave that the feeling is that of a Poitevin hall church. We shall see how in a few more years this partnership was involved, elsewhere in Lancashire, in the building of a more radically planned Catholic worshipping space.

The third of these Liverpool architects was Edmund Kirby, whose large output stretched well past 1900. Some of his work lay in Lancashire, among it a spired church for the Benedictine parish at Parbold. He was particularly favoured in the diocese of Shrewsbury, till 1895 including North Wales.[14] So Cheshire and Shropshire both have Kirby churches; the former, with a large Catholic population in Chester and the Wirral, has the densest concentration. St. Werburgh's at Chester, Early English with an apsidal sanctuary of some dignity, is an early specimen, while from the last phase of Kirby's career Our Lady and the Apostles at Stockport marks a breakthrough from some of the conventions of Victorian Gothicism. An ambulatory lies behind the sanctuary apse, and the continuous clerestory runs boldly all round the church. The giant external arch of the entrance façade recalls Peterborough Cathedral and effectively includes a rose window. It is sad that this fine design is in brickwork of the harshly hideous redness unhappily typical of Prudential Assurance offices.

The years between 1875 and 1920 covered the long clerical cum architectural career of Father (and later Canon) Alexander Joseph Cory Scoles.[15] He was the third son of J. J. Scoles the architect. Like Ignatius his Jesuit brother he qualified in his father's profession before he became a priest; it was as a layman that he designed his pleasant little mock-Decorated church at Trowbridge. His output was large, and though he took his architect's fees he ploughed the money back into the Church. He was a colourful, strongmouthed, eccentric cleric who worked for much of his priestly career in Clifton diocese. But a sharp disagreement with his bishop caused his migration to that of Portsmouth. It was there, at Basingstoke where he was parish priest, that he built, and paid for, the church which some consider his best work. He had already done the same, at Bridgwater and then in Yeovil, for parishes under his care. Both Somerset churches, with their good handling of high Gothic details and in the excellence of the trefoil-headed arcading inside their chancels, suggests that here at all events more money existed for the refinements of design than in most of the churches, whether completed or never finished for lack of money, for which Fr. Scoles was the architect.

Most of Fr. Scoles's churches are in the southern and south-western counties which make up the Roman Catholic dioceses of Clifton, Plymouth and Portsmouth. Many, being built for small country or country town congregations with little money, are small, unambitious buildings. They are, as a rule, in simple Early English or else, as in the Franciscan Friary church at Clevedon, in the later thirteenth-century idiom which allowed for plate tracery. Mid-Victorian polychromy was avoided, so that stone and smooth plaster provide the main internal effects. It was unusual, and on a commission outside his normal territory, when Canon Scoles (along with G. Raymond his partner from 1903) designed an Italianate Catholic church at Kew Gardens. But in general the Canon kept firmly within the historic conventions of neo-medieval-ism. So the nave of the Scoles and Raymond church at Newton Abbot, completed in 1915 and with a well composed, scholarly street façade in the style originally current about 1260, shows how little these partners were in tune with the newer handling of Gothic by then well entrenched in the churches of all denominations.

By the last few years of Victoria's reign ecclesiological revivalism had all but worked itself out. There was, indeed, a sensitive and scholarly reaction against the stiflingly ornate, brassy, polychromatic horrors of mid-Victorian Gothic. So in the closing years of the century some architects showed how Gothicism, more tasteful than most of what had been built in the previous decades and exploiting the merits of late Decorated and the once despised Perpendicular, could still produce excellent work. In the liturgical field this more scholarly approach was aided by the researches and actions of such high Anglicans as the enthusiasts of the Alcuin Club. A real effort was now made to equip churches more nearly as had been done in the late Middle Ages. The second generation of ritualists was thus closer than were the pioneers to the liturgical practices of, say, the fifteenth century. Hand in hand with these developments in taste there came the wider practice of what was held to be the "English" or "Sarum" liturgical use; this was doubly convenient in that it was aesthetically tasteful, and that by so conducting one's choral eucharists one could be "high" without being too "Roman". Some, however, among the Anglo-Catholics preferred such ultramontane displays as birettas, six candles on the altar, and chasubles of the "fiddleback" cut, while in these late Manning and Vaughan days the "Alcuin" or "Sarum" movement found little if any echo in the liturgical practice of England's Roman Catholics. It was in architecture, rather than in the *montage* of the Mass, that the late Victorian Catholic designers moved in sympathy with what one may call the "Bodleyan" school. It was found, moreover, that side by side with this last phase of purely imitative neo-Gothic architecture other currents of taste, in the decorative arts rather than in the structure of churches, suggested that even within an over-riding Gothic formula one could still break new ground.

Just as some of Bodley's churches were wholly or in part decorated by the Preraphaelites, or by Morris and Burne Jones, so the later "Arts and Crafts" Gothic became partially linked with the sinuous, exotic fancies of *Art Nouveau*. But the Arts and Crafts movement was itself as much concerned with furnishing and interior decoration as with the main structure of buildings. The honest, unmechanical, at times escapist craftsmanship of William Morris and his devotees could thus be found in churches built each side of 1900. The architectural interest of the Arts and Crafts movement lay in its largely successful breaking away from the "historic" rigidities which had confined many Gothic Revivalists, and which still appeared in the copyism of Pearson and of the Catholic designers of such undeniably impressive churches as Norwich and Spanish Place. But in two main aspects of Arts and Crafts Gothic originality did appear. The architects of this school courageously tried to break away from the grouping of masses, or the disposition of windows and pinnacles, which the Middle Ages and the stricter revivalists had established as canonical. Their larger late Gothic windows were apt (with two important precedents at Gloucester Cathedral) to be sub-divided not only by mullions of the normal width but by mullions widened out to make buttresses. Though the shapes of these designers' arches, and their tracery designs, were often conventional by standards set before 1530 they included some arched openings, and some windows, which they treated with a fanciful invention unexplored in the pre-Reformation centuries. We have seen how the fittings and decoration of these "Arts and Crafts" churches could include both the honest simplicities of craftsmanship in oak and iron with the lighter fantasy of *Art Nouveau*, this often being expressed in the sinuosities of wrought ironwork or in the patterns of beaten copper.

Some Catholic architects whose career lay between 1880 and 1914 successively worked both in the late ecclesiological discipline and in the less inhibited Gothic of "Arts and Crafts". Others, among whom Giles Gilbert Scott became a leading figure, belonged mainly to the latter school. More significant, for a study such as this, is the position of these designers among the general body of their contemporaries. For while in the high-Victorian period the Catholic designers tended, in part because of a scarcity of funds, to produce work below the standards normally reached by the leading figures working for the Church of England, we now have three at least among the Roman Catholic church, architects—Bentley, Leonard Stokes, and Giles Scott—who were in the top flight.

Before we come to some "ecclesiological" work by leading Catholic architects who also made their names in the later idiom we can briefly notice two churches in Hampshire which suggested how things had changed, in the 1890's, from the basic designs and stylistic flavour of the earlier Gothicists. One is at Southampton, the other at Boscombe. Both are by an otherwise little known architect named J. W. Lunn. St. Edmund's at Southampton was being built in 1889.[16] It was to have had a tall, thinly pinnacled tower at its liturgical North-East corner. It is another church where the ugly redness of its outer brickwork belies a far better interior. The style of this fairly costly church is the late Decorated which was then in vogue. The clerestory windows have well varied tracery. The "West" wall contains an admirable "flowing" wheel window, while above the High Altar another wheel window is kept small, like others we have noticed, so as not to impinge on a tall reredos.

Lunn's church of Corpus Christi at Boscombe is more unusual, both for the identity of its donor and for the handling of its main material. The Von Hügel family were frequent visitors to Boscombe.[17] So this large Jesuit church was built by Baroness Pauline, a sister of Baron Friedrich, the prominent Catholic philosopher.* Commenced in 1895, it is imposing, in a simple lancet Gothic, with an inner arcade and paired lancets round its apsidal sanctuary. The stone arches of its nave are overshadowed, in a church where stone dressings are sparse, by splendid, almost Hanseatic German stretches of exposed brickwork, giving a powerful character to the Baroness' offering.

The career of John Francis Bentley spanned both ecclesiological and Arts and Crafts Gothic.[18] He was born in 1839, the son of a wine merchant in Doncaster. He joined the Roman Church in 1862; by then he had been trained both in engineering and building, and had started his independent architectural career. He had been Clutton's pupil, but that architect's ponderous French Gothic was absent from his own work. From Clutton, however, and some other mid-Victorians he gained the love of colour which he later expressed in *opus sectile* and mosaic. His career was mainly that of a refined Gothicist, with a few excursions into the English Renaissance; one has to remember that his best known work lay outside his normal stream of taste.

Bentley was a sensitive, withdrawn artist, disliking self-assertion and architectural competitions. Much of his work, as in delicately worked altarpieces at Spanish Place and in Holy Name, Manchester, lay in furnishing and decoration. He added some aisles and chapels to existing churches. At the Redemptorist church in Clapham (see page 134) Bentley's addition, in a pure fourteenth-century style, very sympathetic to Wardell's main fabric but out of scale with the rest of the church, amounted to a complete new transept, double-aisled and of considerable length so as virtually to form a second nave. But his completely new churches and chapels were few.

The first of them, "Early English" in the late ecclesiological tradition, is St. Mary's, Cadogan Street, Chelsea. It replaced a simple Regency chapel of 1811-12; this had been built, with help from exiled French royalty and aristocrats, by an emigré priest the Abbé Voyaux de Franous. Bentley had already designed a pulpit, and a new altar, for this chapel, and these were replaced in his new building of 1877-9. The church is simple, and of no special merit. Lack of money restrained the

* A western bay, and an Arts and Crafts Gothic tower with an octagonal top stage, were added in the 1930s.

architect, whose somewhat more ornate initial designs of 1877 were never carried out.[19] They allow, among other points, for an attractive set of three early "Decorated" East windows instead of the four actual lancets. The central opening was to have two lights, the flanking windows being of a single light apiece. We shall see how this grouping recurs in another, more ambitious Bentley church.

Bentley's next church was that of Our Lady and the Holy Souls in Kensal Green. The clergy first opted for Romanesque, but Bentley won them over to an "Early English" design, realised in 1881–82. The mainly brick exterior, with a long nave, transepts flush with the aisle walls, and the short chancel then preferred for Roman Catholic churches in England, is of no special distinction. But the south-western turret and its stone spirelet make an attractive composition, while between the western lancets two shallow, semi-octagonal buttresses are delicately detailed in a nice reaction from coarsely florid mid-Victorian taste.

From 1886 onwards Bentley superintended the first stages of what should have been his greatest Gothic work. The present church of Corpus Christi, Brixton Hill is merely the eastern part of a far larger conception. Its aisled chancel, outer chapels, and shallow transepts lack the nave and the tower which were also planned; they arise in busy southern London as does the vast fragment of the cathedral over the streets of Beauvais. The outside of the church is of red brick, with generous stone dressings; within, the rendering is in stone and pale plaster. The church's style and detail are fairly literally of the English fourteenth century; only in some furnishings, for example in the delicate detail of the brass altar rails, are there traces of the more venturesome Gothic of "Arts and Crafts". The great church was meant to have a complete vault. But over most of the chancel a pointed waggon roof rests on vaulted coving which springs up from each wall. It is at the East end that Bentley's finest architectural effect appears. For in an elaboration of the 1.2.1 fenestration he had planned for Cadogan Street he gave his Brixton church a trio of eastern windows whose central element has three lights, and whose flanking members each have two; below them an exquisite arcade of cusped arches is similarly arranged.

On a smaller scale, but completed without the financial frustrations of Brixton, Bentley's church of the Holy Rood at Watford replaced an earlier chapel. It was financed by a single benefactor. Cardinal Manning presented the foundation stone which was laid in 1889; most of the building was opened in the next year. It is an exquisitely finished and detailed building, mostly in the Perpendicular style and with a strong Hertfordshire character in the handling of its exterior. Some elements of design it borrows from what its architect had done at Brixton. For as in the Brixton church two-tiered arcades part the shallow transepts from the congregational space, while the East windows, like those at Brixton Hill, are arranged in the pattern of 2.3.2. Bentley's "Perpendicular" is much of it rendered in an "Arts and Crafts" Gothic idiom, while his decoration of this type is specially charming in the electric light pendents, in the shallow-bowled font, and in other details of the vaulted baptistry created beneath the tower. This tower, along with the north aisle and the founder's chapel, was built a little later than the rest of the church. In 1900, when it was opened, the architect himself lay stricken in his final illness. It is fitting that here, in the most characteristic of his works, one finds Bentley's own memorial plaque; like some of his chapel fittings, and Junior School Buildings, at Beaumont College it is in the Renaissance taste.

Bentley designed one Anglican church (at Chiddingstone Causeway in Kent) and his unexecuted Catholic schemes included two cathedrals for dioceses in the United States. His actual cathedral lay almost wholly outside the main aesthetic current of his work.

Other Catholic architects of the last years of the nineteenth century did imitative Gothic work as a prelude to more pioneering activity. Leonard Stokes, who became a major figure in a more progressive phase, was one of these, as one sees in his chancel at Exeter and in a poor "Decorated" church commenced in 1884 at Maidenhead.[20] Frederick A. Walters, the son of an architect in London, and articled both to his father and to Goldie and Child,[21] was another designer whose earliest churches did not fully foreshadow his later achievements. Much of his early work was in "historic" Gothic. Among other designs of this type was his scheme, got out in 1888 but never carried out, for a large new church at Winchester, cruciform and with some of its neo-Perpendicular details resembling features of the Priory at Great Malvern.[22] The 1880s also saw Walters working on another notable church, like that at Cambridge much indebted to a single benefactress, and like it too in being an important late ecclesiological work. The first part of the Jesuit church at Wimbledon was opened in 1887, a long, ornate, somewhat crowded building, in elaborate "Decorated" with a continuous clerestory and an imposing apse. Its western façade, of 1901, has a charming pair of flanking turrets which suggest that here was an architect whose other Gothic work could contain new delicacy and freedom.

Throughout his career Walters also had considerable success in the second revival of Norman Romanesque. The first Victorian efforts to imitate this style had as a rule been unhappy. Now, however, there were various designers (for the most part Catholics) who worked more convincingly in this important pre-Gothic style.

One work of this Romanesque revival is at Beccles in Suffolk. The architect of this barrell-vaulted Benedictine church was F. E. Banham, a local man; he worked elsewhere for the monks of the English congregation. The first part of this never completed church was opened in 1889. It was meant to serve a small priory, and in 1901–02 its designer made drawings for an apsidal eastern end[23] which would have housed the conventual part of a monastery church of moderate size. F. W. Tasker was another late Victorian Catholic architect to use Romanesque as well as Renaissance or Gothic. Not long before he died, aged fifty-six, in 1904 he designed two such churches.[24] One, at Catford in South London, was opened soon after his death.[25] The other, put up in 1902–03, is the well designed and detailed Catholic church at Clacton.[26] It is transeptal, with cylindrical piers and scalloped capitals in the twelfth-century manner; its shrine of Our Lady of Light is in one of the transept chapels. Its best feature, recalling some medieval monastic church, is the fine arcade of the ambulatory which circles behind its High Altar.

Another Catholic neo-Normanist, though also an adept at Gothic, was one of our priest-architects. Like Canon Scoles, Fr. Benedict Williamson was something of an eccentric. A student both of law and architecture, and a convert Catholic, he designed several churches and wrote books on mysticism, hagiography, and church art.[27] His most important Romanesque church he built before he became a priest. This is the great church of St. Ignatius, on a busy North London highway, at Stamford Hill; Cardinal Vaughan laid its foundation stone in 1902. With its pair of (liturgically) western towers, a nave and transepts, and a mosaic-clad chancel which has a square end and a passageway behind it, it is strongly French in its idiom and in the style which marked the move from Romanesque to the earliest Gothic. A wheel window and several lancets keep company in its roadward façade, while the eight large arches of the nave arcades are slightly pointed but rest on capitals which are wholly Romanesque. Tunnel vaults of an almost Cluniac character are another striking point in this busy stronghold of the Society of Jesus.

Another of Williamson's churches, from the time when he was a priest and dating from 1911, is the Franciscan Capuchin church down Iffley Road at Oxford. It is a curious, chastely designed mixture of flint rubble and pink granite dressings. At one end of its clerestoried nave a gabled tower has a central spirelet of green copper, while beyond the lofty chancel arch a sanctuary leads on, past the two sacrarium doors, to a concealed choir for the Offices of the friars. The whole church is Romanesque, with correct and reasonably effective neo-Norman details such as cushion capitals. As in the Jesuit church in Stamford Hill there is an inherent anachronism, for the style is that which was current about a hundred years before the Franciscans existed.

The most prolific of these neo-Normanists was F. A. Walters; as with his Gothic churches one finds him kept specially busy in the south-eastern counties comprising the Southwark diocese. His Romanesque church at Deal (an early commission, of the 1880s) and the first part of his design at Sevenoaks, call for no special comment. His church in Battersea is more innovating, with its somewhat Germanic *Westwerk* rising up to a western tower, an octagonal top storey, and a slender, spirelike cap. Better than these are two churches in South Wales and a real masterpiece in the Shires; the two former were commissions from the Benedictines who were Walters's steady patrons.

The church of St. Mary of the Angels, in the Canton district of Cardiff, was started in 1907. Its exterior and its western façade, are well composed and simply detailed. Inside, Walters's Romanesque is more ornate, and the foliate capitals of the double bays in the church's spacious nave are those of the transition to the earliest Gothic; the clerestory windows, whose glass recalls that which once adorned the cathedral choir at Canterbury, are also in the manner of about 1180. A much more evidently neo-Norman church by Walters is his later work, not far away, at Penarth. Here too the exterior design is in the simpli-fied Romanesque much favoured by this architect, and there are plain pilasters on the noble eastern grouping of a squared sanctuary, round-apsed side chapels, and shallow transepts. The nave, with five bays and a little extra length for a western gallery, has a wheel-pattern West window, a clerestory of single openings, squared orders in its arcades, and more capitals of a "transitional" type. The aisles are mere passage-ways, a convincingly Norman arch leads into each side chapel, and the sides of the sanctuary cant inwards, as at Canterbury, towards the High Altar.

The date of this excellent Walters church at Penarth is given as 1915; the same year saw the starting, in the feudal and aristocratic setting of Ashby de la Zouch, of the architect's best essay in Romanesque.

As one enters Ashby de la Zouch from the South one's first archi-tectural encounters are with the Regency buildings of the town's one-time spa quarter, with a finely placed neo-Norman Catholic church, and with a tall Victorian monument in the shape and high Gothic style of an Eleanor Cross. This memorial very appropriately commemorates the tenth Countess of Loudoun who died in 1874. She held three Scottish peerages in her own right, and also achieved the rare gen-ealogical feat of holding in her person the four medieval baronies of Botreaux, Hungerford, Moleyns, and the local one of the Hastings family. Her daughter, Lady Flora Paulyna Abney Hastings, became a Catholic and duly married the fifteenth Duke of Norfolk; it was from her bequests that the Duke started this church. Such is the proud back-ground of a building far superior to most Catholic churches in Midland or southern country towns. Its arcaded tower, recalling the Norman belfry at Bury St. Edmund's and dominating the roadward approach, is at the church's south-eastern corner; behind it the chancel apse has blind arcading and then a set of bold arches along its window stage. Much zig-zag moulding, and other typically Norman ornament, all crisply rendered, appear on this opulent, cross-shaped church. The nave has one aisle, and a stately arcade of five arches whose pillars are clustered or round. The crossing and the main apse are vaulted in the manner of an unusually fine Anglo-Norman parish church. By the time that this church at Ashby was built it was almost too late for such a building to be wholly convincing. It proved, however, that Walters was a fine master of the repertoire of Romanesque.

Before we reach the final phase of revived Gothic, as this appeared in England's Catholic churches, we must glance briefly at a few which in the late Victorian and Edwardian period stayed faithful to classicism. Some of these are in London. The new church at Moorfields, built in 1899–1902 to replace John Newman's famous Regency chapel, was one of them; George Sherrin its architect well used the marble Corinth-ian columns from behind the older High Altar. In Cheyne Row,

Chelsea, the Renaissance classical style of the church of Holy Redeemer, which was started in 1894, came from the direct instructions of Canon Keens the client to a somewhat reluctant Edward Goldie. When complaints came in about the interior's "concert hall" appearance the architect explained that an inevitable narrowing of the site, and lack of money, had prevented him from perfecting a domed, more "Oratorian" design.[28] In Soho Square the new St. Patrick's, replacing a large chapel of the 1790s, was designed by J. J. Kelly in an Italianate Romanesque, and given a *campanile*, which would suit the many Italians in a polyglot congregation. Near Lincoln's Inn Fields the Italian traditions of the rebuilt Sardinian Chapel were respected by F. A. Walters when the cutting through of Kingsway caused the demolition of that church. He gave S.S. Anselm and Cecilia a façade in a freely interpreted, somewhat Flemish Renaissance style, with more Renaissance details in the nave, and behind the rood loft in the strangely narrow sanctuary with its flanking passageways.

In the provinces, the completion of the new chapel at Prior Park was achieved in the early 1880s. Fr. A. J. Scoles faithfully completed his father's forty-year old design, and his splendid Corinthian interior was described as "the most perfect model of a Roman basilica existing in England".[29] The last years of the nineteenth century saw some striking classical decoration and re-painting in St. Charles Borromeo's at Hull, a church already newly ceiled, and given new aisles, by local architects named Smith, Brodrick, and Lowther. The artist employed was Heinrich Immenkamp, a German then living in the Yorkshire port.[30] His work was highly dramatic, a belated version of that done in the lavish Rococo settings of central or southern Germany. A sculptured Trinity was poised above the main altarpiece, with its Dove looking down on the Globe, and on a bank of billowing clouds, from a rich *gloria* of rays. Other paintings were all of them in the most elaborate taste.

The most important new classical church of this period was that built by the Birmingham Oratorians. It was planned as a memorial to Newman, and enshrines a rich marble altar set up in the older church soon after the Cardinal's death. The church which Newman knew was gradually pulled down as its successor was built. The new Oratory was set back, behind a forecourt, from the busy Hagley Road. With its simple pedimented façade, short transepts, a low dome, and a shallow-apsed, marble-lined sanctuary it is in an earlier version of the Renaissance style than its counterpart in Kensington. Its nave is basilican in the true ancient Roman manner, its tunnel roof and horizontal architraves being held up, on each side, by a noble row of six mono-lithic Corinthian columns, unfluted and of Serravezza marble from northern Italy. This admirable basilican Oratory was started in 1903; its completion year was 1909. Its designer was E. Doran Webb of Salisbury. The bulk of his church work was Gothic. He was more typically himself in his Catholic church at Swindon, neo-Decorated, cruciform, with a squat central tower and outer flintwork sympathetic to the neighbouring Wiltshire downlands.

Lastly, in a chapter taking us to the fatal year of 1914, we have the Catholic activity of the Arts and Crafts Gothicists. Not only did these designers render Gothic with a new delicacy, freedom, and inventive-ness, but some of them showed signs of a new approach to the planning of congregational space. No changes, as yet, were apparent in the actions or postures of the Mass, and such innovations as Mass facing the people, or a liturgy largely in English were inconceivably remote. But it was being more widely realised that seats in aisles were pointlessly unliturgical, and that visual co-operation, if not oral participation, was worth striving for when architects designed their naves.

Leonard Stokes was important in these new developments; one may now survey the main elements of his career.[31] Born in Southport in 1858 he came to London as a boy, there entering the office of S. J. Nicholl. As Nicholl had been J. J. Scoles's partner and pupil one may see in Stokes another figure in the Catholic architectural dynasty which had started with the Bonomis. But late Victorian Gothicists like Bodley, St. Aubyn, and Garner were more of an influence on Stokes, and in the secular side of his architectural career his output of excellent, functional telephone exchanges was helped on by his having married a daughter of the General Manager of the National Telephone Com-pany. It was not till late in the 1880s, in the fine Liverpool church of St. Clare, that he propounded the idea that aisles were not meant for seats but were best left as mere passageways.

St. Clare's is a true masterpiece and one of the best churches which I must mention in this book. It was the gift of two wealthy brothers, being placed in the staid residential district of Sefton Park, not far from Pearson's Anglican Church of St. Agnes with its admirable vicarage by Norman Shaw. It soon attracted foreign attention as well as local admiration.[32] It was started in 1888 and finished in two years.[33] It

31 *Walters Neo-Norman*
   (a) *Ashby de la Zouch*
   (b) *Penarth, Glamorgan*
   (c) *Canton, Cardiff*

32 *Downside Abbey*
   (a) *The Goodridge buildings, 1822*
   (b) *The later church*

St Josephs R.C.Church
Penarth
Glamorgan

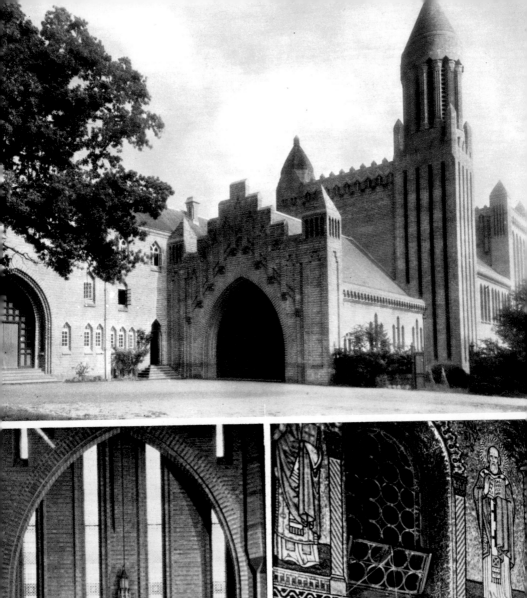

THE HIGHPRIEST RECEIVED MARY & BLEST HE

blends progressive planning, Bodleyan influences, and details from the rich repertoire of "Arts and Crafts". Its roof section, and the "late Decorated" tracery of its windows, recalled Bodley's recent church at Pendlebury near Salford;* the 2.3.2 pattern of its West window made a unified version of the fenestration used by Bentley at Brixton. The lengthy, nine-bay nave has narrow aisles beneath continuous side galleries running just below the upper windows; each aisle widens out into a spacious eastern chapel. The pulpit, with its sides sloping outwards towards the base and with beautiful openwork panels, the confessional doorways, the alabaster font with its rich copper cover behind iron railings in Arts and Crafts Gothic, and other details of this same school in the churchyard gates, all show how an imaginative artist could soar above the conventions of a stiffer Victorianism.

Stokes exploited the idea of narrow nave aisles in other churches of the 1890s. His designs for All Souls', Peterborough[34] show them in an apsidal church whose tracery is a free version of "Decorated", and whose West window has lights in the pattern of 2.3.2. The Holy Ghost, Balham, started in 1896, has a wide North aisle. But that on its Southern side is no more than a narrow passage with a striking series of pointed tunnel vaults, like those in the choir aisles of Bristol Cathedral in that they are placed at right angles to the nave. The church's style is that of about 1360 which was much favoured by the architects of this school, and the simple nave arcades have pillars which are hexagonal and without capitals—a later version of those which Stokes planned for the greatest of his unexecuted designs.† Aisleless churches were also within this inventive architect's scope. His designs for the sturdily composed Arts and Crafts Perpendicular Catholic church at Folkestone were based on this ground plan. He exhibited his drawings at the Academy of 1888 and *The Builder*, in the first of two articles,[35] points out that all of the church's five hundred worshippers were to see the High Altar.

An important church in Salford, designed on the same lines as St. Clare's at Liverpool, gives an insight into the thinking behind these more intelligently designed congregational spaces.

In 1898 the parish of St. Sebastian's, Pendleton was handed to the

* The five-light East window, set high above the great tritych altarpiece, is not as Stokes first designed it. His drawings in the R.I.B.A. (U 3.) show a cross worked into its tracery.

† See the next chapter, page . 172

33 *Downside:*
   nave and choir

34 (a) *Quarr Abbey: church from south-west*
   (b) *Quarr: reordered sanctuary*
   (c) *Droitwich: some nave mosaics*

Dominicans; though the church is now served by secular clergy (with the Priory buildings used as the offices of the Salford diocese) the arms of the Order of Preachers remain, in the West door's tympanum, to recall its history. The designs were by the Liverpool firm of Sinnott, Sinnott, and Powell. They were said to be based on a church in Ostend. But one feels that the designers needed no more for their ideas than some dialogue with the Dominicans and a quick trip up to Arundel Avenue near Sefton Park. Sketches were circulated, for comment, to many members of the Order.[36] One friar hoped for an extra bay to make the church as long as St. Dominic's in Newcastle. Elaborate detail was to be sacrificed to gain more height, and to have a "grand, open, massive church". The Prior of the new friary at Hawkesyard in Staffordshire considered, once the plans were settled, that the church at Pendleton would be "entirely on new lines, different from anything in England up to now". He must have known little of Stokes's Liverpool masterpiece. For in its simple way, and with a somewhat bald exterior, St. Sebastian's is on much the same lines as St. Clare's. The chancel apse, with its inner arcade of marble or granite columns, is disappointing and in the earlier, less happy Victorian manner. But the nave, of six bays, and with an unaisled space to admit its western gallery, is nobly pioneering. Bold arches span it to define its bays. Its trios of clerestory lancets have rear arches on the inside, and on the outside long sloping reveals give emphasis to each trio. As in St. Clare's the aisles are narrow passages, with continuous galleries, connecting bay to bay, just below the clerestory. Shallow transepts come before the chancel whose stalls, with richly designed ends, survive from the church's Dominican days.

F. A. Walters was also prolific in this new aspect of revived Gothic. Much of his work lay in his special territory of Southwark diocese. At Heron's Ghyll, Sussex and at Godalming he built small "Early English" churches which respected local building traditions. For the latter of the two Mr. Ian Nairn has used the odd descriptive phrase of "low-voltage late Gothic Revival".[37] A sketch shows that Walters's "Dec-Perp" church at Petworth, with a flushwork parapet and a slim spike above its turret, was more ambitiously planned, while away in West Wales his church at Tenby is an attractive building of 1892–3, its northern windows being set high in the nave wall, and a canopied statue niche being placed between a pair of eastern windows.[38]

In South London a far larger Walters church is St. Anne's, Vauxhall of 1903-7; it ranks as one of his finest works. Its street façade, with a quartet of bold buttresses, a pair of lancets, and a vesica above them, gains distinction from the grouping and fenestration of a fine gabled north-western tower. The five-bay nave, with its eastern bay canted inwards to lead one's eye to the stencilled chancel with its "Arts and Crafts" stalls, combines the newer planning with some late Gothic Revival refinements. There are passageway aisles, and as the church has no clerestory the aisles are lofty; their arches die gently into the small capitals of the piers. "Early English", of an economical simplicity, is the dominant style.

Another South London church with passageway aisles and an "Early English" idiom is that of the English Martyrs, Walworth. It was started in 1902, and F. W. Tasker was its architect. It is an admirably simple Gothic work, of yellow brick outside and red brick within. Narrow arches pierce its piers to make the passageway, and over each bay of the nave a steeply pointed transverse vault runs at right angles to the main direction of the nave.[39]

Giles Gilbert Scott, hard at work on his Anglican cathedral at Liverpool, found time for some Edwardian Gothic commissions for his own church. We have noted his Sheringham building; another work, remarkable for the grouping of its masses as well as for the free handling of its tracery and the Arts and Crafts detail of its iron and woodwork, is his church of the Annunciation in Bournemouth's inland suburbia. Its variation of roof levels was unconventional to the verge of revolution. A very low nave, with side windows so deeply recessed that passages run through the piers of their rear arches, has a low-pitched roof. A central element rises dramatically, as it were like a tower. But the sanctuary continues beyond it at the same height. The light which falls on the High Altar is strikingly concealed. There is no East window, and the "tower" only has windows in its sunny western and southern sides.

Arts and Crafts Gothic, sensitive and attractively planned, also appeared in some unexecuted Catholic designs. One finds it in the plans by Eastwood, the architect of the new cathedral at Leeds, for churches at Bridgeford near Nottingham and at Hemsworth in the Yorkshire coalfield.[40] Leonard Stokes also planned an exquisite unachieved church. He had designed the two new school wings, with beautifully rendered detail, which were put up at Downside in 1910–12. His complete plan was much more ambitious, and would have swept away the old house and Goodridge's additions.[41] So when the monks projected a new permanent church for their nearby parish at Radstock they naturally turned to Stokes for designs. His drawings[42] are for an aisleless, cruciform building, lying low along its site with a wheel window in its West wall, and with Arts and Crafts Perpendicular as its general style. The date on the drawings, explaining the church's non-commencement and marking the end of an era, is that of 1914.

Chapter X

CATHEDRALS AND CONVENTS CONTINUED

Along with the late Victorian or Edwardian Catholic parish churches a few cathedral and conventual churches contributed to this country's sum total of architectural aspiration and achievement. The available Gothic styles, with a few exceptions, made the stylistic running.

One existing church, moreover, attained cathedral status at the very end of last century. In 1895 the whole of Wales, bar Glamorgan and Monmouthshire, was made a separate Vicariate. Three years later it became a full diocese, its title being Menevia, which was the old Latin name for St. David's. But the bishop's headquarters was as far as possible from the village-city in its remote corner of Pembrokeshire. It was set at Wrexham, and Edward Pugin's church of Our Lady of Sorrows became a cathedral. Opened in 1857, it is a respectable work of its architect's early period. It was built, by a private donor, as a parish church of moderate size. It has quatrefoil columns and fine foliate capitals in its clerestoried nave. In its chancel the East window only has tracery, and no vertical mullions, in a space which is only the upper part of a Gothic arch. We shall see how this small Cathedral has of late been adapted both to its status and to the needs of its large parish congregation.

Our next cathedral, a late ecclesiological work of red brick and stone, is that at Portsmouth. The project, for what was already described as a new cathedral,[1] was afoot in 1877. Though the new Roman bishopric of Portsmouth was not formally created till 1882 the Vatican machinery had for some time been at work on the idea of partitioning the Southwark diocese. The new building, replacing the enlarged late Georgian chapel in Portsea, could be planned from the start on cathedral-esque lines though on a scale which was modest by the cathedral standards of the Middle Ages.

A competition was held. Plans came in from various architects, Joseph Hansom and C. G. Wray being among them. The chosen designer was a London architect named J. A. Crawley, already responsible for Catholic churches at Havant and elsewhere in the Southwark diocese, and in 1880 the author of some elaborate neo-Decorated plans for a diocesan seminary which was projected at Clapham but never built.[2] His plans of 1877 were for a church of some pretension. He allowed for the use of all the available site in Edinburgh Road. His building was to be cruciform, 181 feet long inside, early "Decorated" in style and with a tower and spire just over 200 feet in height.[3] The Duke of Norfolk gave money both for the site and for the building work. Operations started about 1879.[4] In 1882 five bays of the nave were opened on the very day when the first Bishop of Portsmouth was enthroned.[5] Crawley had died in 1881, his practice being taken over by Joseph Hansom and his son Joseph Stanislaus. It was the latter, after his father's death, who finished the transepts, the side chapels with their two-arched arcades contained in a single structural bay of the chancel, and the apsidal chapel which in a way resembles that of Our Lady and the English Martyrs at Cambridge; the likeness is reinforced by the Gothic *baldachino* above the High Altar. Early this century the nave was lengthened westwards by Canon Scoles.[6] The tower and spire were never built, but some compensation came, in the West front, in the two corner turrets whose spirelets with their sheathing of green copper rise up among the other copper-clad features which brighten the sky-line of central Portsmouth.

Those who completed Crawley's work were faithful to his intentions, and the Cathedral at Portsmouth is very much as he planned it.[7] Its early "Decorated" detail includes a good wheel window, with tracery of a late fourteenth-century flamboyance, in its southern transept, and the whole interior is of some dignity. In the nave and chancel roofs the hammerbeam idea of Crawley's sketches made way for coved vaults along each side, with a barrel ceiling along the cathedral's centreline.

Another Gothic Cathedral in a Catholic diocese was brought about by conditions more familiar nowadays than in the earliest years of the motor age. Dislocations in 1901 caused the building, by 1904, of what is, perhaps, the most attractive of all England's Roman Catholic Cathedrals. The Corporation of Leeds had plans for important street improvements. These led to the compulsory purchase of St. Anne's Cathedral, built in 1839 and only since 1878 in the enjoyment of its new status. The new Cathedral, on a nearby site was by J. H. Eastwood of London; one wishes that more churches had been built from his designs.[8] The building is short, but of a fair internal height beneath roofs of low pitch; where it gains is in the uncumbered width of the seating space in a three-bay nave whose short tower arises on its northern side. The transepts are of no great note, but beyond the nave the choir has its own passageway aisles, with galleries above them, and is of four delicately handled bays. Arts and Crafts Gothic is inventively displayed in the pinnacles of the tower and of the West front, in the tracery of several windows, and in some fittings which keep company with Augustus Pugin's "ecclesiological" altarpiece, transferred from the older Cathedral to its successor's Lady Chapel.

By the time that the new Cathedral at Leeds was started the Metro-politan See was well on the way to the belated acquisition of a really large and spacious cathedral.

After Cardinal Wiseman had died there were many who felt that a fine cathedral would be a worthy memorial to Westminster's first Archbishop. Cardinal Manning was not, in principle, opposed to such a scheme. But a new cathedral, when set against various other pastoral needs, came low in his order of priorities. So Our Lady of Victories in Kensington continued, for some thirty years, as the "pro"-Cathedral of the Westminster archdiocese.[9] We may be thankful, architecturally speaking, for the long delay, for the first projects for a Catholic cathedral in Westminster were far from happy.

In 1867, within three years of Wiseman's death, a cathedral site was bought; it was closer to Victoria Station than is the actual cathedral. Henry Clutton was appointed cathedral architect. He designed two successive buildings. The first was long and narrow. The second, when more gound had been bought to widen the site, was for a vast building which would have given London's Catholics their French Gothic equivalent to St. Patrick's in New York. A sketch[10] shows that it would have been an unhappy answer to the genuinely French Gothic Abbey at the other end of Victoria Street. Its length would have been 450 feet and its extreme breadth the tremendous distance of two hundred and fifty. Two western towers would have been crowned by lofty spires. Then in 1882 there came an even more alarming scheme. The idea was that Westminster Cathedral should be a flamboyant Gothic structure, with openwork western spires and an abundance of pinnacles to harbour the London grime, closely modelled on Baron von Ferstel's comparatively new *Votivkirche* in Vienna. Nor was this the end of Gothic notions. A. M. Dunn got out plans which were eventually described and illustrated.[11] Their cost was reckoned at about £200,000; I do not know if what he designed was for the past or the present site. For the ground in Carlisle Place was sold when in 1884 four acres, in what was known as Tothill Fields and which were the site of the demolished Middlesex County Prison, were bought but never used in Manning's lifetime. The convert Cardinal died in 1892. His successor, Cardinal Herbert Vaughan, at once decided to give London's Catholics their permanent cathedral.

Herbert Vaughan came of a leading and devout Catholic family, reasonably well to do and connected to many of the most important families who had come through from penal times. It was natural for a Vaughan to "think big"; we have seen how the Cardinal's uncle did this when as bishop of Plymouth he built a cathedral for his western diocese. The new Archbishop saw that now at all events Britain's capital should no longer lack a worthy headquarters for a religious body which was growing in consequence and which had, by the time of his accession, been free, for just over a hundred years, to worship in public. He was specially keen to ensure that here at all events among England's modern Catholic cathedrals the *opus dei*—the choir offices and regular High Masses—should be rendered as had been normal in the Middle Ages. He first hoped that his new cathedral could be served by Benedictine monks, and that modern London should have a cathedral monastery like medieval Canterbury, or Belmont in his own time. In this idea he was frustrated, but found compensation in the gathering of a body of secular canons and chaplains large enough to perform the same services. So Westminster Cathedral's régime is closer to that of Old St. Paul's than it is to medieval Westminster Abbey.

The Cardinal decided against a competition for his cathedral's designer. From various quarters he heard well of Bentley, so Bentley was appointed. From such a choice, and from nearly all the architect's previous work, one could have looked for yet another Gothic design, perhaps of the Arts and Crafts type, leading up to an earlier equivalent of Scott's Anglican cathedral at Liverpool whose commencement date made it nearly a contemporary of Westminster. But the Cardinal's firm preference was for Byzantine. Vaughan saw that a Byzantine cathedral would be cheaper than one built in any Gothic style, that it could be more quickly built, and that a Byzantine church of the type he had in mind could not be started and then, in the manner of so many elongated Gothic naves, left incomplete. Herbert Vaughan, not Bentley, is the man we must thank (or blame, if we dislike his cathedral) for the stylistic choice at Westminster. Bentley was thus led on to the one great non-Gothic achievement of his career. It was as if almost every building by Wren, bar St. Paul's, had been in the style of Tom Tower at Oxford. Bentley was, indeed, an admirer of Byzantine. He had, as a young man, made designs for a Byzantine church.[12] He had designed a Byzantine basilican church to replace the chapel at Warwick Street, and some alterations were in fact made according to his plans.[13] In an altar at Warwick Street he had used mosaic in a Byzantine manner. But he had, as yet, carried out no major Byzantine work. He now thought it wise to visit Italy, there to study such buildings as St. Mark's at Venice and the appropriate churches in Rome and Ravenna.

Bentley's cathedral was started in 1895. The architect died in 1902; Cardinal Vaughan's death in 1903 almost coincided with the main fabric's completion. What was built is not a lengthy, many-pillared basilica like Old St. Peter's, several others in Rome, or S. Apollinare in Classe near Ravenna. Nor was the new cathedral "centrally planned" in the manner of S. Vitale in Ravenna or St. Sophia at Constantinople. A closer model for its basic planning lay in the great vaulted halls of some *thermae* in Rome, and still more in the spacious Basilica of Maxentius, or Constantine, in the same city. For as in this great assembly hall of the fourth century the congregational nave at Westminster is composed of only three vast bays. Each of these is lit, above its flat aisle roofs, by semicircular lunettes like those which once gave top light to the ruined basilica in Rome,[14] while at Westminster the windows just below the lunettes recall those which lit Constantine's lofty aisles. Where Bentley's cathedral differs from Constantine's basilica, and where it comes closer to the kindred churches of St. Mark's Venice and St. Front at Périgueux,[15] is in its roofing. For instead of the richly coffered barrell vaults of Constantine's basilica the Cathedral at Westminster has a sequence of great saucer domes, one to each bay and apparent from outside as well as within. The transepts of the cathedral flank the easternmost nave bay; unlike those in the cruciform early Christian basilicas, and in most medieval cathedrals, they are screened from the nave by a gallery and a colonnade—a neo-Byzantine version of Bentley's Gothic transept screens at Watford and Brixton Hill. Beyond the nave another bay is flanked by large apsidal chapels and contains the choir stalls, the High Altar beneath its famous canopy of yellow marble columns, and the archbishop's throne, not set as in early Christian times behind the High Altar but in the more normal modern position on what one used to call the Gospel side. A choir space, apsidal, arcaded on the outside, and apologetically small for the bulk of the whole building, completes the cathedral. Bentley had wanted a pair of flanking towers; the campanile which was actually built rises high and slim, above the cathedral's north-western corner, to the little dome which crowns its topmost turret.

As the outside of Westminster Cathedral, with its red brick profusely striped with stone dressings, has been finished it is easier to judge than is the partly decorated interior. The building's main impact, when one compared it with the Gothic cathedrals thought normal by most Englishmen in 1903, lay in its clifflike bulk, and in the silhouette of its successive saucer domes. In its corner turrets, in the patterned brickwork over the windows of its side chapels, and in the unusual grouping of elements at its west end, it displays much beautifully wrought detail. The 284 feet of its slender campanile made, and still make, a fine element in West London's skyline. Yet for all its grandeur the cathedral is not, when seen from outside, a complete success. It soon had some fiercely outraged critics. The biographer of Ambrose Phillipps de Lisele, being faithful to his hero's Gothic propensities, called it "a sort of pre-Heptarchical evolution—Byzantine-Babylonian, bizarre", going on to the opinion that the building was "the creation of a circle . . . a huge indigested mass of unshapely agglomerations, a megalomaniac hulk in a sea of unsightliness".[16] That disgruntled Catholic Frederick Rolfe, alias Baron Corvo, referred to it as a "pea-soup and streaky bacon-coloured caricature of an electric-light station."[17] But Corvo being what he was his comments would probably have been no less waspish had Cardinal Vaughan's choice been for Gothic, neo-Norman, High Renaissance, or Baroque.

The interior of Westminster Cathedral is unfinished, and is still controversial. Of its architectural grandeur, and of the fine thinking behind its design, there can be no doubt. Nor, despite its semi-darkness, its incrusted London grime, and the dinginess of its great expanses of brown brick and grey plaster, can one dispute an effective magnificence in an interior which still awaits the full reality of its creator's vision. But had Bentley designed his interior so that his brickwork should be seen he would probably have chosen less gloomy bricks, and his plaster would have reflected more light than that which still awaits its coating of gleaming mosaic. But what Bentley intended, in the manner of St. Mark's at Venice, was an interior whose great piers should be clad in marble to correspond with the deep green of its gallery columns, and whose upper surfaces should be slowly covered with neo-Byzantine mosaics. Such a policy was bound to take time; it has actually been as much bedevilled as this country's economy by the expediencies of "Stop and Go". The marble sheathing, for the most part in dark red, white, and attractive shades of green, is virtually complete. So too are most of the mosaics in the chapels off the nave aisles, while they are finished, and most effectively so, in the large chapels of Our Lady and the Blessed Sacrament. A few of these finished mosaics were by Bentley's collaborator Christian Symons. Others, in a convincingly Byzantine idiom, are by Anning Bell, Boris Anrep, and Justin Vulliamy. The largest, with a somewhat unhappy background in varying blues and a central figure of Christ in Glory, is that in the "tympanum" above the sanctuary. The artist, for a large expanse completed in 1933, was Gilbert Pownall. More effective than most of the mosaics, and better known as works of modern art, are the reliefs of the Stations of the Cross which were carved by Eric Gill.

The mosaic decoration of Westminster Cathedral is now suspended. The cost of its continuance would be very high. It is felt that there are other pastoral and charitable purposes for which the money must at present be used. Yet one should aim, in essentials, at the fulfilment of Bentley's scheme, for which he contrived his brickwork as he did. A building such as Westminster Cathedral, like that of the Anglicans at Liverpool, must needs take many years to complete, and by the time that it is finished it cannot fail, in these days of a revolution in architecture and building, to be something of a period piece. But at Westminster as in Liverpool due piety to a great designer's memory means the carrying out, aesthetically if not in all constructional points, of that designer's master plan. This is being done at the southern end of Rodney Street in Liverpool. The inevitable abandonment of another great architect's project near the other end of the same street does not mean that Bentley's more nearly finished cathedral should for ever remain without the full scheme of decoration which its architect worked out in the last years of his life.

In addition to his activity at Westminster Bentley worked in delicate mosaic, and in his much favoured *opus sectile*, in the convent chapel which he designed and decorated at Braintree. Leonard Stokes's chief conventual commission was not for nuns of his own faith, but for the Anglo-Catholic sisters at London Colney in Hertfordshire. He also made some striking designs for the church of a Catholic Order of male religious; his sadly unfulfilled conception would have given this country one of its noblest Arts and Crafts Gothic buildings.

The mission of Corpus Christi, in the Miles Platting area of Manchester, was started, in 1889, by the Premonstratensian Canons Regular. The modern growth of this Order has largely lain in Belgium, so Belgians were among the canons at Miles Platting. Abbot Geudens, who built the church, was from the important Belgian abbey of Tongerloo. The canons soon got designs from Leonard Stokes. The date on his sketches is 1891;[18] *The Builder* soon published an article on his splendid project.[19] It was sad for Manchester that lack of money prevented the building of Stokes's church.

Stokes's designs allowed for a short sanctuary and, as at St. Clare's in Liverpool, for a long nave with narrow aisles. In those aisles a continuous gallery was to run, below the windows, along each wall, almost touching the outer side of each pillar in the nave. Across each aisle, some way below its transverse tunnel vault, a sculptured panel would have represented a Station of the Cross. Plain pillars, hexagonal like those which Stokes later built at Balham, would have supported a simple nave vault. Only at the sanctuary's entrance, in the moulding and the canopied pairs of statues of the chancel arch, would more elaboration have appeared.[20] More fanciful touches were planned for an inventive western end. A Crucifixion group was to have been set just below the curved top of the main gable, while at intervals along the coping little balls were to have been perched on uprising classical plinths. The other details in the proposed façade are free late Gothic, with curvilinear tracery and a great west window of eleven lights.*
In this window a transom, curving upwards in the middle, would have contained much tracery of its own. The whole of Stokes's design

* Grouped thus: 2.1.5.1.2.

showed that in the last decade of the nineteenth century the Arts and Crafts Revivalists had made their own distinctive contribution to the Gothic repertoire.

The actual church of Corpus Christi in Miles Platting was started in 1906; its nave was opened in another two years. It is impressive if somewhat graceless, and its clerestoried interior is very lofty inside. It is by an architect named Ernest Gunson,[21] and the style is Romanesque. This character is best expressed in the external shafts of the clerestory, in the somewhat Byzantine grille pattern of a western lunette, and in the moulded arches and varied cushion capitals of its seven-bay nave. But it is a somewhat disappointing substitute for Stoke's noble conception. The chancel, with eleven windows round its apse, was delayed till the 1930s. Appropriately enough, when one considers the Belgian links of the White Canons, it was by an architect from Belgium.

The building and enlargement of England's Catholic seminaries continued along with the work done on convents and cathedrals. Though nothing came of the scheme for a new seminary at Clapham the Southwark diocese found its compensation when in the 1890s F. A. Walters worked in a Flemish Renaissance vein on the large new seminary at Wonersh in the south-western Surrey countryside. Up in Lancashire, on the other hand, a large Gothic complex was opened, in 1883, as the new seminary of Upholland on its far-seen hill near Wigan. In the older colleges the main architectural event was the building of a larger new chapel at Ushaw.

By the 1870s Augustus Pugin's chapel in the Durham seminary was far too small. Dunn and Hansom of Newcastle were consulted in 1878, reporting that the building was already in poor condition, and that it could not be so extended as to double its accommodation.[22] It was pulled down, and the same architects replaced it, between 1882 and 1884, with their noble new chapel whose cost was £14,430.[23] Some buttresses, and the mullions and tracery of several windows, were neatly "cannibalised" for reuse; the west window, and the top halves of two in the apse, are still the early "Decorated" work of Pugin. Many fittings, such as stalls, some glass, some of Pugin's brasswork, and the earlier mural monuments (by Green of Newcastle) to Vicars Apostolic and college notables could also be transferred.[24]

The present chapel, like Pugin's, is T-shaped, the northern transept of its antechapel being somewhat shorter than that on the southern side. It is in this southern transept that a chapel lies behind a screen, in reasonable late Victorian Gothic and by the non-Catholic architect Basil Champneys, which was given to Ushaw, in memory of his son Henry, by the poet Coventry Patmore.*[25] The great screen, enlarged to fit the greater width of the new chapel and with chapels beneath its side arches in the manner of the fourteenth century, is of Pugin's time. The main chapel is arranged collegewise and is "early Decorated". It is impressive, particularly in the rich canopy work and vaulting of its apse. The whole interior has only lately been cleaned and lightened by a modern scheme of painting and redecoration. With its apse, and in its general style, this great chapel at Ushaw has much of the feeling of the chapel built by George Gilbert Scott, some twenty years earlier, at St. John's College, Cambridge. If one disregards the fan-vaulted twin chapel which was built, in the 1920s onto its antechapel's West end it is only some twenty feet shorter than its Cambridge equivalent. It is certainly a masterpiece of Victorian collegiate building.

The seminaries were not the only places for late Victorian collegiate projects or buildings by England's Roman Catholics. A feature of Manning's rule at Westminster was the swiftly frustrated project for a Catholic University College in Kensington. The Archbishop and Mgr. Capel were those mainly responsible; it was for the Monsignor that Goldie and Child made designs for a sumptuous chapel which were published in 1877.[26] Had this chapel been built the Earls Court district would have seen an Oxford collegiate building in the late Perpendicular of about 1500, with an arch-braced and hammerbeam roof and a series of chapels along its northern side. When the project collapsed the designs were stored away, reappearing in another twenty years in Edward Goldie's plans for an important Dominican church.

The estate in Staffordshire now known as Hawkesyard was called Armitage Park when in 1839 it was bought by the widow of the third Josiah Spode, whose family had become famous for fine pottery and porcelain. Towards the end of his life the fourth Josiah Spode became a Catholic. When in 1893 he died he left the Romantic Gothic mansion to the Dominicans. They built the church in 1896–9; the priory buildings were slowly finished in the years before the first World War.

The buildings at Hawkesyard are smaller, and less finished in detail, than their architect intended. Edward Goldie's first designs[27] were for

* This screen was not Champney's only Catholic work, for in the early 1880s he designed the vaulted, apsidal church of Our Lady, Star of the Sea, at Hastings. Patmore was a leading benefactor of the work.

a complete quadrangle. But the western range, with its tall central gate tower, was in practice omitted. So too was a long cloister which would have led to an ornate, polygonal Chapter House. The actual priory, like the church in red brick with stone dressings, is unexcitingly late Gothic. The merits of Hawkesyard are concentrated in its church; there one finds the most convincing "Oxbridge" chapel outside Oxford and Cambridge. Its intended buttresses, and its pinnacles bar those at the four corners, were never built. The choir absorbs five bays, and the antechapel takes four. The side windows of the chapel, in the late Perpendicular accepted among the Gothic Revivalists of the 1890s, are transomed, and a large window of seven lights fills much of the West wall. But behind the High Altar the East wall, as in New College at Oxford, is blank to allow for the tiers of statues, and the surmounting Crucifixion group, of a towering late Gothic reredos. Two little chapels, one of them delicately vaulted, lead out of the antechapel. A more unusual feature is the organ which once stood in the Spodes' mansion. For its fine Baroque case, very much akin to those set up, in the Restoration period, in many English cathedrals and other churches, was once that of the organ in the college chapel at Eton. It was installed in 1700–1,[28] and here in this modern Dominican choir one sees displayed the arms of William III, the King under whose rule legal restraints again fell upon the worship now conducted to this organ's accompaniment.

Another Friary of this period is that built for the Franciscans at Chilworth near Guildford. Its architect was F. A. Walters; some critics consider it to be one of his most successful works. The main dates are 1890–1, and the grouping is conventual in a strongly medieval manner.[29] A three bay choir runs en suite with a "nave" which actually contains dormitories; the Chapter House, the refectory, and a library at the south-western corner are grouped round a cloister court. The gabled central tower and its slender spirelet give the main impression of "Arts and Crafts". But the remaining buildings are simply and correctly late Perpendicular. As these modern Franciscans had continuity with the Observant Franciscans of the fifteenth century, and as these friars were much in favour in the reign of Henry VII, the style chosen for the buildings at Chilworth was that which then prevailed.[30] Some untraceried windows in Walters's design are indeed like those installed, in the years soon after 1497, in the reconstructed nunnery buildings which then became those of Jesus College, Cambridge.

My last passages in this chapter concern the achievements, and some projects, of the various Congregations of the Benedictines.

As the monastery and the school at Downside increased in numbers it became clear that the old mansion, Goodridge's additions, and the buildings by Charles Hansom were no longer sufficient. Ambitious ideas were entertained for a large new church and for new blocks for the monastery and the school. The story of the church's gradual building, piecemeal and with five architects successively at work on the main structure, its tombs, and its fittings, resembles in its interest the building sequence of a genuinely medieval monastic church. Edward Hansom, an old Downside boy, was chosen to design the complete new complex of buildings which was started in 1873.[31] Priority had first to be given to his monastery block, to the large refectory, and to the Petre cloister which connects the two. It was not until 1878 that Prior (later Cardinal) Gasquet resumed work on the North transept of the Newcastle architects' great cruciform church. The main building process, on an abbey church whose West end has never been finished, took sixty years. Twice over the main designs of the church's architects were carried out in a way which differed from their drawings. The final result was of the greatest importance as an ambitious masterpiece of revived Gothic; it has been called "the most splendid demonstration of the renaissance of Roman Catholicism in England", and "Pugin's dream of the future of English Catholicism come true."[32] Another consideration helps us to place Downside Abbey in its right place within the whole vast corpus of imitative or "period" Gothic. The great Anglican cathedrals projected for Manchester and Liverpool were never built, and we have seen how frustration overtook the Catholic schemes for Southwark, Liverpool, Birkenhead, and Westminster. The achievements of Pearson at Truro, and of Edward Hansom and his main followers at Downside, thus emerged as the noblest, most spectacular churches built in essentially Victorian Gothic rather than in that of the Arts and Crafts movement.

Edward Hansom's plans of 1872 allowed for a cruciform, traditionally monastic church, whose nave of five bays would have been much shorter than that eventually built.[33] But the ground plan of its eastern portion would have been very much that of the existing building. The tower, adjoining the South transept as Abbot Huby's tower abuts onto the northern one at Fountains, was to have been crowned by a tall spire. The choir limb, designed to have an apse and

35 *Four Catholic Architects*
(a) *A. W. N. Pugin*   (b) *J. F. Bentley*
(c) *Leonard Stokes*   (d) *Sir Giles Scott*

with polygonally ended chapels off its ambulatory, would have been more French in feeling than the actual eastern end. The interior, as one sees from a sketch[34] and from the actual fabric, was designed in a somewhat heavy mid-Victorian idiom, less pleasing than Dunn and Hansom's later work at Cambridge and in Newcastle. It has a clerestory consisting of pairs of two-light openings, and the early "Decorated" windows in its aisles and in the clerestory are of two lights. A large wheel window is set above an ornate altar which first did duty as the High Altar of a temporary church aligned crossways to the main length of the abbey's design. For all that first happened was the building of the central crossing and the transepts, of the lower stages of the tower and of one bay each of the intended nave and choir. In the last years of the century work progressed on the chapels off the choir aisles, and on the crypt and upper structure of the apsidal Lady Chapel. The placing of this chapel was a stroke of ecclesiastical cunning. For its position, far to the East of the crossing, made it inevitable that when in time the intervening space was filled in the resulting eastern limb had to be long enough for a large choir and an ample sanctuary. In a medieval manner the design of some chapels was changed as work went on. For when in 1887-9 the large southern chapels of St. Benedict and St. Isidore were built they had square East ends, and the style was Perpendicular, not that of about 1300.[35] By the time of Edward Hansom's sad suicide in 1900 F. A. Walters, and the Anglo-Catholic artist Ninian Comper, had been commissioned for some tombs, and for much furnishing and decoration.

About the turn of the century the monks of Downside took in hand the filling in of the long space between the Lady Chapel and the crossing. The architect chosen was Thomas Garner, a pupil of Sir George Gilbert Scott who had been Bodley's partner.[36] He had lately joined the Church of Rome, considering then that he would the less embarrass his High-Anglican partner if in future he worked on his own. In 1900 he supplied drawings for the completion of the tower. By 1902 he had made designs for the reasonably faithful continuance of Hansom and Dunn's church.[37] His nave was to be of six bays instead of their five, his sanctuary was to finish in a squared end, and his tower would have been closer to Somerset traditions than the spired steeple projected in 1872. But Hansom and Dunn's notion of a pronounced triforium, and of an "early Decorated" clerestory, would have been kept, and the whole building would still have had a mid-

36 *Post-War Traditionalism*
  (a) *Wallsend on Tyne: St. Bernadette's*
  (b) *Plymouth: Christ the King*

M

Victorian stamp. What was built, however, is closer to the late ecclesiological Gothic of Bodley and Bentley than to the earlier scheme. Garner's task was an awkward one. The buildings put up since the 1880s, and the changes from the originally chosen style, had made for irregular settings, so that no pillar of the new work was quite opposite its fellow.[38] Yet the eastern limb built between 1902 and 1905 was superb, giving the Downside Benedictines a vaulted choir without a peer in the revived monastic architecture of this country. The suggested triforium was cut out, and above the arcades (of six full bays and a smaller one) whose character is that of about 1300 the choir's upper structure is that of the late fourteenth-century imitations favoured by some late Victorian Gothicists. The clerestory windows, large and transomed, are in tune with this brilliant change of design. It is said that Garner intended to insert a large East window.[39] If so, he changed his mind, and above the three arches which stand behind the High Altar Comper's splendid glass glows out from a trio of windows whose central element has three transomed lights, while the flanking windows are of one apiece. The disposition of these windows, and their tracery with its idiom of the late fourteenth century, recall Bentley's plans for his East ends at Cadogan Street, Brixton, and Watford.

The work done on the eastern limb at Downside by 1905 made it little more than the shell of a fully furnished choir. Later designers designed much of what was finished by the early part of the first World War. F. A. Walters, for several tombs and the initial arrangement of the sanctuary, was prominent among them. He was also the architect for Downside's daughter priory at Ealing. His drawings of 1890[40] show a large Perpendicular church whose flush-work battlements are of an East Anglian type. A five-bay eastern limb runs out past flanking towers whose placing recalls the cathedral at Exeter. No such choir limb was ever built, but the eastern part of the nave at Ealing, devoid of a clerestory and with tall arches in its arcades, was opened in 1899.

Other projects by Benedictines of the English Congregation were at Ampleforth, and in the new home in rural Berkshire of the community of St. Edmund's which had once been in Paris and later at Douai.

I have mentioned the monastery block at Ampleforth, and the limited competition for a strung-out sequence of buildings to include a church as well as new quarters for the monks and the school. Bernard

Smith thus designed a new church as well as his still existing monastic block.[41] The Georgian house, and Charles Hansom's church, were to disappear; Smith's church was to be fitted into part of the space thus cleared. It was to have been a fine cruciform building in a not very venturesome "Decorated" Gothic. A tall central tower and spire would have given a note of architectural ambition to Ampleforth's broad valley below the North Yorkshire moors. The nave and choir, of five bays apiece, would have run out East and West of the tower. Yet the cleared space, and the bulky monastery block to the West, would only have allowed the moderate length which is that of the church eventually built.

In 1903 the community of St. Edmund at Douai was forced to leave France by the edict of an anticlerical Government. The monks took up quarters in what had been the Portsmouth Diocesan School at Wool-hampton near Newbury. The site had a history which included a long spell of penal Catholic ownership. Once again we find that an important English college or monastery is placed where it is because its ground had once been owned by some recusant family. When in the 1780s the Earl of Fingal sold his Woolhampton estate the mansion chapel had been closed, but land and money had been left for the survival of the local congregation. In 1833 a school was founded; the "handsome and appropriate" chapel of that year was soon replaced by the aisled Gothic church of no great note which still stands near the abbey.[42] Other scholastic buildings were replaced, in 1884-85 and soon after the founding of the Portsmouth diocese, by new ones of warm red brick; their style is the good, plain, "educational mid-Tudor" much favoured for such purposes at that time.* Other buildings followed by 1900, of higher aesthetic quality and designed by F. A. Walters. They included the Haydock wing with its refined late Gothic detail. and the boldly collegiate gate tower which greets one's approach up the lane from the main Bath road.

Once the monks decided to stay at Woolhampton new monastic buildings were put in hand. Despite his Benedictine connexions Walters was not the chosen architect. The firm of Pugin and Pugin (under Sebastian Pugin Powell) was responsible for the brick and stone, late Gothic blocks built soon after 1906; they were also the designers of the neo-Decorated, unventuresome church of St. Gerard

* The wing of 1885 has a Tudor main doorway inscribed with that date, and the monogram of Bishop Virtue of Portsmouth.

Majella which the Douai monks built for their parish in the southern suburbia of Bristol.

Designs for a church at Douai Abbey were also got out in the Edwardian years. Messrs. Pugin and Pugin made complete plans for a new monastery and its attendant church. Pugin Powell's alabaster reredos, with its panels showing scenes from St. Benedict's life, was intended for such a building; it is palpably too large for its actual position in the small sanctuary of 1848.[43] Two Pugin and Pugin schemes survive, from this period, for a possible abbey church at Woolhampton.[44] One of 1907 allows for an aisled and apsidal church, ornately "Decorated" and with a southern tower and spire. The other is for a very large structure, cruciform and with double-aisled transepts. The stalls were to have been in the eastern limb, and as at Downside a large Lady Chapel was to have run out behind the High Altar. Another plan at Douai, perhaps, from this period before 1914, is by F. A. Walters. His church would have been square-ended, with five eastern chapels behind a five-bay choir. Walters allowed six bays for his nave, his style for the church being more fully Gothic than in the actual abbey for which he is best known.

The Benedictine monks of Pierre-qui-vire in Britanny were in 1880 ejected from France by an anticlerical Government. Two years later they took over the castellated late Georgian mansion built over part of the foundations of the western range of the Cistercian abbey of Buckfast in Devon. At first a French community, and later with many German recruits, they have, since 1960, formed a unit of the English Benedictine Congregation.

Soon after 1882 the monks planned to build a modern abbey on this old monastic site. They chose Frederick Walters as their architect; what they hoped to do was to build a new church on the long empty Cistercian site. Walters's sketch of 1886[45] is for a complete monastic complex, on traditional lines and in the "Transitional" style, combining Romanesque with incipiently Gothic elements, which had been in vogue soon after the completion of the previous Buckfast Abbey. His suggested tower was lower than the one which now exists, and a four-bay eastern limb was longer than the twelfth-century Cistercian norm. His eastern Lady Chapel was to be of three bays, in a more developed Gothic than that planned for the rest of the church. Some of the monastic buildings designed by Walters were the first to be put up, and when in 1907 the present church was started it differed both from its architect's first design and from the previous Cistercian building. Excavation had now uncovered the ground plan of the medieval church. The new one largely rests on the old foundations and reproduces much of the earlier plan. Its nine-bay nave is of the medieval length, and as in the old Cistercian churches (and some used by the Benedictines) the choir of the modern Buckfast monks is in the easternmost bays of the structural nave. But beyond the presbytery its eastern extremity diverges from what the excavators revealed. Walters found that the original rectangular East end had five chapels, with the central one running out a fair distance beyond its fellows.[46] But the new church was given a sextet of eastern chapels, so arranged that they made a T-shaped eastern limb whose plan recalled those at Fountains and Durham. The style is that of the early Kirkstall or Fountains—a painstaking Transitional Norman, but with a triforium stage added in, and giving a cramped feeling to a none too lofty interior. The exterior, despite the unhappy heightening of the central tower,[43] is more successful than the inside, and the fittings are in their way more exciting than the architecture. For the great pavements of the sanctuary and the crossing are brilliant modern examples of geometrical *opus Alexandrinum*, while the painting of the tower ceiling is of an austere Byzantine splendour. The front and the reredos of the High Altar, the great sexfoiled candelabrum, and the font are all virtuoso reproductions of the German Romanesque metalwork of such cities as Coblenz, Aachen, and Hildesheim. Given the need, in such a church, for antiquarianism in the fittings their style was appropriate in view of the German origin of Abbot Vonier who commissioned them, and they make an interesting change from the neo-Gothicism of Comper, or of Walters in his tombs at Downside. Benno Elkan's bronze candelabra, and his great memorial plaque to Abbot Vonier, are, however, a refreshing contrast.

Another Benedictine community which left France for political reasons was that of Solesmes. They reached England in 1901, rented a house in the Isle of Wight, and then in 1907 they followed the Buckfast example and moved, within the island, to the estate of Quarr Abbey which had, in the Middle Ages, been the site of a Cistercian house. As at Buckfast monastic buildings came first; the new church was built in 1911–12. For its date it was an innovation in England, and in the whole setting of our religious architecture it is more significant than any antiquarian copy, or the tail end of Arts and Crafts Gothic. The abbey's designer was Dom Paul Bellot, a monk of the Quarr community who had trained in Paris as an architect at the 'Ecole des Beaux Arts, and who later designed churches and monasteries in France and the Netherlands.* He was familiar with the simple, massively grouped brickwork of some new buildings in the Low Countries. Despite its Gothic references, and the strong, simple pointed arches in the church and in the monks' living quarters, Bellot's work at Quarr belongs to the modern architectural movement. Patterned Flemish brick, expressive in its simplicity and with no stone dressings, was his chosen material. The church is severely functional for its essential purpose of housing the monks' choir offices and their conventual High Mass. A rectangular choir has its stalls against the plain side walls, and a squat, solid tower contains the sanctuary. Only at the junction point below the choir and the low, short nave does a screen-like erection of brickwork break out, with its pillared turret at one end, in a touch of uprising ostentation.

Before the building of the new Quarr Abbey the monks of another community from abroad had been strictly revivalist in a major building project. About the turn of the century the Beuron Benedictines at Erdington had ideas for the replacement of Charles Hansom's church by one of monumental size. At some time before his death in 1906 Thomas Garner made designs[48] for a cruciform Abbey church which would, had it been built, have been some 270 feet long inside. It would, bar Downside and St. John's at Norwich, have been the largest revived Gothic church built in England for Roman Catholic use. Its style was to be elaborately late Decorated, with no triforium stage in its nave of nine bays or in its eastern limb of three. Two towers and a low narthex would have stood at this great church's western end. But no work on it was done before the outbreak of the great conflict whose course, and whose aftermath, made it convenient for these monks of Beuron to return to their native land.

* Mr. Peter Anson has pointed out to me that his work was also a strong influence on that of other Continental architects.

Chapter XI

THE YEARS BETWEEN THE WARS

The World War which started in 1914 delayed the churchbuilding work of all denominations. A few Catholic projects, like that at Ashby de la Zouch, were completed while it raged, and the creation of two new Catholic sees before 1918 caused the elevation of two churches to cathedral status. But most of what we must notice in this chapter dates from those years from 1919 to 1939 when Britain saw vast changes in the housing, and in the general distribution, of her urban and suburban population.

The diocese of Newport, confined since 1895 to Glamorgan, Monmouthshire, and Herefordshire, and still having Belmont as its cathedral priory, became that of Cardiff in 1916. St. David's, not far from the business and shopping centre of Cardiff, was for four years a co-cathedral along with the church at Belmont; since 1920 it has been a cathedral on its own. It is by Peter Paul Pugin and was first built between 1884 and 1887, replacing Scoles's church of the early 1840s. Its style is the late Geometrical of about 1300, and its large West window has a low-set transom. Of more interest was the design of its spacious eight-bay nave, laid out with no real aisles so that those in it could all see the High Altar. This plan, being congenial to modern liturgical ideas, was retained when in the 1950s the cathedral, unroofed and largely gutted by bombing in 1941, was restored by Messrs. F. R. Bates of Newport.

In 1917 an Essex diocese was carved out of that of Westminster; it was the only one of England's Roman dioceses to coincide with one county. Brentwood, being geographically convenient and tactically well placed for the county's railway services, was chosen as the bishop's headquarters. Its Catholic parish church became a cathedral. It had been built in 1861, succeeding a brick building, in simple late Perpendicular and now used as a school, which still stands close by its northern side. Lord Petre gave the site, and some of the money, for the new church. Gilbert Blount the architect produced a parish church of moderate size, with a four-bay nave, a low clerestory of convex triangles to suit the church's early Decorated style, and an attractive little octagonal spire above a square tower at the north-western corner.[1] No one could have foreseen that this modest church would ever attain such a dignity. It well proves that what makes a cathedral is not size or architectural grandeur but the housing within its walls of a particular piece of ceremonial church furniture.

The next parish church honoured with cathedral status was more obviously cathedralesque. For in 1924 St. Peter's at Lancaster (see pages 136–7) became the cathedral of the new diocese of that name.

Elsewhere in Lancashire a more exciting project was launched in the years between the wars. Only now, and in a manner not envisaged by the architect first chosen, is it coming to completion.

The long delayed building of a permanent cathedral for Liverpool's Catholics was seriously mooted soon after Archbishop Whiteside's death in 1921. Some years passed before the spacious site of the Brownlow Hill Institution could be bought, and in 1933 the new cathedral was started. Neo-Gothic ideas, and rivalry with Sir Giles Scott's great Anglican cathedral, had now been laid aside. Sir Edwin Lutyens's design, in what he called "Wrenaissance" was for a stupendous building, in load-bearing brick and stone.[2] A great dome would have stood above its crossing, the grouping of its masses would have had a modern flavour, and many strictly Renaissance references were in the architect's detailed drawings. Lutyens's concept paid tribute to Wren as well as to Bramante and Vignola. Had his cathedral been finished it would, at a time when period architecture was ceasing to be credible, have been the greatest of England's "period" churches; it is certainly the noblest and most splendid of this country's Catholic "might have beens". Work slowly proceeded on the crypt of this mighty cathedral; it was nearly finished, and had been used for Mass, when the second World War broke out. Off one side of its long, narrow side compart-

37 *Bootle: St. Alexander's, by F. X. Velarde*
38 *Pinner: St. Luke's, by F. X. Velarde*

ment, it includes the severely Doric Mausoleum chapel whose trabeation supports the sarcophagi of Archbishops Whiteside and Downey. This chapel derives from the Mausoleum at Stowe. In its solemn beauty it is one of the choicest interiors in any Catholic church in England. The crypt's whole interior, and the massive Renaissance splendour of its masonry façade, make one sadly realise how great a building we have missed.

A Lutyens commission which was fully carried out was in a place where many can see its results. Campion Hall had been established, as a Jesuit house of studies at Oxford, for some years before 1934 when its present buildings were started. Their merit lies not only in the stylistic success of Sir Edwin's blend of Gothic and Renaissance, and in the simple traditionalism of this Jesuit chapel in Campion's University, but in the brilliant way in which the buildings of a small College have been squeezed into a narrow site which is cramped even by the standards of central Oxford. The more spacious purlieu of St. Giles contained, by 1929, the Dominican priory which Doran Webb designed as a Renaissance cum Gothic neighbour to the more fully Gothic Anglo-Catholic stronghold of Pusey House. The church, with its wide nave and choir, and including a row of tiny chapels off one side of its nave, is unadventurously late Perpendicular. One is surprised, in these days of more daring modernities, to know of the stir which Oxford's Blackfriars originally caused. But its simple furnishings, and its lack of coloured windows, were in their time an austerity of a primitive Cistercian stamp.

The Cistercians themselves completed the church at Mount St. Bernard between 1935 and 1939. They needed to build the central portion, and to add an East end. They employed a Leicester builder named Bradford.[3] His drawings exist for a few schemes which differ from what was eventually done. One is along the traditionally Cistercian lines set out in Pugin's drawings almost a century before. A low tower, with a tall turret at one corner, was to have stood above the crossing; beyond it a short choir would have led to an eastern sanctuary. Other Bradford drawings show various rejected schemes. One allows for a tower rather more ornate than the present one, but not unlike the open-arched structure, with its late thirteenth-century references, whose designer was Mr. Alfred Herbert of Leicester. What the church in fact received was a five-bay eastern limb. Its style is that of Pugin's nave, and it is used to seat lay visitors. Below the eastern arch of the

39 High-Peaked Roofs
  (a) Knebworth, Hertfordshire
  (b) Harlow, St. Thomas More

40 Leyland, Lancashire, by
    Weightman and Bullen
  (a) Exterior (b) Inside

finely vaulted tower, so placed that it serves monks and laity alike, a simple central altar was in the 1930s a comparative innovation.

Another important monastic church, designed in the 'tween-war period to have its High Altar in the crossing, was that started, in 1922, at Ampleforth Abbey.[4] The nature of the site, and the presence of existing buildings, enforced modest dimensions on this important new building; its total length is only 175 feet. The private altars are mostly in the crypt. Above that level the main structure of each limb was planned to be of an equal length on each side of a central tower. The windows are all of an early lancet Gothic type; the details, too, are from the transitional time between Gothic and Romanesque. What made this replacement of Charles Hansom's Victorian church of special note was its roof construction. What Scott designed was not a timber-roofed or rib-vaulted church, but a version of the quasi-Byzantine, saucer-domed Romanesque churches which give distinction to the architecture of south-western France. His row of three saucer domes, one each for the nave and choir and one below the tower, and the arrangement of his arcades and windows, owe a clear debt to the church at Cahors and St. Front at Périgueux. The choir limb, with its arches and other details in beautiful blue-green stone from Hornton in Oxfordshire, was finished by 1924. The High Altar, designed for use on either side, is from this first period of Ampleforth's refashioning, a masterly work in a version of Arts and Crafts Gothic. Its high canopy is not really a *baldachino*, but a composition of two closely spaced arches.

Saucer domes were also a main feature in a more monumental monastic design by Scott; it was a sad architectural tragedy that the church he planned for Douai Abbey was never built.

Soon after 1918 the Benedictines at Woolhampton again turned their thoughts to the building of a large abbey church. In 1923 Sebastian Pugin Powell got out a scheme[5] for an ornate cruciform building in strongly traditional "Decorated" Gothic, with no central tower above its crossing, and with extremely slender pillars in the arcades proposed for its nave and choir. Scott's design,[6] more innovating in its structure and austerely Early English in its fenestration, must date from this same time when he was also busy at Ampleforth and on his school chapel for Charterhouse. Had his church been built at Woolhampton it would have been something of a cross between the two. Its rectangular plan, with no tower of any kind, would have been that of a college chapel and seemed too un-monastic, in the traditional sense, for this community of Benedictines. A saucer dome would have been poised above each of its five double bays. Narrow processional aisles would have had private chapels leading out of them, confessionals were to have been cleverly fitted into the great buttresses, and the monastic choir was to have filled the second bay from the eastern end. But the Douai community missed its chance with Giles Gilbert Scott, turning instead to J. Arnold Crush of Birmingham, an architect born in 1885 and at one time articled to Lutyens.[7] But his Gothic was more in the tradition of Giles Scott, and his designs for a church at Woolhampton, conventionally cruciform and with a tall central tower, were in the late medieval tradition. His style was the late Decorated of Bodley and of Bentley the Gothicist. His initial designs for the Douai church allowed for lofty aisles and high arcades in something of the manner of the choir at Bristol Cathedral.[8] What was actually built between 1928 and 1933 was somewhat different. A fine apsidal Lady Chapel lies East of a fragment (one full bay and a shorter one) of the intended choir limb. There is no triforium, but a clerestory is included, and in the aisles each compartment has its sharply pointed transverse vault. The outside of Crush's church blends flintwork, dressed stone, and rich red brick. Inside, the whole rendering is in creamy stone, of an uncoloured purity not unlike that in the nave built at Downside by Sir Giles Gilbert Scott.

More work by Arnold Crush for Benedictine clients was built in 1929 for the nuns at Colwich. An early scheme was for an ambitious "Decorated" priory church, projecting nearly a hundred feet from one side of the Regency Gothic mansion.[9] A four-bay choir was to have led to an attractive gabled tower, whose general design, and whose surmounting spirelet, would have recalled Walters's Franciscan work at Chilworth. Beyond this central feature a four-sided apse would have contained the altar, while a large Lady Chapel was planned to complete the design. The reality was far less imposing—a projecting sanctuary of a single bay and a three-sided apse. The tracery in its windows resembles some of Crush's work at Woolhampton.

Scott's nave at Downside is another Catholic building on a major scale, in the grand manner of Edward Hansom and Thomas Garner, and more in tune with their work than most of Scott's achievements. Soon after the Armistice Scott was asked to plan a nave which would grandly complete the abbey church and commemorate Old Gregorians who had died in the war. Two of his schemes omitted the clerestory windows and a triforium stage, providing for low passageway aisles and for arcades of giant arches which would, as in Liverpool Cathedral, have reached nearly to the vault.[10] So great a break with the existing building was too much for the Downside community. They rejected the plans as being "in too violent contrast" with the style and proportions of the earlier choir and transepts. What the monks wanted was a nave harmonising with Garner's choir, but including a triforium stage consistent both with Hansom's transepts and with Garner's early designs (see page 177) for the entire church. Scott met their wishes, so that the seven bays (of his projected ten) which were finished in 1925 have early Perpendicular arcades, a triforium like that envisaged by Garner, curvilinear windows in the fourteenth-century idiom, and a plain quadripartite vault. But when after Cardinal Gasquet's death in 1929 Scott designed a noble canopied tomb for the one-time Vatican librarian his idiom was the splendid Arts and Crafts Gothic he had so brilliantly used in the furnishings at Liverpool. Other fittings in the eastern limb at Downside followed the unrelenting neo-medievalism of the great church's fabric. For when in 1929 new choir stalls were planned their richly canopied design reproduced that of the stalls set up, in the fourteenth century, by the Benedictine monks of Chester. They were, however, carved by craftsmen in the Tirol. The last addition to this great church was again by Scott. The upper stages of the tower were finished in 1939 as a Gasquet memorial; their idiom is that of the great Perpendicular towers of the county of Somerset wherein Downside lies.

What greatly affected the building of parochial churches in these years after 1918 was the spreading out of this country's urban population. All denominations faced the same problem, and many Catholic parishes started from nothing with the building of large new housing estates. Another factor, very noticeable in the Home Counties, was the slow suburbanisation of what had once been countryside. Small towns, or villages which had no Catholic church, or where Mass had been said in makeshift private accommodation, found that permanent Catholic churches or chapels of ease became part of their scene. Much was also done, in provincial dioceses where new Catholic activity was now started, to provide Mass centres in houses, inns, and public halls, or in some cases to build permanent churches or church halls. Nottingham and Clifton were among those where this policy was briskly pursued. In the former, simple and inexpensive churches, each built to hold some 200 people, were in favour; some of these were by the Leicester builder F. J. Bradford who also worked at Mount St. Bernard. In Wessex a few churches, inoffensive, undistinguished, and useful, were designed by a Taunton architect named J. H. H. Wilman. Nearer London, many churches of larger dimensions were designed by Mr. Thomas Birchall Scott.*

Coming to style one finds, as with most churches built in England by other denominations, that traditionalism prevailed; this was no surprise in the heyday of "Stockbrokers' Tudor" and "Bankers' Georgian". Neo-Gothic churches, often of great stylistic sterility, were much to the fore. Renaissance classical pastiches remained fairly rare, and English churches in communion with Rome seldom echoed the neo-Baroque Anglo-Catholicism of Mr. Martin Travers and the Society of St. Peter and St. Paul. Neo-Byzantinism was, however, considerably more popular in Catholic circles; here one clearly sees the influence (not confined to churches of the Roman obedience) of Westminster Cathedral. Though a "period" style, and in many ways outdated as the "contemporary" movement slowly made headway, this revived Byzantine of the 1920s and 1930s had about it a certain timeless dignity. It thus seemed fuller of meaning and purpose than the more pathetically backward-looking efforts of the last Gothic Revivalists. A striking church of this Byzantine—Romanesque stamp, by a Dublin architect named Charles Powell, was the new one built at Lowe House, St. Helens; it replaced the much altered building of the 1790s. Completed in 1930, it has such Continental features as round-ended transepts, a dome above its crossing, an ambulatory, a vault of hollow brickwork put up by Belgian contractors, and windows from a studio in Ghent.

Few of these Byzantine or Romanesque churches were centrally planned, or had single domes like those of Sta Sophia or S. Vitale. Those built at Ludlow, and at Abergele in North Wales, were in this respect unusual among their fellows. Both are by an Italian architect named Rinvolucri, who settled in this country and had two other commissions in the Menevia diocese. One of these was his church at Amlwch in Anglesey which was an innovating building when opened in 1937. Its tall, narrow nave and sanctuary are of reinforced concrete on a base of stone, while the nave bays are boldly defined by a succession of lofty parabolic arches.

Rectangular, strictly basilican planning was that most favoured for

* Mr. Peter Anson has listed at least twenty-three of his buildings.

the churches built in the Byzantine or Romanesque styles. The long arcades, numerous pillars, and simple timber roofs of the more conventionally constructed basilicas were more in evidence than the few bays and ambitious vaults or domes of Westminster Cathedral. Economy dictated a general use of brick for these fabrics. But marble columns, as one finds them in many early Roman churches, gave a more opulent feeling to the nave of the church of the Blessed Sacrament in the Heavitree suburb of Exeter; the same church has the odd feature of a Corinthian portico not at its narthex end but along one of its sides. The church of the Holy Name in the Jesmond district of Newcastle, Corpus Christi at Weston-super-Mare, and Holy Cross in the Bedminster district of Bristol are but a few of the more ordinary basilican churches built (mainly of brick) in the 1920s and 1930s; their Romanesque details are apt, however, to be worked in stone. A more ambitious building of this type, with its tall, neatly designed campanile commanding a stretch of Queen's Drive which surrounds Liverpool's outer suburbs, is the great church of St. Matthew. It was the first church, and one of the more "traditional" achievements, of F. X. Velarde who now emerged as an important Catholic architect in England. Then in Bath one has the one Romanesque basilican work of Sir Giles Gilbert Scott, the exquisitely detailed church of St. Alphege which was put up by the Downside Benedictines not long before they relinquished the city's chief Catholic parish.[11] Its simple stone arches have finely carved capitals, while over the High Altar the pillared *baldachino* derives from that in S. Clemente in Rome.

Two Byzantine-Romanesque churches, mainly in sensitive brickwork, were now built in the Portsmouth diocese. Both were by Mr. W. C. Mangan of Preston; the same architect worked elsewhere in this diocese and also in his home area. The first of these churches is at Totland Bay, in the western end of the Isle of Wight. Though it was built in 1923 its "founder" was Edmund Granville Ward, a son of the well known convert Wilfrid Ward who had lived, near his friend Tennyson, at Freshwater and had there built a smaller church.[12] The other, at Newbury, dates from 1928. The church at Totland Bay is a long, rectangular, apsed basilica, with an outer narthex approached by five open arches. Its internal design is slightly unorthodox, for each arch of its main arcades is segmental, not round, two pairs of clerestory windows being contrived above every arch. The Newbury church is cruciform. One enters its narrow, aisleless nave by a graceful semicircular porch. A low, gabled, central tower, with a lunette in each gable end, stands strikingly above the High Altar. This is of marble, below a curved *baldachino*, on green marble columns, which conveys a Westminster impression. Both churches are distinguished for the nice patterning and good colours of their brickwork. The Wards' church at Totland Bay has a slender campanile, striking if not wholly attractive in the dramatic overhang of its shallow-pointed cap. At Newbury too the campanile is very slender. Its upper composition, topped by a small copper dome, is an obvious borrowing from Bentley at Westminster. Where neither of these churches emulates the Metropolitan Cathedral is in the possession of mosaic decoration.

Yet mosaics of the Byzantine type were occasionally applied to the interior walls of churches. At Rochdale the sanctuary, and the apsed altar recess, of St. John the Baptist's had a fine set completed in 1933, the designer being Mr. Eric Newton. Far more striking are those which were gradually installed in the new Catholic church at Droitwich. The church itself is a brick-built basilica in the exact Ravennate or early Roman manner. It was built, to designs by Mr. Barry Peacock, between 1919 and 1921. Like many of the better churches described in this book it has fabric, decorations, and fittings which were mostly due to a single donor. A campanile stands on one side of its narthex; inside the church Byzantine idioms appear in such details as the cushion capitals, the pulpit's panels, and in a fine copper sanctuary lamp. All pales, however, before the astonishingly authentic splendour of Mr. Gabriel Pippett's mosaics; here indeed we find Ravenna in the English Midlands. This church differs from Westminster Cathedral in that nearly all of its mosaics have now been finished. They cover the tribune arch and the wall above it, the conch of the sanctuary apse, the clerestory walls, the long stretches of walling below the clerestory, the very arches of the nave, and the whole western wall. They appear in the aisles, in the baptistry, and in all but one of the chapels. Many of these mosaics display the life of St. Richard of Chichester who was born at Droitwich. Others are of subjects like the Sacred Heart, St. Teresa of Avila, and some English post-Reformation martyrs, which could not have occurred in Byzantine times. Yet the mosaics as a whole, particularly in the main apse and above the arcades, are truly in the Byzantine tradition, if of varying quality. Those in the vault of St. Catherine's chapel are of special brilliance, while some details in that of St. Richard recall those in Ravenna's Mausoleum of Galla Placidia.

A few churches were still built in the Romanesque of western or north-western Europe. Sidney Brocklesby was an architect who had some striking successes of this kind. When in 1920 his church of St. George at Derby was built its Romanesque idiom came as a pleasing relief from the prevalence of Gothic. Two of his churches form a striking pair and can be discussed together.

St. Augustine's at Nottingham dates from 1921 to 1923. At Ashton-in-Makerfield in southern Lancashire Brocklesby's new church replaced an earlier one and was built between 1925 and 1930. Neither church was finished exactly to the architect's designs. Yet both of them, in particular the Lancashire building which Cardinal Bourne is said to have considered the most beautiful Catholic church in England, are masterly achievements. As at Ampleforth the churches of Périgueux and its neighbourhood provided obvious inspiration. For each church is mainly of two large structural bays, each bay having a saucer dome, and three side arches with a small window above each arch. In the Nottingham church the low pillars of these subordinate arcades vary between square ones in the western bay and quadruple clustering in the bay nearer to the altar. In each church the designer allowed for a great retaining arch as the main feature of his western façade; only at Ashton-in-Makerfield was this conception fully carried out. Boh churches are fortunate in the noble treatment of their apsed East ends. For arcades of five Romanesque arches part the sanctuaries from the ambulatories behind them. In both churches the windows have fine glass in the manner of about 1200, that at Ashton-in-Makerfield being richly tinted work by Harry Clarke of Dublin.[13]

Most 'tween-war Catholic churches of England were, however, less exciting than these varied essays in Romanesque. We have noted a prevalent Gothicism in their style. Greater interest lay in the new trends behind some of their furnishing. Though many churches were still given statues, and other fittings, produced by repository art at its most banal some priests came closer to the genteel good taste then common in new or refurnished Anglican buildings. The movement for the installation of "the liturgical altar", inspired as it was by the book of that name by Geoffrey Webb, was a belated Catholic counterpart to the work already fashionable under such Anglican influences as the Alcuin Club and the activities of Dr. Percy Dearmer. At Seaford in Sussex a new church, by Geoffrey Webb himself and J. O'Hanlon Hughes, had an interior in which an Anglo-Catholic of the less

41 *Liverpool: St. Ambrose, Speke, by
Weightman and Bullen*

"spikey" stamp could well feel at home, while at Sudbury in Middlesex Leonard Williams's neo-Perpendicular church of St. George, opened in 1928 with a flat tester above an "English" altar, gave a Roman answer to Comper's East Anglian glories in St. Cyprian's, Clarence Gate. By and large, the greater light and softer colours of many new Catholic churches made a change for the better from the gloomy obfuscations handed down by the Victorians.

But of real modernity, as this was understood in some new churches in France, Germany, and elsewhere on the Continent there were as yet few traces, and the work of such architects as Auguste Perret and Dominikus Böhm found little echo among the Catholic churches put up in England. Little was done to use new constructional techniques, or to display the dramatic groupings of masses now fashionable among architects of the modern school. F. X. Velarde of Liverpool was prominent among the few Catholic architects whose work was distinctive of his own time.

Velarde was born about 1898, so that in 1928 his great basilica on Queen's Drive at Liverpool was the achievement of a young architect. He travelled abroad with that famous Liverpool architectural mentor Professor C. H. Reilly. He studied Romanesque churches, came under Beaux Arts influences, and much admired the Dutch tradition of fine building in brick. Exposed, and almost unrelieved brickwork was a strong feature of his work; he thus followed the example of Dom Bellot at Quarr. Professor Reilly became his staunch admirer, declaring in 1938 that Velarde's work was "always dignified, and, to my thinking, deeply religious" and that the best of it had an austere beauty which seemed "beyond the powers of all but a very few". The Professor felt that here was "something vital and of our own time".[14] In no church were these qualities clearer than in the building, finished in 1936, which is reckoned to have been Velarde's masterpiece.

St. Monica's at Bootle is set in the more demure part of the borough lying back from the dockland zone. Despite Ionic and Romanesque references it is mainly a building of the "contemporary" school. The church's structure is in an attractive greyish brick. At its liturgical western end a broad tower has statues on its outer face and then opens, by a wide arch, into a great six-bay basilican nave. Tall arches, with pairs of small windows above them, connect with the aisles; one of these is a narrow passageway, but that on the old Epistle side is wider, with higher and broader arches, to allow for a Lady Chapel. The most

42 (a) *St. Ambrose, Speke: exterior*
   (b) *Thames Ditton: by F. G. Broadbent and Partners*

modern effects are in the lofty, flat-ceiled sanctuary. There the modern sculptured angels on the blank East wall blend with eight slim pilasters, in a pattern of 2.1.1.1.1.2, whose capitals are a stylised version of the most archaic Ionic designs.[15] Despite its age of thirty years, St. Monica's remains very much a church of our own time. One sees this point as much in its Stations of the Cross, in low relief on a green backing, as in the austere strength of its structural brickwork. Only in the plan of its sanctuary is it somewhat dated by the standards prevalent in the mid-1960s.

Just as "contemporary" architecture was slow to make headway in the building of English churches, so the religious buildings of this country only slightly displayed the new ideas on liturgical planning now gaining ground on the Continent. In the late 1930s, only two Catholic churches were designed for the innovation (or revival) of the centrally placed altar.[16] One was at Bradford in the West Riding, where Fr. John O'Connor (G. K. Chesterton's original for "Fr. Brown") built the small octagonal church of Our Lady and the First Martyrs. The architect was Mr. J. H. Langtry-Langton, a local man who has since had many other Catholic commissions in Yorkshire. He set a small central altar beneath a boldly cantilevered dome. The other centrally planned church was at Gorleston in Norfolk. It was by Eric Gill, better known as a decorative artist, and for his reliefs of the Stations of the Cross not only at Westminster Cathedral but also for Fr. O'Connor in another church in Bradford. His church has a cross-shaped congregational space, and its altar stands in the crossing. The church was planned, so its designer tells us, from the altar outwards, and as from that point onwards he trusted to luck the results, on his own admission, were "gawky and amateurish". The completion date was 1939, a year which ushered in a spell of time when destruction, not increase, was the governing factor among the religious buildings of all denominations in England.

Chapter XII

CHIESE AGGIORNATE?

I

In the years since the end of the Second World War Catholic church-building in this country has had time to go through at least three phases. It has become more interesting, and sometimes more exciting, than could once have been expected. What was first a matter of proceeding, and where possible of expanding, on lines that seemed traditional in 1939 has in fact become a process more stirring, and more innovating, than most previous efforts to provide places of worship for the English and Welsh spiritual subjects of the See of Rome. The practical action taken in the last few years has also been ventured in a religious atmosphere, of friendliness among the denominations and of growing respect in this country for the Church which two centuries ago was hardly more than a remnant of the despised, that would have seemed almost beyond imagination as late as 1939. One also sees how churchbuilding, and the ordering of churches, have themselves changed, at an almost breathless rate, since 1960. Decisions made at the formal sessions of the Second Vatican Council, and by the bodies asked to give practical shape to those decisions, have by now had a strong bearing on the basic design, and still more on the internal arrangement, of the new buildings covered by this chapter.

Immediately after the Second World War all denominations were severely restrained in their churchbuilding. Building priorities, and the licensing of such structures as new churches, meant that little could be done but the replacement of the buildings entirely lost, or most severly

damaged, in the war itself. In those initial post-war years, and from the
end of licensing till its return in the mid-1960s, many Catholic Schools
(sometimes with halls which have served as churches) have also been
built, competing with a large output of churches for money and
materials. Heavy outlay on Catholic schools has often meant post-
ponement, or cramping economy, in the building and fitting out of
churches. Add to these factors an evolution of taste towards the
"contemporary" style, and the gathering impact of liturgical change
and new two-dimensional design, and one finds that the last twenty
years make a difficult story for an architectural chronicle.

As soon as possible after 1945 some tasks of repair and restoration
had to be taken in hand. Where churches had been destroyed or
damaged they were replaced or repaired. The replacements of such
wholly obliterated churches as St. Alexander's in Bootle are best
treated along with the completely new foundations, and with those
that have been built to replace temporary buildings, or churches whose
growing congregations had made them too small. Major repairs, as in
the rebuilding of the South aisle of St. John's at Bath, tended to mean
that the new work was much the same as that which had existed
before. Few churches (of any denomination) were repaired with such
harsh boldness as that which in Germany might produce modern
concrete construction on one side of the centreline and traditional
Gothic on the other.

Though my main subject is the new buildings put up since 1945 for
the public, or private conventual, worship of Catholics in England and
Wales one must also notice a vast work of repainting, redecoration,
and internal re-ordering in previously existing churches. In the last
few years these changes in present buildings, and in particular the rearrangements planned or carried out in some of their sanctuaries, have
been closely linked to the great liturgical changes, unforeseen by most
observers as late as 1955 and so drastic as to give a "dated" feeling to
High Altars set up as late as 1960, which have been and are being made
as I write this chapter.

The liturgical changes themselves need explanation. They aim at a
closer, more intelligent participation in the Mass by lay people who
tend to be more literate than their forbears, and whose taste, in their
homes as well as in their places of assembly, has veered towards more
luminous colours than those accepted by the Victorians. Lighter and
brighter churches can thus be allied to a clearer apprehension of what

happens inside them. They can also, to some extent, be adapted for a closer sharing, by the ear as well as by the eye, in services whose wording has now to be conveyed, as never in the past few centuries, in the language of those present. At a Catholic Mass in England the priest does not only read the early part of the service (the Liturgy of the Word) towards the people and from a lectern or desk well down in the sanctuary. He is also more likely than before to say the offertory and consecration prayers, and those which follow them, from behind the altar and facing his congregation. Some of these changes date from the Spring of 1965. We shall see how great an effect they must have on the design and internal planning of completely new buildings. They are also reflected, more or less, in the refurnishing of those which most Roman Catholics in this country actually use for worship.

By no means least, in its own theological importance and for its effect on people accustomed to the dingy gloom of Victorian interiors, has been the redecoration and fresh painting of hundreds of this country's Catholic churches; other denominations too have played their full part in a wide process of ecclesiastical defuscation. The cleaning of brickwork and stone, replastering and the application of new distemper in various light-reflecting shades, and the repainting of roofs and other woodwork in lighter and more cheerful colours, all these have wrought wonders in such interiors as those of the chapel at Ushaw and at Kemerton, of Holy Cross, St. Helens and St. Vincent de Paul's at Liverpool, of St. Walburge's at Preston and also (despite a certain oddity in the subdued red of its pillars) in that vast church in London's East End, S.S. Mary and Michael, Commercial Road.

Yet in these Victorian churches, and in most later ones of essentially "basilican" or rectangular plan, there are limits on the refurnishing that can fitly be done, or on the acceptable re-location of High Altars away from their eastern walls and reredoses. One cannot easily adapt these buildings for a liturgy which is, for the purposes of seeing and hearing if not for its underlying theology, much changed from that in which most of this country's Roman Catholics have been trained. In most churches built before 1955 more can be done by way of good amplification, and still more by the training of the clergy to read clearly and audibly in the English language, than by trying to arrange things as if long rectangles were circles, ovals, or squares. It has also been proved that many churches of the Catholic Survival, in other words those built between the last decades of the eighteenth century and about 1840, are more suited than aisled "ecclesiological" buildings to the new scheme of things. Where, as at Chipping Norton, adaptations are being made the changes are smoother than in the Victorian churches. We have seen how most of these immediately "post-penal" churches were closer in their design to Nonconformist Chapels than to the aisled and normally medieval fabrics of the Established Church. Since the early Nonconformist churches, like many of those built in London by Wren, were laid out for a more "auditory" purpose than aisled, late medieval churches with their far-receding sanctuaries it is no surprise that these late Georgian Catholic chapels are more convenient than the churches of the Puginites for the offering of Masses whose teaching prologue, and whose sacrificial prayers, are now meant, as never since Cranmer's time, to be understood by the people.

Apart from the building of new churches much has also been done to enlarge those already standing, and in some places to convert for Catholic purposes churches or chapels once used by other denominations. These endeavours are part of a wider process, aimed at solving a general problem. For the Roman Catholic Church in England and Wales continues to grow. Natural increase, conversions, the lasting settlement of "refugee" Catholics from Poland and other countries in eastern Europe, and continued immigration from Ireland, Italy, and elsewhere have added to the total. Despite much non-attendance at church and many losses from total lapse, and despite the fact that not more than about sixty per cent of this country's nominal Catholics are at all regular in the public practice of their religion, the worshipping Catholics of England and Wales are more numerous now than at any time in four centuries. Catholic churchbuilding is certainly more, in relation to that done by other denominations, than it was during the great Victorian outburst, all religious bodies being more apt than they were to relate the new church seatings they provide to those who actually fill them than to those nominally on their membership rolls. Not only are Catholic churches built, in New Towns or new housing areas, where none existed before, but increasing congregations have forced the clergy of many existing churches to add, as best they may, to their indoor worshipping space.

In some places the needed room has been provided by the simple process of adding to the western ends of existing naves. Many churches were designed for such elongations, or were left incomplete with lengthening allowed for when the money came in. The churches so extended are apt, in the new liturgical climate, to be too narrow for their length. As a rule, however, it was the obvious thing to do. Where one or more bays have been added to these earlier naves the style of the new work as a rule continues that of the old. One finds it thus in the Byzantine Bristol church of Holy Cross in Bedminster, while Sir Giles Scott's naves at Bournemouth and Broadstairs have been lengthened in the late Gothic of their architect's first designs. But at Leicester, when the Dominicans added a large nave to the chancel and transepts of their priory church the style of the addition was a Gothic rather later, and more modern in feeling, than the correct Perpendicular of the original work.

Another method of extension has been the sideways expansion of previously unaisled naves. At Reading Pugin's neo-Norman church has so been treated. In a few other towns these changes have meant the somewhat delicate task of widening aisleless buildings of the immediately post-penal years. As these churches were "auditory" from the start they are better suited for the liturgical needs of the 1960s than many of those erected by the ecclesiological Victorians. They also need careful treatment as being churches of historic interest and architectural merit. At Tamworth the recent changes have included both a westward lengthening and the adding of a North aisle. Though the work has been sympathetically done it has left little that one can readily see of Potter's church of 1829–30. An extension, plus a western gallery to give yet more accommodation, has been contrived at Thetford, while at Grantham the charming classical church of 1832 is being restored. The work is under the direction of Mr. Gerard Goalen, an architect well known for some wholly new Catholic churches. This building at Grantham is to be drastically changed. For while the tower, its cupola, and the Ionic doorway below them are all to be kept as main elements in the classical West end the southern wall is to make way for a large apsed extension. This extension, in a complete re-orientation of the congregational space, is to contain the free-standing altar now required by the latest liturgical directive, while what was at first the church's sanctuary is to become its baptistry.[1] In Guernsey, another church of about the same date has been wholly transformed. For when drastic reconstruction became necessary in the charming French Catholic church in St. Peter Port its lovable though jumbled interior was gutted and then replaced, under M. Alain Séguin of Paris, by a courageously modern and simple auditorium whose glass and paintings are also in the "contemporary" French taste.[2]

Priests and people have alike found that wide aisles with seats, and the arcades which part those aisles from the naves of their churches, severely impede the laity's visual sharing in the liturgy. In new rectangular churches, with no aisles at all or with their aisles only planned as passageways, this particular trouble has been easily and widely avoided. But in Victorian or later churches which have their aisles full of pews, with substantial pillars and arches to block the sightlines from those pews, a solution is less easy to find. One can, of course, sweep the pews from the aisles. But this, in churches already apt to be overcrowded, is a somewhat desperate remedy. Under modern conditions of construction one can, however, lessen the blockage by removing the arcades. This method, unattractive but harmless and most useful in a church which must have had little architectural charm, has been followed in the Birmingham church of St. John the Evangelist, Balsall Heath.[3] The Gothic arcades of a late Victorian building have been cleared away. The architects, Messrs. Jennings, Homer and Lynch who have had other Catholic commissions in the Midlands, have replaced those arcades with horizontal architraves of structural steel, supported in their turn by thin steel columns which cause no more impediment than the iron ones set up, in 1840, by J. J. Scoles at Newport. The seating in the church has gone up from about 350 to over 500, a useful addition in a building used, each Sunday, by over two thousand people.

Extra worshipping space for the Catholics of some towns has also been found by taking over buildings once used by other denominations. The process is by no means new. As far back as 1861 the New Meeting Unitarian Chapel in Birmingham was sold to become the attractive Catholic church of St. Michael, Moor Street.[4] Built in 1802, with a pedimented façade adorned by pairs of Ionic pilasters, its interior keeps many old pews and a gallery, on Tuscan columns, along three sides of its auditorium. With later changes along its sanctuary wall, this typically late Georgian Nonconformist interior remains wholly suitable for the Catholic uses of our own time. The same process of purchase and adaptation has continued since 1945. A Presbyterian chapel in Shepherd's Bush has become an additional church for London's large Polish community. In 1965, on Bristol's eastern outskirts, a one-time Methodist chapel at Soundwell became a Catholic chapel of ease. More interesting still, and the means whereby an old and historic building of much merit was saved from total decay, was the action taken, some ten years ago, at Bewdley. The Unitarian chapel in that charming Severnside town had been built in 1778, with its walls of mellow brickwork and designed to have short straight stretches to form the sides between two ends which are gracefully elliptical. The cornice, and the round-headed Georgian windows, are rendered in the grey sandstone of the locality. The Unitarians of Bewdley having abandoned their chapel it was for some years a furniture store, that phase in its career being fatal to its benches but not to the gallery on its Roman Doric columns. Now, however, it has been bought, and in part reconditioned, as a most characterful chapel of ease in the Catholic parish of Kidderminster.

The buying of Nonconformist chapels for secular uses, or for such other religious purposes as Catholic worship, is comparatively straightforward. Denser legal thickets, and more awkward emotional and ecclesiastical shoals, beset the notion that disused Anglican churches might have the same future career as the chapels at Soundwell and Bewdley. A project, which may perhaps become a precedent with results, has been mooted at Aylesbury; the scheme's outcome remains uncertain.[5]

The new churches which have been finished since 1945 include some, started before the outbreak of war, whose building was halted for obvious reasons. St. Edmund's, in the Waterloo suburb of Liverpool, was one of these.[6] In such buildings it was natural enough that the later stages were in the style (as a rule traditional) of the initial plans. Traditionalism has also, less excusably, been the idiom of some new churches commenced from the beginning since peace returned. This was specially true in the first few of the post-war years; it is part only of a complex, baffling, and fascinating process of liturgical and aesthetic ferment, a story incomplete as I write and likely, in the late 1960s and beyond, to encounter a newer, more formative stage.

We shall find, in our brief survey of Catholic parish churches built since 1953, that the rate of their building increased steeply from that year till the middle of the 1960s. One may, however, expect a slower rate of new commencements in the period of the current building squeeze. By October, 1966, neither the details nor the duration of this were clearly known. The architectural interest of these new buildings has risen fairly steeply in the present decade. Since the autumn of 1964 new sanctuaries have been planned from the start for the recently decreed placing of the High Altar, and for some at least of the other new arrangements flowing logically from the recent rule that all such altars must be usable from either side. But before we take critical, if somewhat generalised note of the parochial building work of the last twelve years one class of existing buildings is of enough importance, in the strictly ecclesiastical sense, for their renovations, extensions, and re-orderings to be noticed on their own.

The Roman Catholic cathedrals of England and Wales now number nineteen, for in 1965 St. Philip Neri's at Arundel became the ceremonial headquarters of the Arundel and Brighton diocese which was then parted from that of Southwark. Those at Cardiff and Southwark were gutted in air raids. Re-conditioning and re-colouring of the normal type has brightened the interiors of some others. In two of them internal re-ordering (in one case with some useful extensions) has gone deeper. Two other dioceses are at work on schemes for entirely new cathedrals, more likely than most other Catholic cathedrals in this country to emerge, within this century's church architecture, as buildings of national note.

At Cardiff the re-roofing and renovation of St. David's produced a sanctuary more spacious and dignified, and better planned for major ceremonies, than that which existed before the bombing. Many new furnishings were installed, among them some curious conical canopies and Mr. Adam Kossowski's attractive ceramic Stations of the Cross. The Archbishop's Throne is not, however, a new piece of furniture, but is the canopied oaken chair, richly panelled in its mock medievalism, which once served the same purpose in the monastic cathedral of Belmont. The whole restoration was, however, done too early in time for it to enshrine the latest ideas for the placing of such items as the High Altar, canons' stalls, and the bishop's throne. Basic conservatism was also a main point in the restoration at Southwark which was done by the summer of 1958. Here too the sanctuary was enlarged so that it includes the eastern bay of the nave. The outer walls of Pugin's church were kept, and in the aisles Mr. Romilly Craze's new vaulting has "flying" ribs on the model of those in the fourteenth-century sacristy at Bristol Cathedral. The plans, as published, allowed for the building up of Pugin's truncated western tower into a great pinnacled structure, Perpendicular and without Pugin's spire.

The reconstruction at Southwark has also brought in new features, so that the renovated cathedral is lighter, a little loftier, and more cathedralesque than the building which served from 1848 to 1941.[7] A bay of each aisle has been heightened to make a shallow transept, while all along its length the nave is now lit from above by a clerestory, much as Pugin intended though in a later Gothic idiom than that of his plans. To carry the weight of this clerestory, and of the new ceiling with its painted panels and sequence of cross arches, the new arcades are sturdier than those which did duty before them. Like the clerestory windows they are unmistakably early Perpendicular, while in the new southern Lady Chapel the Gothic idiom of the new side windows is so late as to be "debased".

We have seen (page 102) how at Northampton Edward Pugin's cathedral nave has now been extended, by adding transepts, a central tower, and a lancetted chancel, into a building about as long as that originally planned.[8] The finished church is more "cathedralesque", in the manner of a small medieval cathedral or a priory church, than Bishop Amherst's unfinished building. In another Catholic cathedral by Edward Pugin some ingenious additions to the building have also gone hand in hand with much re-ordering. For at Wrexham the cathedral of the Menevia diocese has obtained new, more spacious sacristies, in contemporary style and arranged in a separate block lying East of the chancel wall. A new vestibule connects them to a side chapel of the Victorian church, while on the chancel's northern side a much enlarged chapel, faithfully repeating much of Edward Pugin's Gothic, will give extra congregational space, and new housing for the reserved Sacrament. For the High Altar is now beneath the chancel arch, and on that altar's original site the bishop's throne looks down a small choir whose canons' stalls line each of the sides.

In one other cathedral drastic and enlightening re-decoration has also brought with it some important re-ordering. In Pugin's cruciform building at Nottingham the High Altar is now beneath the central tower, so that those who use the transepts now look inwards to the sanctuary. As at Wrexham the site of the old High Altar has become that of the bishop's throne, a modern canopied structure having ousted a throne of Victorian Gothic design.[9] But at Plymouth the badly needed redecoration of another cruciform cathedral has been done without drastic refurnishing or liturgical adventure. The building is, however, vastly improved when one recalls the dinginess which once pervaded it.

The Religious Orders of men and women have also done some church and conventual building, in addition to much work on their schools, since 1945. Many convents of nuns have been founded, or have built themselves new chapels and living quarters to replace earlier and smaller buildings. The chapels of these nunneries need not, for the most part, call for our special attention, though at Waldron in Sussex Mr. Justin Alleyn's new buildings for the Visitation nuns make a "contemporary" group of enterprising merit. Among the friars the Dominicans have not, so far, built a church so strikingly a modern masterpiece as that of their Irish colleagues at Athy in Co. Kildare. The most important Carmelite achievement is the restoration for religious purposes of the buildings which survived from their Order's medieval priory at Aylesford in Kent. The old church had been destroyed. The survivals from the original priory lay in two heavily restored ranges of the domestic quarters and in the more spread-out buildings of an outer court running down towards the Medway. Chapels for the community have been fitted up in the medieval ranges; here and elsewhere in the present-day friary paintings by Mr. Adam Kossowski and sculpture by Lindsey and Michael Clark add touches of modernity to a generally traditional scene. No attempt has been made, in the manner of Buckfast, to build a large new church on the foundations of the one started in the thirteenth century. The present priory serves as a leading pilgrimage centre. For this purpose, and for the gathering of large outdoor congregations, an unroofed piazza faces a group of new buildings which themselves form three sides of an apse. Enclosed, polygonal chapels, an arched and vaulted canopy for an altar visible from outside, and some connecting vestibules make up a grouping of buildings whose ground plan is ingeniously novel. Their Arts and Crafts Gothic style makes them mannerly if unexciting neighbours to the medieval survivals a short distance away. Their architect was Adrian Gilbert Scott. His brother Sir Giles had in the meantime worked for the Carmelites on their church in Kensington, replacing a building wiped out by bombing. Despite the noble boldness of its great cross arches the pointed shape of those arches, the late Perpendicular idiom of the clerestory windows, and the Gothic detail of the towering altarpiece combine to give a traditional feeling which was outmoded by the time of the church's building and unnecessary on so completely empty a site.

Since 1960 the monks of England have commissioned more "contemporary" building work than have the friars. The Cistercians, it is true, have had no such developments, for no more work was needed on the church at Mount St. Bernard, and at Caldy the community still uses the church first built on that island by the Anglican Benedictines. For a truly modern Cistercian abbey one must go North of the Border, to Nunraw near Haddington. In England itself the conventual achievements and projects of the Benedictines are, however, of varying, and considerable, significance.

At Ealing, first a daughter priory of Downside but now an independent abbey, the work on the church done since 1945 has largely lain in the replacement of wartime destruction. The nave's eastern section was devastated by bombs. Its fabric has now been repaired. The nave has been lengthened, and the transepts and the crossing of a cruciform church have been added, along with the stump of a central tower. The architect for this work has been Mr. Stanley Kerr Bate, now in charge of the architectural practice once that of F. A. Walters. The style of his additions is the neo-Perpendicular of Walters's original work, and of the turretted western facade which was added by Edward John Walters his architect son.[10] No more eastward lengthening is expected for several years; new liturgical developments, such as the growth of the concelebration of Mass by several priest monks at a time, are likely to affect any building that may eventually be done.

At Buckfast, now an abbey of the English Benedictine congregation, another monastic church by F. A. Walters has been augmented by other architects. But here the style of the addition differs much from that of the old building. The result of what was finished in 1965 has been that the eastern Blessed Sacrament Chapel is the part of the church most worth seeing by the thousands who throng the abbey. The style of this rectangular chapel, by Messrs. Walls and Pearn of Plymouth, is wholly of our own time, with a concrete structure so planned that its roof rises from the west and then slopes gently towards the altar end. The walls are the setting for four large, richly coloured windows, designed by Dom Norris of the Buckfast community and made in the abbey studio, whose reputation in this art grows apace. The whole chapel is entirely of this century, contrasting with the pseudo-Romanesque of the main church and succeeding in just the manner of the late Gothic towers or chapels which were added to mainly Norman abbeys or cathedrals.

At Ampleforth the tower, the transepts, and the nave bay of Sir

Giles Scott's stocky church were built between 1958 and 1961. The need for economy caused some differences between the post-war additions and the work done in the 1920s. The deep southern transept is lower and less impressive than that originally planned. The crossing arches, and those in the saucer-domed nave, are of simpler stonework than in the earlier portion of the church, with plaster replacing the Hornton stone of the choir. But the nave was given a short extension, and a deep gallery, to contain the large lay congregation composed by the boys of the school.[11]

The most ambitious building venture now in hand among the English Benedictines is at Douai Abbey. It was too costly, aesthetically pointless, and liturgically inconvenient to complete the late Gothic church as designed by Arnold Crush. Mr. Frederick Gibberd has made plans not only for the continuance of the church as a "contemporary" building, but for new, comprehensively planned monastic quarters which can free the existing monks' blocks for the uses of the school.[12] It is on some of his monastic accommodation blocks that work was started in 1964. Two ranges of study bedrooms have been built of load-bearing brick whose rich redness will tune in with the older buildings nearby. Their layout and appearance are those of accommodation blocks built nowadays for various places of corporate and communal living and study. They could as well serve a new University or a teachers' training college as a community of monks and novices. The better to catch the sunlight their rooms are planned behind the zig-zag, or successively serrated, profile lately used for new sets of rooms built by Clare and Jesus Colleges at Cambridge.

Mr. Gibberd's plans for a new abbey church at Woolhampton recall the recent success at Buckfast in that they boldly combine Crush's unfinished building with new work in a wholly different style. The two Gothic bays of the choir limb are to be given two more corner turrets, thus becoming a low central tower above the High Altar. As at Ampleforth this altar will have the monks' choir on one side, arranged (as it is now) in what was planned as the Lady Chapel. On the tower's other side a new nave, severe and boxlike and shaped as a broad rectangle, will run out to the west. Chapels and a narthex are planned to envelop its congregational space, while tall slit windows are to admit the light.

In 1928 the largely convert Benedictine community of Caldy Island near Tenby moved to the old hillside manor house of Prinknash near Gloucester. The house had, from about 1520, been the country mansion of the abbots of St. Peter's in that city. Though the previous lay owners had added an apsed sanctuary to the chapel, and though some hutted monastic buildings and a charming pseudo-Gothic laity chapel have been added to the picturesquely rambling old house these were, and are, inadequate for the purposes of a much grown community. In the 1930s the late Abbot Upson chose the sloping, view-commanding site for a vast cruciform church which ranks as the greatest "might have been" of this country's revived Benedictine monasticism.* The late Mr. Goodhart-Rendel was the architect who produced designs for a huge church whose Romanesque style, and whose general feeling, would have had about it a neo-Cluniac grandiloquence; the attendant living quarters, traditionally arranged on a strictly claustral plan, would have been no less ambitious. The steepness of the ground below the choir end of the church made the architect plan a large and lofty sub-crypt as well as a main crypt above it. It was this sub-crypt which was started in 1939, being finished by the early 1960s when Abbot Upson retired.

It was then clear that the great church of Abbot Upson's dreams was financially impossible, as well as being out of date in its style and out of tune with liturgical thinking in this age of *aggiornamento*.

The community decided to abandon the full project and to use the sub-crypt as an element in any buildings eventually to arise on this beautiful site. Mr. F. G. Broadbent, who had been a partner of Mr. Goodhart-Rendel and who had taken part in the preparatory work for Prinknash, was asked to design monastic buildings, and a church for later erection, on a far more modest scale than the abbey which had been started. The most pressing need was for new living quarters for the monks. The sub-crypt, being large enough to serve as a temporary church, is proposed as the base for a monastery block, to be built in a restrained "contemporary" style and faced with Cotswold stone.[13] Many difficulties have followed this decision of the early 1960s. Not only has there been trouble over mounting costs, but the new Prinknash Abbey had to go through the inevitable entanglements of official planning consent. The Gloucestershire County Council formally rejected two schemes by Mr. Broadbent. Both of these included domestic buildings partly resting on the sub-crypt which is due, for several years to come, to be used as the Abbey church. They also allowed for a

* It would have been a little longer than Gloucester Cathedral.

rectangular permanent church, with a transept for visiting laity as well as the appropriate worshipping space for the monks; this church is planned for building when finance allows. An appeal against the County Council's second refusal was made to the Ministry of Housing and Local Government, but both of Mr. Broadbent's schemes were taken into account when the appeal was heard. In the upshot, the Minister approved the second of the submitted designs. Its domestic blocks were adapted from those indicated earlier, but rather more change was suggested for the church which will, none the less, be rectangular, with chapels on one side of its central altar and the monks' choir on the other, and with a large laity transept running out (as does the present laity chapel at Prinknash) at right angles to the monastic sanctuary. The design which has come through the ordeal of appeal is thus the one we may expect to see rendered in this lovely estate of the modern Benedictines on the Cotswold escarpment, looking as it does over Gloucester and the lower valley of the Severn which were once so eminent a centre of Benedictine monasticism.

The great monastic church at Downside has had no more additions since 1945, and the buildings so far put up to the designs of Messrs. Brett and Pollen have mostly been provided to meet the needs of the school. Now, however, work is afoot on a new building, by the same architects, which will alike serve monastic purposes and fit the Abbey's growing position as a centre of religious studies for those of all faiths. A scientifically designed library is being built, on a site east of the monastic complex which corresponds to that of the polygonal chapter houses of such medieval monasteries as Westminster and Abbeydore. A square podium will serve as a book store, while above it an octagonal structure will arise, in three storeys, to a peaked and copper-clad roof whose height will be about that of Edward Hansom's Lady Chapel. Access to the library, for the many and varied readers likely to use a collection of University calibre, will be from outside as well as from within the *clausura*, and ample ground exists, next to the site, for eventual extension.

Early in the 1930s, the Downside Benedictines bought "Paddock-hurst", a mansion near Worth in Sussex, as a preparatory school. The house was lavishly extended, in 1895, by the first Lord Cowdray. It is a remarkable period piece, ornately Gothic with some Renaissance and Mexican undertones. A winter garden, with an opulently vaulted vestibule and in general of a remarkably ecclessiastical appearance was

43 *The Rectangular Plan*
    (a) *Heston*   (b) *East Acton*

fitted out as a chapel, and a simple monastery block was built out from one side of the mansion.

Worth has now become independent of Downside. It has been graded as an abbey and has its own large senior school. Schemes are afoot for monastery buildings more commodious than those now on the site, and for a church large enough for new and expanded needs. Designs by Mr. Francis Pollen allow for the lengthening of the present monastery block, for the facing of the new southern frontage in a mixture of concrete and grey brick, and for two extra monastic blocks to complete a square of buildings recalling the traditional monastic plan. No specially religious impression is planned for these living, sleeping, and eating quarters for a modern community of Benedictines; their general aspect could be that of any contemporary buildings, such as the blocks of study bedrooms in teacher training colleges, which are designed for corporate living. Where tradition is overridden is in the position of the church, and of the crypt which may extend beneath part of its area. For whereas in a medieval abbey the church would more than fill one side of the claustral square, here at Worth Abbey the inner square itself is reserved for a church whose interior planning (allowing for the uncertainties of current liturgical moves) is to be "central", and whose ordering may not be unlike that of Ampleforth's daughter priory at St. Louis, Missouri.[14] A circular dome is proposed as the covering for this square auditorium for worship. Its silhouette will resemble that of certain types of sunhat, or some people's conception of a flying saucer. Planning approval has now been given for what promises to be a monastic church of some novelty and excitement, and the hurdles of official consent have proved easier to surmount in the forest ridges of northern Sussex than they were on the wooded slopes of the Gloucestershire Cotswolds.

Another important non-parochial project is that for a westward extension of the Old Palace Chaplaincy at Oxford. The large nissen hut which now serves as a chapel is due for demolition, and the new buildings planned by Messrs. Ahrends, Burton, and Koralek are to be something more than replacements for facilities which now exist. They should also form a leading element in the much needed redevelopment of the sleazy St. Ebbe's area of the city. One corner of the compact, somewhat massive complex of "contemporary" buildings proposed by the architects will face out, with a grouping of vertical walls, and of turrets to mask the top lighting of the chapel, onto a secluded little

44 *Cardiff: St. Francis, Ely*
  (a) *Nave and ceramic frieze*
  (b) *Sculptural Group*

o

square whose other sides will also consist of modern work. Inside the new buildings the worshipping space will be split between an essentially octagonal main chapel and a much smaller, more intimate Blessed Sacrament Chapel whose congregational space will be embraced by two curving walls. Outline planning permission for these extensions has now been given. But many details are still to be settled, in particular for the internal finish and furnishing of what should be a considerable contribution to Oxford's modern architecture. The starting date for any actual building work is still unknown.*

II

Published statistics are a somewhat misleading guide to the hundreds of new Catholic churches built in England and Wales since the end of the Second World War. The 1955 issue of the *Catholic Directory* shows that the combined total of parochial and other public churches, and of private chapels with Mass at least once a week, was then 3,952. For 1965 the equivalent figure was 4,470. Yet of the 518 places of worship added in those ten years many are neither permanent nor architecturally important. In some places Sunday Mass is said in such buildings as schools, hired rooms, or village halls; these buildings can hardly be ranked as "churches". One finds, moreover, that many new Catholic churches, at Leyland for example or at Chichester where a T-shaped building by Messrs. Tomei and Maxwell has replaced one of 1855 by Wardell, replace buildings long reckoned among the markings on a modern Catholic map of England. Yet the clear fact remains that since 1945 some hundreds of new buildings have been put up for the public worship of the Roman Catholic body in England and Wales. At least in theory these buildings should have added something to our riches of church architecture.

I have shown how in Kensington the Carmelites employed Sir Giles Gilbert Scott, towards the end of his life, to build them a largely Gothic church to replace that which had been bombed. Farther west in the same borough the new Our Lady of Victories was started in 1957. Mr. Adrian Gilbert Scott's wide interior has none of the bold cross arches of the Carmelite church, or of the large new church of Our Lady of the Rosary in Marylebone Road. But Gothic arches lead into

* Information for this passage on the Oxford Chaplaincy has been kindly conveyed and the drawings and model shown to me, by Rev. Michael Hollings, M.A.

the sanctuary and into the western organ space. New windows are in a stylised late Gothic; one's whole feeling, when one bears in mind the date of this act of replacement, is of the sad missing of "contemporary" chances. Another, more successful replacement church by the same architect is near London's dockland, where Wardell's cruciform church of S.S. Mary and Joseph in Canton Street was obliterated. The new building is planned as a Greek cross, with some Georgian references in its loggias, elliptical shapes for some window heads and for the main arches of its octagonal central space, a neo-classical baldachino, and some excellent modern glass. This church is a less obviously modern building than those in the Lansbury precinct not far away. Yet one feels that it may still be admired when they are "dated".

Another seaport district where bombing brought destruction to some Catholic churches was that of Merseyside. Augustus Pugin's re-located church of St. Mary's, Highfield Street, was among those destroyed. Its successor, built between 1950 and 1953, was among the first post-war Catholic churches in England whose building was officially allowed.[15] By the standards of those somewhat distant days, and despite some Romanesque reminiscences, Mr. A. G. Bullen's rectangular, clerestoried church was a decidedly modern building, and in its sanctuary the wall behind the High Altar gains character from its great heraldic display of the arms of Downside and other monasteries of the English congregation of the Benedictines. Further out on the way to Blundellsands St. Alexander's, by Edward Pugin and in the dockland zone of Bootle, was also pulverised. Its brick-built successor has a large, open, rectangular interior by F. X. Velarde. The street façade has a high-rising western wall, deep-set between two towers whose top stages are capped and have tiers of round-headed windows. The composition recalls the sturdy western terminals often built by the masters of Germanic Romanesque.

Many new churches built in the 1950s, and a few since 1960, are traditional in style. Pastorally they are valuable, but they are not buildings of the type one finds mentioned in books on modern church architecture. In the context of this country's "contemporary" religious architecture they have little meaning. Many such churches are in the north-eastern counties, while at Billingshurst and East Worthing in Sussex one has neo-Perpendicular and neo-Byzantine in two Catholic churches, by the same architect who practices in that county.[16] In the East Anglian sector of Northampton diocese Mr. Sebastian Comper has used the early Romanesque style for his strictly traditional churches at Newmarket and in Norwich. Of the latter he has said that he does not for a moment believe that traditional building is played out for religious buildings,[17] while of the Newmarket church I have heard it said that its idiom, recalling the neo-Romanesque style of many new churches across the Irish Sea, was chosen to ensure that the Irish jockeys and stable hands in its congregation should know at a glance that here is a church.

This same desire for a place of worship which would "look like a church" seems to have decided a donor's choice of style for the new church of Christ the King in the reconstructed area of Plymouth.[18] The site, on the slope where Windsor Lane used to run up to the Hoe, is narrow and rectangular, dictating the building's shape. That fact need have brought no disadvantages, for a rectangular church can be as good a piece of modern building as one which is polygonal, circular, or square. Where this church in Plymouth has failed is in the outdated neo-Gothicism of its idiom, and in its inclusion of aisles and arcades which lessen its effective liturgical width. Hangings, and fumed oak of the type that was popular between the wars, help out with the fittings of this Arts and Crafts Gothic interior. The church, carried out after his death, was among the last executed projects of Sir Giles Gilbert Scott. It is not always easy to realise that here is some of the work done in Plymouth since 1960 and not an agreeable confection of the 1930s.

When we come to the more obviously modern Catholic churches built in England and Wales since about 1960 we find that shape, as well as style, is apt to be a new factor in their design. After a hesitant start, and after some typically British caution over the full acceptance of new architectural ideas this country's Catholic churches are now caught up in the changes made fashionable by the Liturgical Movement, and in the new ideas on internal ordering evolved after the liturgical deliberations of the Second Vatican Council.

The Liturgical Movement has, of course, stirred the Anglicans and Protestant Nonconformists of this country as well as Christians whose loyalty is to the See of Rome. The design and inner ordering of churches have caused much controversy, and have generated some heat, within the past ten years. Not all of the prophets of change have expressed their views in wholly courteous terms, and it is surely wide of the mark to suggest, as has been done over such buildings as Sir Basil Spence's Anglican Cathedral at Coventry, that a rectangular or basilican church automatically incurs a kind of damnation. Within the Catholic field such views are refuted by the obviously high quality of St. Aidan's, East Acton, designed by Burles Newton and Partners and including, among several works by modern artists, ceramic reliefs by Adam Kossowski and a striking Crucifixion painting by Graham Sutherland.[19] Yet it seems that few more long, rectangular Catholic churches are likely to be built to house liturgical arrangements which assume that no one should be remote in distance from what is both a table for the Eucharistic meal and an altar of sacrifice.

This new movement in the building and reorganisation of churches, with its urge to break physical barriers within the auditorium for worshipping, has its close parallel in the modern theatre. For in present-day theatrical planning the proscenium arch, cutting off the audience from the stage, is much less favoured than it was. Designers have returned to the projecting, or "apron" stage which was normal in Shakespeare's time, or in some theatres to "arena" stages where those who attend the play are even more obviously gathered round and in close contact with the actors. There is thus more sympathy of purpose than one would at first suspect between such a building as the new theatre at Chichester and the Catholic church only lately built in the same city. The extremity of theatrical innovation has come with "Theatre in the Round", where those present are seated all round a stage set in the middle of the auditorium. Mr. Stephen Joseph, the chief advocate of this plan, has claimed (I suspect with his tongue in his cheek) that all existing theatres should be burnt down; one senses a kinship between his views and those of the advanced liturgists whose feelings on most churches built before their time seem no less incendiary.[20] Churches with their altars in the centre, and with their laity seated all round the resulting circle, are among those urged, and in some places built, by some of the Liturgical Movement's enthusiasts. I have never attended such a church, but having endured the acoustic and dramatic drawbacks of "Theatre in the Round" I can understand how it is that churches so ordered are now somewhat discredited. If circular or polygonal churches are built their lay congregations are less likely than before to use all 360 degrees of a circle, and their main altars are closer than dead centre to the circumference of the roofed enclosure. One also finds that if the laity sit round more than half a circle the celebrant's position, as that of one who presides over an assembly of God's people, is more awkward to arrange.

Other shapes than that of the circle have been used for many of the most recent Catholic churches of England and Wales. One is aware, at this same time, of more care and reflection over church-building problems than was given, in previous years, by those responsible. More discussion, is apt to occur, between church architects and their patrons, on the theological, liturgical, and aesthetic sides of the tasks in hand. We shall see how the precise ordering of the churches now built is much conditioned by the work of the Second Vatican Council, and by the Liturgical Instructions issued from Rome as late as September of 1964.

We therefore find, in the English and Welsh dioceses, that square and broadly rectangular churches are not unknown. Polygonal buildings are in essence the same as those built to a strictly circular plan. At Burnham on Sea in Somerset Mr. Peter Ware, a young Bristol architect, is building a new church whose High Altar will lie towards one of the oval's long curves; the oval shape is also being used by Mr. Gerard Goalen for a new Catholic church at South Ruislip.* A square church, arranged diamondwise inside and with a hyperbolic-paraboloid roof, has been built in the Denton district of Manchester to the design of Walter Stirrup and Sons,[21] while at Bath one more church on this plan has been finished, and another is being built, by Mr. Martin Fisher.[22]

Some other churches are in the shape of a wedge or a fan, the sanctuary being at the narrow end. In a few of these churches, as in some others built in recent years, the laity's vision of the altar is improved by the arrangement of their benches so that the seating slopes upwards from the sanctuary. Other churches have their auditoria planned in the shape of a T, with three blocks of seating converging on a sanctuary set in the middle of the crosspiece. Such buildings recall many of those put up in Ireland in the immediately post-penal years and in the aftermath of Emancipation. For this arrangement occurs both in the chapels of country congregations and in sophisticated classical Dublin buildings like the church of St. Nicholas of Myra or Boulger's masterly composition of the 1830s in Westland Row. These T-shaped Irish churches were built so that large congregations could be better contained than in enormously long rectangular auditoria. Those lately built in England express the more deliberate liturgical purpose of gathering everyone as near as possible to the altar. They thus reflect the same ideas as do the other buildings laid out on what

* His designs were exhibited in the Royal Academy Exhibition of 1965.

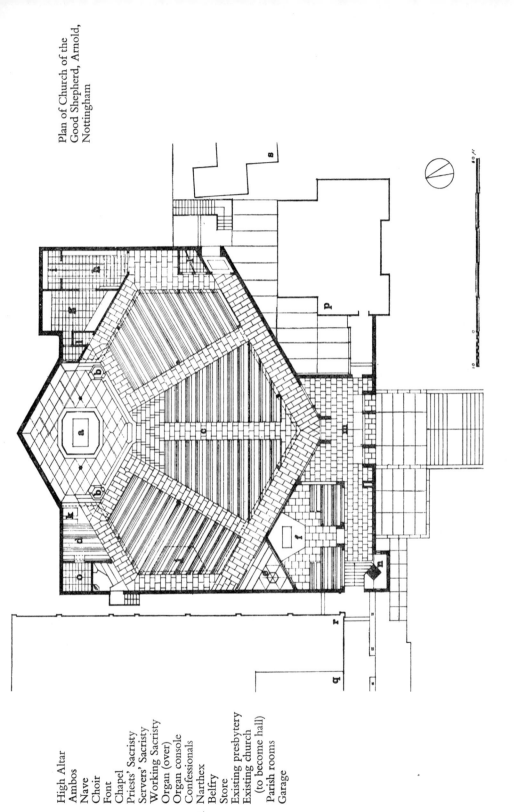

Plan of Church of the
Good Shepherd, Arnold,
Nottingham

a   High Altar
b   Ambos
c   Nave
d   Choir
e   Font
f   Chapel
g   Priests' Sacristy
h   Servers' Sacristy
i   Working Sacristy
j   Organ (over)
k   Organ console
l   Confessionals
m   Narthex
n   Belfry
o   Store
p   Existing presbytery
q   Existing church
    (to become hall)
r   Parish rooms
s   Garage

were revolutionary plans as late as the 1930s. A striking example of a T-shaped church is that of Our Lady of Fatima at Harlow, designed by Mr. Gerard Goalen. An extremely slender, copper-covered spire rises high above the intersection of its limbs, while the large upper wall spaces of its nave and transepts glow splendidly, if at times a little harshly, with the colours of the stylised windows by Dom Charles Norris and his glassmaking colleagues of Buckfast Abbey.

Mr. Goalen has had other Catholic commissions since his church at Harlow was finished. One of these, with a fan-shaped auditorium converging on a simple sanctuary whose concrete-set glass (like that in the nave) is by Mr. Patrick Reyntiens, is the church of the Good Shepherd at Arnold near Nottingham. The slim concrete pillars of its interior recall Perret's church of Notre Dame du Raincy in Paris; the architect has, however, told me that he was not directly inspired by that pioneering work of the 1920s.[23]

Mr. Goalen is one of many architects who have worked, since 1945, on Catholic buildings. Not all of these designers have themselves professed the Roman Catholic faith. Their patrons are less automatically inclined than once they were to employ architects of their own denomination. Careful briefing, now at all events, is more likely to occur, whatever the religion of the chosen designer.

The late Mr. F. X. Velarde was responsible for some important churches in the last years of his life. He was, perhaps, the last convincing exponent of the basilican Byzantine manner; his churches were in essence traditional, but with a real individuality. Most of these Velarde churches are in Lancashire and in the Shrewsbury diocese. But in the London area St. Luke's at Pinner has again proved that a rectangular church, with low Romanesque arcades parting the nave from its passageway aisles, can still be architecturally effective. Mr. Velarde still excelled in the simple handling of monochrome brickwork. One sees this point as well in his new side chapel at Hindley as in the low-set, slightly pointed chancel arch of his small chapel at Alsager in Cheshire.[24] Distinctive points in Mr. Velarde's work are his use, in such churches as Holy Cross at Birkenhead,[25] of mosaics on his walls and pillars, the Rhenish Romanesque flavour of his bell towers with their peaked caps and groups of round-headed belfry openings, and his curious, somewhat restless fenestration wherein plain rectangular windows alternate, in close-set rows, with those whose tops are rounded. Mr. Julian Velarde and his colleagues of the F. X. Velarde partnership

45 (a) *Woodthorpe, Nottingham,*
    by Gerard Goalen; interior
  (b) *Buckfast Abbey: Blessed Sacrament Chapel*

46 *Modernity in Wales*
  (a) *Briton Ferry*
  (b) *Machynlleth*

NORTH ELEVATION

FRINAKASH IDDEY CLOB
START FOR CHURCH L ABBEY

continue this Liverpool practice. Their church at Boreham Wood near London has a simplified, stylised version of the twin-towered *westwerk* which Mr. Velarde Senior had designed in Bootle.[26] But their most recent work breaks out along bolder lines, most notably their Catholic church at Woodchurch in the Wirral, where a high-peaked structure, with glass to fill its western side, rises high above the sanctuary and throws light, unseen by those in the nave, onto the High Altar.

In so short a survey one can only name a few of the other architects who have lately worked on Catholic churches, or of the buildings in England or Wales which they have actually designed. Among those whose churches, whether lingeringly traditional or more "contemporary", have been finished in this decade there are some whose work mainly lies in particular areas. Messrs. Harrison and Cox* have worked considerably for the Birmingham Archdiocese. Their churches in Birmingham itself include the circular, somewhat gasometric bulk of the new St. Catherine's, lately finished in the Horsefair to replace the Victorian Gothic building whose nave lay in the path of a wider thoroughfare from Bristol Road to the city centre. Messrs. Jennings, Homer, and Lynch, with a good polygonal church to their credit in Walsall, have worked for the same ecclesiastical authorities, while at Lillington near Leamington Messrs. Reyner and Federski's cruciform church has attracted much attention; it has kinship with Mr. Goalen's church at Harlow in that its laity sit in the three arms of a T. Though based on Manchester, Mr. Desmond Williams has also done Catholic work in the Midlands, his least conventional achievement being a fine circular church at Dunstable which has a strikingly patterned aluminium ceiling; the brick panels of its curved walls are spaced out between tall windows of tinted glass.[27]

Coming further west, we find that Messrs. Ivor Day and O'Brien have had much of the work available in the diocese of Clifton. They have not, however, enjoyed a monopoly, for Mr. Peter Falconer and Partners of Stroud have been commissioned for two churches in their own county; one of these will be an octagonal building, with a striking spire above the apex of its roof, on the western outskirts of Chelten-

---

* From now onwards I normally refer to architects by their business titles. I am, however, well aware of the importance in these matters of the actual "project architect"; as with the vexed question of the division of credit between Vanbrugh and Hawksmoor this will sometimes be a teaser for the architectural historians of the future.

47 (a) *Prinknash Abbey: the allowed design*
   (b) *Douai Abbey: a domestic block (model)*
   (c) *Liverpool Cathedral: Mausoleum Chapel*

48 *Liverpool Cathedral:*
   nearly complete

ham.[28] In the Archdiocese of Cardiff the diocesan architects, Messrs. F. R. Bates, Son, and Price, have designed most of the churches put up in the last few years. Of their buildings in Cardiff St. Teilo's out at Whitchurch replaces a smaller, earlier building. Its auditorium is wedge-shaped, and in its western façade a sturdy, outward-curving central pier parts two doorways and two large window expanses of concrete mullions and tinted glass. The south-western corner of St. Francis' at Ely has a modern sculptural group of the Crucifixion and the patron saint. Inside, a rectangular nave is narrowed, at the altar end, by the inward canting of a large gallery's two ends. The front of that gallery is continuously adorned by a Way of the Cross, designed and rendered in ceramics by Mr. Adam Kossowski.

The Home Counties, with their vast immigration from other regions, have added greatly to their Catholic population. They have thus seen an outburst of churchbuilding, giving work to several architects. Mr. F. G. Broadbent and his partners have designed some churches as well as many schools. Their church at Thames Ditton, opened in the autumn of 1965, is an addition to the growing total of those with circular auditoria. Among their smaller buildings those at Knebworth in Hertfordshire, and at Aycliffe near Dover display a basic design widely favoured for small parish churches and some chapels of ease. A high-pitched roof, with its main supporting members in steel or concrete, rises sharply above low or almost non-existent side walls; the building's section thus becomes that of an acute-angled triangle.

Messrs. Tomei and Maxwell have had some commissions in what was, till lately, the undivided diocese of Southwark, while Mr. Justin Alleyn has designed churches for sites in several directions from London as a centre. His rectangular church at Ewell, and one at Horley on a polygonal plan, may rank among his best works; the former has clean, simple exterior brickwork, and both have windows by the French glazier Pierre Fourmaintreaux.[29] Messrs. Burles, Newton and Partners of Southend have designed several churches in Essex and elsewhere near London. Their large aisled basilica at Hayes shows that such a plan can still be architecturally alive if its aisles are narrow; like their church at East Acton this building is of some note for works, by modern artists, which include a painting by Annigoni. The same architects' church at Harlow, with its high-peaked triangular section on a low rectangular base, has been praised in an organ of the architectural press,[30] while at South Benfleet in Essex they are now supervising a square church, arranged diamondwise but with a triangular projecting baptistry and a large separate chapel of Reservation.

We turn, at last to Menevia diocese, and to the great Catholic stronghold of Liverpool. Messrs. Lionel Prichard and Son have worked on Catholic churches in South Lancashire, and on an octagonal one near Chester. But the most prolific Catholic architects in this area are Messrs. Weightman and Bullen of Liverpool. They are also the architects for the diocese of Menevia. At Overton in Flint, at Welshpool, and at Bethesda they have finished what seem to be excellent little churches with low bases and acutely pointed triangular roof structures; their size and quality are suitable for the small Catholic numbers and "missionary" conditions in most of northern and central Wales.

Polygonal churches by Weightman and Bullen have been built at Lowton near Warrington and at Thornton on Liverpool's northern outskirts. St. Ambrose's at Speke is an important rectangular work. Slender concrete piers part the congregational space from an "aisle" running behind the sanctuary as well as along the sides of the nave. The patterned concrete vault, and the clerestory lighting from a succession of arched windows round all four sides of the church, resemble the upper structure of Mr. Denys Lasdun's hall in the new Fitzwilliam House at Cambridge.[31] Similar planning, but with a more modest inner height and low triangular-headed clerestory windows, occurs in the Weightman and Bullen church of St. Margaret Mary Alacocque in Pilch Lane, Liverpool. As at Speke the High Altar stands clear of the East wall, and its Communion rails enclose a square. Almost exactly above the altar an octagonal dome structure lets more light onto the sanctuary, becoming a modern equivalent of the domes which surmount Renaissance or Regency churches of earlier Catholic times.

The best known Weightman and Bullen church is that built by the Benedictines of Ampleforth for their parish at Leyland near Preston. In its own field it has become as famous, internationally as well as in this country, as the vehicles for which Leyland is also renowned.[32] The project architect here was Mr. J. Faczynski; as the church also has important ceramics by Mr. Adam Kossowski it is another which well illustrates the great contribution which Polish immigrants have made to Catholic churchbuilding in the land of their adoption. Its success

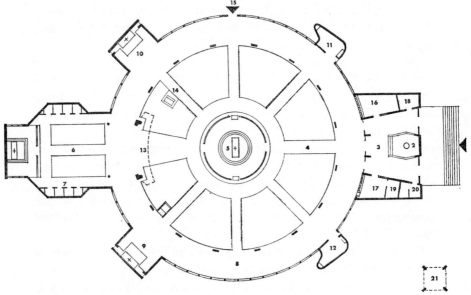

Plan of St. Mary's Church, Leyland, Lancashire

1. Main entrance 2. Baptistry 3. Narthex 4. Nave 5. High Altar 6. Blessed Sacrament
Chapel 7. Confessionals 8. Ambulatory 9. All Souls Chapel 10. St. Benedict's Chapel
11. St. Joseph's Meditation Chapel 12. St. Anne's Meditation Chapel 13. Organ over
14. Organ console 15. Entrance from Sacristy and Priory 16. Children's Room
17. Warden's Room 18. Book Shop 19. Store 20. Toilet 21. Bell Tower.

also displays the merits of direct architectural commissioning, and of
careful briefing discussion between priests and their chosen designers.

This church replaces a somewhat barnlike early Victorian building
not far from what is still a picturesque old village centre at the southern
end of Leyland. The "garden city" setting of the new building is near
what is now the middle of a township much expanded by the booming
success of its staple industry. More important, in the context of the
year 1959 when it was planned, was the forward-looking nature of its
plan and liturgical ordering. The High Altar stands in the centre of the
nave, but as the organ console and the choir seats are "behind" it the
congregation does not, in normal practice, gather all round the sanctuary
in its downward-sloping blocks of pews. The many-angled concrete
roof, the triangular clerestory windows, and the nave's drum with its
walling of warm brickwork, rest on fourteen Y-shaped concrete piers
whose angles hold the controversial, somewhat spidery cast-bronze
Stations of the Cross by Mr. Arthur Dooley. Across the aisles the outer

windows have *dalle de verre* panels of symbolic glass by Mr. Patrick Reyntiens. The church is important for its various works of modern art as well as for its basic design and fine construction. None of these works is more satisfying than the tapestry behind the altar of the large Blessed Sacrament chapel which projects from the circular body of the church. Its subject, against a glowing red background, is the Trinity and the project architect was its designer. As one looks from the church's main entrance, beyond the central altar, this chapel and the colours of this splendid hanging give a focal point not always achieved if one opts for a "central" plan. That plan has itself proved less than perfect in practice, and seems outdated by the changes of position introduced into the Mass since the church at Leyland was planned.

The opening of the church at Leyland was in the spring of 1964. Since then the Catholics of England and Wales have seen many liturgical changes. These arise from decisions made at the Second Vatican Council; they affect the text and language of the Mass, the positions, at various parts of the service, of the officiating priest, and the ordering of the churches in which the Mass takes place. The new changes are important both for newly built churches and for the reorganisation of those which already exist.

The most important changes concern the exact placing of a church's main altar. Since September of 1964 it has been laid down that in new churches this altar must stand clear of the sanctuary's eastern wall, and far enough from that wall to be usable for the increasing (though not rigidly enjoined) practice whereby a priest says the sacrificial part of his Mass with his face to the people.* As in a room where the moving of one piece of furniture may lead to more rearrangement, this instruction means that much else in a new or reordered sanctuary must be in different places from those long thought normal. It involves a "dated" appearance for the inner layout of a new church such as that of St. Anne's at Wrexham, where an octagonal building, with a shallow circular dome, has its altar close against the wall which faces the doorway. The positions of such furnishings as the celebrant's chair, the lectern, the pulpit and the *ambo* (if such are still found as separate items), and the seats for acolytes are all affected by the one major change in the placing of the altar. Precise positions for all these things, consistent with the theological-cum-liturgical ideas which now hold sway,

* This "facing" posture is already normal in this country for the earlier, instructional portion of the service.

are likely to vary according to such circumstances as the exact design of churches and the knowledge and taste of those who plan and build them. Of special importance, and to some beholders of surprising novelty, will be the place chosen for sacramental Reservation, and the actual way in which this is contrived. In some large churches this can be done by the building of a side chapel which is also used for Mass on weekdays. Where a single sanctuary exists the problem is less easy. The arrangement which has long (though not perpetually) prevailed is that the tabernacle of Reservation stands on, or close above the middle of, a High Altar set near to the sanctuary's eastern wall. But once an altar is used for consecration *versus populum* such a tabernacle is distinctly inconvenient. So too, to say the least, are some of the suggestions for dealing with the problem. One or two of these, including the idea that the tabernacle should rest on a ledge in front of the altar but at a lower level than its *mensa*, and one by which the tabernacle descends, like a Jack in the Box, into the body of the altar, are discouraged by some commentators[33] and are flatly forbidden by some overseas bishops.[34] A solution which seems to have advantages, and which goes back to the "Sacrament House" which occurred in medieval Scotland and Germany, is to have a separate shrine or altar of Reservation, conspicuous from the nave and containing a free-standing tabernacle or recess in the sanctuary wall. For the sake of a good sightline from itself to the people in the nave such a shrine must be set on one side of the main axis of the worshipping auditorium. In England and Wales no final sanction has as yet been given to any particular arrangements, to the Comments from Bologna, or to the Pastoral Directory in force in Montreal. However one regards the process, the building of new Catholic churches in this country, and the more or less drastic reordering of those gradually accumulated since Georgian times, finds those engaged on these tasks in a fluid, exciting situation. It is one in which, to mention a point in Cardinal Lercaro's Comments, the status of the Liturgical Movement has been reinforced and, so to speak, canonised by the Second Vatican Council which ended in December of 1965.

CATHEDRAL EPILOGUE

Despite the great activity now seen in the building of this country's Roman Catholic parish churches, and despite the modest standards of most of its present Catholic cathedrals when one compares them to those which flourished as such before the reign of Henry VIII, the word "Cathedral" still carries a mystique and conveys significance. So my final words in this chronicle of churchbuilding must be on two current schemes for wholly new cathedrals. One of these buildings is nearly finished. The other has yet to be physically started. Another difference between the Roman Catholic cathedrals of Liverpool and Clifton is that one was designed and started before the first session of the recent Vatican Council, while no building work was done on the other before that Council ended; the final gatherings in the nave of St. Peter's were held at the same time as the preliminary briefings and discussions for a new cathedral in the city of Bristol. One notes, moreover, that at Liverpool the cathedral's designer was chosen after a heavily entered competition, while at Clifton the Bishop and his advisers commissioned their architect direct.

By the middle of the 1950s it was clear that whatever the aesthetic promise of Lutyen's great project for Liverpool, its completion was by now a financial chimera. The Lutyens plan was abandoned, and Mr. Adrian Gilbert Scott got out a reduced version of the design. His dome, with its obvious debt to that of St. Paul's in London, might have improved on that of Lutyens. But by and large this redesigned cathedral would have been a poor shadow of the one first projected; it would likewise have been too expensive. Mr. Scott's designs were set aside, and the way was clear for a cathedral of our own century on its site between Brownlow Hill and Mount Pleasant.

The new Archbishop, who is now, as Cardinal Heenan, the Archbishop of Westminster, held a competition for what was hoped would be a truly modern cathedral, up to date in its style and enshrining recent liturgical thinking. Nearly three hundred architects sent in designs. Gothic traditionalism, neobrutalism, reminiscences of the opera house at Sydney, and sheer fancy were found in those rejected.[1] Mr. Frederick Gibberd was chosen as the architect for the most important Catholic commission given out in twentieth-century England. His design, with some changes made since it was first made known, has been rendered and is now (September 1966) nearly finished.

Had the winning design been for a rectangular cathedral the building might have been fitted on to the top of the retained Lutyens crypt. But as Mr. Gibberd's plans were for a great circular church, nearly two hundred feet across the main axis of its porch and its largest side chapel, his cathedral is too wide for the Lutyens base. The new building has thus been planned to arise on a large space between the existing crypt and the lower reach of Mount Pleasant. Only at one point, where an outdoor altar commands a piazza laid out above the crypt, will the circumference of the new building impinge on Sir Edwin's work. Below its auditorium the new crypt will be used as a covered car park. Above that level one has the concrete roof structure, and the worshipping space, of the actual cathedral.

The design of the new Catholic Cathedral at Liverpool resembles that at Leyland in that it is based on a central High Altar, with chapels of various shapes and sizes leading off the surrounding ambulatory, and with the choir, the canons' stalls, and the congregational space so arranged that the laity will not sit all round the sanctuary. To enclose such a space the architect has rejected the completely vertical walling found at Leyland, in Dunstable, and in most other round or polygonal churches. He has opted for a great conical or tentlike structure, not rising to a pointed apex but with its top horizontally cut off so that the lower part of the cone supports the almost vertical uprights of a great lantern; such a lantern has been used already by Mr. Gibberd in his designs for a polygonal chapel in a Catholic training college at Middleton in Lancashire.[2] At Liverpool the lantern is plastic capped by slim pinnacles which are to support a metalwork corona symbolic of Christ's crown of thorns. The main structural elements of the whole composition are the sixteen great concrete struts (thicker than those shown in the original designs and due to be coated with white mosaic) which in a way resemble the taut ropes of a tent, but which clearly project from the roofing of the cone. This roof is itself made of concrete panels coated with aluminium. As the walls of the somewhat oddly assorted chapels are to be vertical, the lowermost section of each concrete strut runs clear through the air, in the manner of a Gothic flying buttress or of the great stone struts which sustain the late medieval tower of the parish church at Cirencester. Much natural lighting will come from the lantern directly above the sanctuary. The great panels of concrete-set glass have been designed by Mr. John Piper and Mr. Patrick Reyntiens and have now been hoisted into place. Their light will be increased by more glass of the same type, set in a narrow, horizontal band just above the chapels and at the base of the sloping cone.

The shape and structure of Mr. Gibberd's cathedral are what tempt a comparison with Oscar Niemeyer's far more graceful concept for a round cathedral at Brasilia. But the beautifully curved and splayed supporting members at Brasilia are to uphold no lantern; they themselves are to do all the work of sustaining a covering for the worshipping space. The poetic, plastic beauty of Niemeyer's structure makes one think of it as concrete sculpture; a sad contrast between it and the cathedral being finished on the slopes above central Liverpool may arise from the Brasilia project's being so caught up in the vagaries of Brazilian politics that the new cathedral amid the tropical jungles may never be completed. At Liverpool the stiff angularity of what has been likened to an oast house, and has been called "the Mersey Funnel" suggests that here we have carpentry in concrete. A parallel to this cathedral's construction does indeed come from the structural carpentry of the fourteenth century. For if one looks at the wooden model of the complicated timber structure upholding the octagonal lantern of Ely Cathedral,[3] one sees that the master carpenter William Hurley's device of upward-slanting timbers carrying the great vertical baulks of the lantern has its equivalent in the conical "tent", and its surmounting lantern, of Mr. Gibberd's design. The parallel is strengthened by the change of plan whereby the uprights of the lantern at Liverpool are now more nearly vertical than was first announced.

Other external features of this new Cathedral at Liverpool are the canopy spreading out over the outdoor altar, and the unconventional combined structure of the main entrance porch and the belfry. The triangular side section of this large projection recalls the tail of a fish or of an aeroplane. Its profile, facing out towards Mount Pleasant, was also to have been triangular. But now, in a sense recalling the Benedictines' belfry at Collegeville in Minnesota, it presents a large rect-

P

angular expanse. Four openings, for bells of differing sizes, are near
the top, while below them, in the triangular space first planned, a
decorative relief has three crosses and three crowns.[4] This element of
Liverpool's Roman Catholic cathedral is the portion of the building
lying nearest to Sir Giles Gilbert Scott's Arts and Crafts Gothic masterpiece which is its Anglican opposite number. No two buildings could
differ more sharply as they scowl at each other, in stylistic incompre-
hension, across the late Georgian zone which is traversed by Hope and
Rodney Streets.

One will need, however, to visit the finished interior of Mr.
Gibberd's great building for a final judgment on its quality. Much will
depend on the goodness of its fittings, and on any works of modern art
which may aid the effect of its structure and liturgical ordering. One
will then see whether the chapel of Reservation, behind the High
Altar as one enters the cathedral from its principal porch, will be as
good a focal attraction as its long equivalent at Leyland. It may be that
the inside of this great building for Catholic worship will be more
appealing than the undeniably imposing, but somewhat angular bulk
and silhouette which has risen into the Liverpool skyline seen from
Birkenhead, or from the upper deck of a ferry coming over the Mersey.
If the cathedral at Brasilia is never finished that at Liverpool seems sure
to be the main example in the world of this type of centrally planned
church. It may, however, be a less influential building than was first
thought possible, and imitations of its inner ordering are less likely than
could have been expected six years ago. For however much one may
aim, theologically speaking and as a liturgical exercise, at the "gathering
round" of those present at Mass that gathering is less likely than it was
to involve a complete circle of the faithful round an altar in their
geometrical midst.

For some years there had been a strong desire to improve the Pro-
Cathedral at Clifton, and to lessen or abolish the dinginess and clutter
which make the interior unworthy of its purpose and dignity. Some
degree of liturgical reordering also became a sharp necessity. Plans
were therefore made by which the interior could be brightened and
improved, and for the sweeping away of many ugly and incongruous
objects of devotion. Some liturgical refashioning could also have been
achieved. But Charles Hansom's ingenious if unattractive roof supports,
with their resemblance to the train sheds of some early railway stations,
held serious problems of long term stability. It could still have hap-

pened, after the spending of many thousands of pounds, that the inner structure of the renovated cathedral would have been well below the standards of stability and public safety which are now required. At a time of somewhat puzzled bewilderment some local benefactors came forward with a generous offer which has wholly changed the position.

In 1965 some Catholic businessmen resident in or near Bristol anonymously offered to build an entirely new cathedral; they stressed that their offer was for this purpose alone. Their proposal was gratefully accepted, and the choice of an architect and a decision on the site have been the first steps taken. No competition has been held. The commission, for what is bound to be an important new building, and for what may be the most up to date of such churches in England, has gone direct to the firm of Sir Percy Thomas and Son. The partner in charge of their Bristol office is Mr. Frederick Jennet. The project architects are Mr. Weeks, and Mr. Poremba who is a Pole by birth and was a competitor at Liverpool. The eventual building must combine the functions of a cathedral and of the parish church of a large congregation.

The next decision was whether to pull down the building started to the designs of Goodridge, fitted out by Charles Hansom, and then so much altered by the same architect that all chances were lost of completing the original neoclassical conception. One could then build a new cathedral on the foundations and substructure started in the 1830s. The other possible expedient was to start afresh on a wholly new site. The second policy has been adopted. A site has been chosen, in the demure and leafy suburbia of Clifton Park, amid fine early Victorian classical villas and close to some terraces in the late Regency idiom. The site itself was first developed, in 1844–45, for a classical mansion. It would well have suited the erection of the neoclassical church of the Apostles as designed by H. E. Goodridge.

Outline planning permission for the building, on this site, of the new Catholic cathedral was given in the spring of 1966; the approval then granted covered such items as vehicular access, crypt-level car parking of the type one will see at Liverpool, site coverage, and the upward impact of the building on the skyline of an area of Bristol where sensitivity and restraint are important, and where any new church must both sympathise with the dignified period architecture of Clifton Park and must also, without question, be a creation of its own age. The ground plan of the new Cathedral is likely to be an irregular hexagon, and its liturgical layout may now be said to have been mainly determined, taking full account of what is needed, and enjoined, for the late 1960s and the decades beyond. The sanctuary is due to be notably spacious and the bishop's throne should look down, in the manner of Nottingham and Wrexham Cathedrals as now rearranged, onto a free-standing High Altar. Since the spring of 1966 several changes have been considered for the elevation, the roof structure, and the general outward appearance of the church; one has to bear in mind that its third dimension will be as significant as the internal disposition of its worshipping space. The final design had still, in September of 1966, to be submitted to the Bristol authorities for their detailed planning approval. But whatever may be the exact external appearance of this new cathedral in Clifton Park one can say that this new headquarters of the Clifton diocese has its chance of being more up to date, for its particular purpose, than other such buildings in Europe. It will certainly be less anachronistic than the costly, massive cathedral which has lately been finished in Galway. Like Mr. Kenzo Tange's new cathedral in Tokyo, and like the striking cathedral recently started at Rockford in Illinois, it can hardly fail, in the entire setting of modern Catholicism, to be truly historic.

NOTES

CHAPTER I

1. The "Humble Request" of Brother Leo of St. Mary Magdalene to the Fr. Provincial; MS at Oscott College.
2. Calendar of State Papers (Domestic), Vol. of 1619–23, p. 593.
3. John Summerson, *Architecture in Britain, 1530–1830,* 1953, p. 80. See also drawings in R.I.B.A., Burlington / Devonshire Colln, I, 9/8–12.
4. Summerson, *op. cit.,* plate 44B (from Isaac Ware, *Designs of Inigo Jones,* 1735)
5. A. S. Barnes in *Downside Review,* XX, pp. 158–65.
6. A. S. Barnes, as above, pp. 232–49.
7. Margaret Whinney and Oliver Millar, *English Art, 1625–1714,* 1957, pp. 299–300 and plate 79a.
8. *The Diary of John Evelyn,* Everyman Library, 2 vols., II, p. 263.
9. For altar silverware, etc., see Charles Oman, *English Church Plate, 597–1830,* 1957, p. 262.
10. Catholic Record Society (henceforward referred to as CRS), Vol. XVIII, pp. 98–235, and *Archaeologia Cambrensis,* 6th series, viii (1908), p. 290.
11. Rev. W. Vincent Smith, *Catholic Tyneside,* 1930, p. 48.
12. Oscott MSS, Introduction to Register Book of St. Peter's, Birmingham (printed in Warwickshire Parish Registers, 1904 – Franciscan Mission, Birmingham 1657–1824).
13. See copy of Thomas Eyre's will (made in 1788) in the Presbytery at Hassop.
14. See MS at Oscott referred to in note 1 above.
15. E. R. Kenyon, *Gibraltar under Moor, Spaniard, and Briton,* edn. of 1938, and H. W. Howes, *The Gibraltarian,* 1951.
16. Lancs. County Record Office, Preston, RC Fe 2/1.
17. J. A. Williams, *Bath and Rome,* 1963, p. 30.
18. *Lloyd's Evening Post,* No. 1406, July 11–14th, 1766, p. 1.
19. Oman, *op. cit.,* p. 261.
20. Bryan Little, *The Life and Work of James Gibbs,* 1955, pp. 19–25.
21. Rev. (later Bishop) Bernard Ward *The Dawn of the Catholic Revival in England,* Vol. I, 1909, p. 25.
22. CRS, Vol. IX, pp. 184–5.
23. See R. W. Billington and John Brownbill, *St. Peter's Lancaster,* 1910.
24. Rev. H. J. Coleridge, S. J., *St. Mary's Convent, York,* 1887, p. 177. For Atkinson see Howard Colvin, *A Biographical Dictionary of English Architects, 1660–1840,* 1954.

Miss Meredith, of The Derbyshire Record Office, has found that he was the architect of the new streets laid out in Sheffield, c. 1780, by The Duke of Norfolk.

25. Daniel Defoe, *A Tour through England and Wales*, Everyman Library, 2 vols. Vol. II, p. 249.

26. Details from photographs shown to me at Woodchester.

27. Information kindly communicated by Miss Katharine Longley, Assumption Convent, Holme Hall.

28. See A. L. Humphreys, *East Hendred; a Berkshire Parish*, 1923, pp. 295–6.

29. Christopher Hussey in *Country Life*, Jan. 9th, 1926.

30. Dorset County Record Office, Weld papers, folder of plans p. 54.

31. W. Watts, *The Seats of the Nobility and Gentry*, 1779, plate XVII and text.

32. Nikolaus Pevsner, *Wiltshire*, 1963, p. 492.

33. J. A. Williams, *op. cit.*, p. 114.

34. British Museum, Addl. MSS 35617, f. 243.

35. 18 George III, c. 60.

CHAPTER II

1. *Felix Farley's Bristol Journal*, June 10th, 1780.

2. Downside Archives, Box 8, A 415.

3. *Felix Farley's Bristol Journal*, June 17th, 1780.

4. J. A. Williams, *op. cit.*, p. 80.

5. See note 3 above.

6. *Felix Farley's Bristol Journal*, June 17th, 1780.

7. Downside Archives, Box 8, A 445 and 415.

8. Rev. (later Bishop) Bernard Ward, *The Dawn of the Catholic Revival*, Vol. I, 301.

9. See Bryan Little, *The City and County of Bristol*, 1954, pp. 201–2.

10. Dorothy Stroud, *The Architecture of Sir John Soane*, 1961, pp. 25 and 34 and plate 39.

11. Soane Museum, London, *Precedents in Architecture*, 1784, f. 78v and f 80 r.

12. Dorset County Record Office, Account of Thomas Weld, I, AF 8–9; information kindly communicated by Mr. N. Drinkwater, F.S.A. of the Royal Commission on Historic Monuments; see also building accounts in Dorset Record Office, Weld papers, D 10/ AE 19.

13. Drawings in Lulworth Estate Office.

14. Weld papers, D 10/ C 116; letter to Thomas Weld I from John Thorpe, Oct. 30th, 1786. For Fanny Burney see her *Diary and Letters*, ed. Austin Dobson, 1905, Vol. IV, p. 308.

15. Western Vicariate Archives (in the Bishop of Clifton's house, Leigh Woods, nr. Bristol) Vol. of 1789–90, f. 146 (letter of June 28th, 1790).

16. Western Vicariate Archives, Vol. of 1791, f. 40 (letter of March 22nd., 1791).

17. Lancs, R. O., Preston, *Account of Expenses attending the building of Mr. Duckett's Chapel in Hindley, 1788–90*.

18. 31 George III, c. 32.

19. Lancs. R. O., Preston, RC CL 2/49.

20. Lancs. R. O., Preston, RC CL 2/15.

21. Details from the reproduction of one of his sketches kindly lent to me by Mr. Peter Anson.

22. Illustration in Rev. Norman Waugh, *A Short History of St. Anne's Cathedral and the Leeds Missions*, 1904.

23. See Mrs. Bryan Stapleton, *A History of Post-Reformation Catholic Missions in Oxfordshire*, 1906.

24. Sketch in Guildhall Library, London, reproduced in Rev. Bernard Bogan, *The Great Link*, 1948, Chapter II.

25. Rev. (later Bishop) Bernard Ward, *The Dawn of the Catholic Revival in England* Vol. I, 1909, p. 308.

26. See her memorial tablet in St. Thomas' Catholic church, Newport, I.O.W.; also Rev. Canon R. E. Scantlebury, *The Catholic Story of the Isle of Wight*, 1962 Chapter II.

27. Letters in Western Vicariate Archives, Vol. of 1772–88, xlvi.

28. Lancs. Record Office, RC CL 2/56.

29. CRS XLIX (Portsea Registers), frontispiece and pp. 5–6.

30. From notes of Oct. 1964 by Rev. E. G. Dunn of East Greenwich, S.E.10 (shown to me at St. Edmund's College, Old Hall Green).

31. CRS VI, p. 367.

32. John Hutchins, *History of Dorset*, Vol IV ed. Gough, p. 351, quoting *Monthly Magazine*, Oct. 1800).

33. Dorset R. O., Weld papers, D 10/ R 17; letter from the Bishop of Bristol, Feb., 8th, 1796.

34. See Rev. (later Bishop) Bernard Ward, *History of St. Edmund's College*, 1893.

35. Drawings at St. Edmund's College.

36. Rev. David Milburn, *A History of Ushaw College*, 1964, pp. 100, 104.

37. John Milner, *The History and Antiquities of Winchester*, 1798, Vol. II, pp. 229–48.

38. See Catholic Section of Mackenzie and Dent, *History of Newcastle*, 1826.

CHAPTER III

1. CRS XXXV, p. 6.

2. CRS XXXV, p. 328.

3. Benjamin Poole, *History and Antiquities of Coventry*, 1870, p. 226 *et seq.*

4. Site plan in Birmingham Diocesan Archives, C. 1763.

5. See Charles Hadfield, *A History of St. Marie's Mission and Church, Sheffield*, 1889.

6. Details from a sketch kindly made for me by Lady Crathorne.

7. See leaflet, reprinted from *Heritage*, Jan. 1956.

8. For these details on Parndon and Bosworth, see Dame M. F. Roskell, *Memoirs of Francis Kerrill Amherst*, 1903, p. 10, p. 40.

9. For these details on Costessey, see the later chapters of *A Great Gothic Fane*, 1913, an anonymously written book on St. John's at Norwich. For Jerningham, see Joseph Gillow in *St. Thomas' Priory* (Stafford), publ. after 1885.

10. For these details see Provost F. C. Husenbeth's book on the history of Sedgley Park.

11. St. Edmund's College Archives VII, f. 15.

12. Milburn, *op. cit.*, p. 104.

13. For these details, see "Old and New Oscott" in the Jubilee issue of *The Oscotian*, 1888.

14. Dom Augustine (later Bishop) Baines's MS Journal (at St. John's Presbytery, Bath and shortly to be printed by the CRS), entry for Oct. 22nd, 1817.

15. George Oliver, *Collections towards . . . the History of the Catholic Religion in Cornwall, etc.*, 1857, pp. 30–31.

16. These details, including those of Bishop Poynter's visit in 1827, are from a booklet on the Leicester church shown to me at Woodchester.

17. Extract from will in the Presbytery at Hassop.

18. The accounts are in the Presbytery at Hassop.

19. Margaret Durkin, *A Short History of St. Mary's, Burnley*, pp. 6–9.

20. Richard Trappes-Lomax, *A History of Clayton le Moors*, Chetham Society, 1926, p. 142.

21. See Rev. J. G. Macleod, S.J., *History of the Mission of the Society of Jesus in Wigan*, 1900.

22. Details kindly communicated by the Parish Priest, Rev. John Gore.

23. J. G. Macleod, *op. cit.*

24. Details from accounts at the back of the Register Book, 1818 onwards, in Lancs. County R.O., Preston.

25. See note 24 above.

26. Details kindly communicated by the Parish Priest, Rev. T. Croghan.

27. Details from a file of invoices, etc., Lancs., R.O., Preston, RC Ma 4.

28. Reproduced in John O'Dea, *The Story of the Old Faith in Manchester*, 1910.

29. Many of the invoices (see note 27) are made out to, or countersigned by, him.

30. John Summerson, *Georgian London*, 1945, p. 214.

31. Dom Cuthbert Almond, *The History of Ampleforth Abbey*, 1903, p. 283.

32. All the above details are from Baines' MS Journal (see note 14 above). An article on this Journal appeared in *The Downside Review*, Vol. XIX, pp. 182–8.

33. Norman's *History of Cheltenham*, ed. John Goding, 1863, p. 470.

34. Details from papers at Douai Abbey, Woolhampton, Berks.; for the tramway, see Bryan Little, *Cheltenham*, 1952, p. 51.

35. From a brochure of 1853, appealing for money to build the present St. Gregory's, at Douai Abbey.

36. See a booklet on St. Gregory's, by Very Rev. J. S. Marron, O.S.B., and the *Cheltenham Guide*, 1818.

37. Baines Journal, Oct., 23rd, 1817.

38. See a history of this church by Very Rev. Canon Stark, 1902.

39. *Ordo*, 1819.

40. *Laity Directory*, 1826.

41. *Ordo*, 1823.

42. *Laity Directory*, 1827; for the subscription list, and a picture of the façade, see the Centenary Year Book of St. Peter's, Leamington, 1964, pp. 3–4.

43. Dom Cuthbert Almond, *op. cit.*, p. 269.

44. For these activities see the *Downside Review*, Vol. IX, pp. 125–55.

45. Details from historical booklet on Hinckley by Rev. Martin Harrison, O.P., 1958.
46. See *A Great Gothic Fane*, 1913.
47. See entry in H. M. Colvin, *A Biographical Dictionary of English Architects, 1660–1840*, 1954.
48. See Peter Fleetwood-Hesketh, *Lancashire*, and the *History of St. Patrick's*, 1911.
49. See entry in Colvin, *op. cit.*
50. Birmingham Diocesan Archives, C 2181.
51. Birmingham Diocesan Archives, C 2493.
52. See note 51 above.
53. See note 51 above.
54. See article on St. Peter's in the *Midland Weekly News*, July 11th, 1885.
55. Letter of Bishop Walsh, Oct. 9th, 1828; (Birmingham Diocesan Archives, C 2539).
56. See note 54 above, also letters of March 31st and April 13th, 1829 on the Tamworth chapel (Birmingham Diocesan Archives C 2557 and C 2558).

CHAPTER IV

1. Information from the transcripts from the Northern Vicariate Archives made by Rev. W. Vincent Smith, and kindly shown to me by Fr. Smith.
2. The *Hull Packet*, July 29th, 1829 (extract kindly sent by Mr. J. A. Williams).
3. Rev. Canon J. Knowles (1961); collection of MSS etc. on the Catholic Church in Hull, 1772–1850.
4. Knowles Colln.; copies of accounts from Northern Vicariate Archives, 1835 (information from Mr. J. A. Williams).
5. J. G. Macleod, *op. cit.*
6. Lancs. County R. O., RC Cl 4–6.
7. Information from Rev. T. Croghan.
8. See Rev. Reginald Riley, S.J., *St. Mary's, Lowe House, 1793–1940*, 1940; the book includes useful illustrations of the old church.
9. See a print in the *London and Dublin Orthodox Journal*, Oct. 17th, 1835, and H. A. Leicester, *Catholic Worcester*, 1929.
10. Information kindly communicated by Mrs. E. M. Unsworth of Grantham; see also, on Willson, Colvin, *op. cit.*
11. See Mrs. Bryan Stapleton, *A History of the Post-Reformation Catholic Missions in Oxfordshire*, 1906. Further information kindly communicated by the Parish Priest, Rev. G. V. Peulevé.
12. See Shane Leslie, *Mrs. Fitzherbert*, 1939, pp. 323–5.
13. For his obituary, see *The Builder*, March 14th, 1885.
14. CRS Vol. VII, p. 260 *et seq.*
15. Hugh Honour in *Architectural Review*, Sept. 1957, pp. 198–200.
16. For Harper see Colvin, *op. cit.*, and Richard Trappes-Lomax in Chetham Society, Vol. of 1926 (Clayton le Moors).
17. First report of Committee of St. Anthony's Society, Feb. 26th, 1832 (Liverpool Diocesan Archives).

18. Notes from Liverpool Diocesan Archives.
19. R.I.B.A. Library; box of "Drawings for XVIIIth and XIXth century churches"; drawings by Broadbent for a classical St. Anthony's.
20. See note 17 above.
21. St. Anthony's Committee, 2nd. Report (on dimensions).
22. Committee Report, July 14th, 1833.
23. Report, with detailed accounts, Aug. 18th, 1834.
24. For this church, see Anthony Holden, *History of St. Ignatius', 1833–1933.*
25. See Anthony Hewitson, *History of Preston*, 1883.
26. A copy of this letter is in St. John's Presbytery, Bath.
27. Baines Journal, August, and Sept. 22nd, 1817.
28. Newsham Correspondence, Ushaw,; letter of Oct. 8th, 1840.
29. See Western Vicariate Archives, Vol. of 1818–37, letter of Aug. 19th, 1836.
30. Western Vicariate Archives, Vol. of 1818–37, letter 91, Nov. 17th, 1830 and letter of Dec. 1st, 1830.
31. See Western Vicariate Archives, letter of May 1st, 1837 and Dom Gerard Spencer, O.S.B. *Catholic Life in Swansea* (Centenary of St. David's church), 1847–1947.
32. *Downside Review*, Vol. XXIII, pp. 212–13.
33. *Felix Farley's Bristol Journal*, July 8th, 1843.
34. Colvin, *op. cit.*
35. Colvin, *op. cit.*, and booklet on the church's history, 1843–1943.
36. Mrs. Bryan Stapleton, *op. cit.*
37. George Oliver, *op. cit.* (of 1857), pp. 31–2.
38. See Consecration brochure, 1947, with illustrations.
39. Illustrations, and other details, in Nottingham Diocesan Archives.
40. See Rev. Nicholas Ryan, S.J., Centenary Book, 1848–1948.
41. Details from the very complete building accounts preserved at the College.

CHAPTER   V

1. See Terence Davis, *The Architecture of John Nash*, 1960, p. 1.
2. For this, see Mark Girouard in *Country Life*, Nov. 24th, 1960.
3. See E. S. Purcell, *Life and Letters* of Phillipps de Lisle, Vol. I, p. 62. For Railton, see Colvin, *op. cit.*
4. *Letters and Diaries* of John Henry Newman, ed. Rev. Stephen Dessain, C.O., Vol. XII, pp. 219–22.
5. Dessain, *op. cit.*, XII, 212–13, 216–17, 219–22.
6. Purcell, *op. cit.* I, 314.
7. Dessain, *op. cit.*, XIII, 460–2; Newman to Miss Holmes.
8. Dessain, *op. cit*, XII, 302–4; Newman to R. A. Coffin, Oct. 22nd, 1848.
9. Dessain, *op. cit.*, XII, 219–22.
10. Dessain, *op. cit.*, XII, 215; Newman to Miss Giberne, June 6th, 1848.
11. See note 10 above.
12. Dessain, *op. cit.*, XIII, 460–2.
13. CRS Vol. IX, pp. 191–2.

14. Information from Mr. S. C. Kerr Bate, L.R.I.B.A.
15. Gloucs. Record Office, Quarter Sessions Certs. under the Catholic Relief Act, 1791.
16. See his obituary in *The Builder*, July 8th 1882.
17. See Dom Hildebrand Lane Fox, O.S.B., *Chronicles of a Wharfedale Parish*, 1909, p. 31 *et seq.*
18. Building Accounts and other documents at Downside.
19. MS ledgers and account books at Downside.
20. Rev. Bernard Basset, S.J., Centenary Booklet, 1949, p. 6.
21. *The Builder*, Nov. 13th, 1847.

CHAPTER VI

1. Bernard Ward, *The Sequel to Catholic Emancipation*, Vol. II, 1915, p. 182 *et seq.*
2. In the R.I.B.A.
3. Bernard Ward, *op. cit.* (see note 1 above).
4. For a description, with a cross section, see *The Builder*, Sept. 9th, 1848.
5. Bernard Ward, *op. cit.*, p. 185n.
6. A sketch of Edward Pugin's design is reproduced in the Souvenir Booklet produced at the opening of the crypt of the Lutyens Cathedral.
7. See Rev. Norman Waugh, *A Short History of St. Anne's Cathedral and the Leeds Missions*, 1904.
8. Rev. W. Vincent Smith, *Catholic Tyneside*, 1930, p. 77.
9. *Andrew's Weekly Orthodox Journal*, Feb. 21st, 1835.
10. See W. B. Stevenson, Handbook to Nottingham Cathedral, published later than 1948.
11. See note 10 above.
12. For this and later points see *Diocese of Shrewsbury, 1851–1951* (Centenary Record).
13. Sketches and plans in R.I.B.A.
14. Sketch of the full design among the E. W. Pugin drawings in the R.I.B.A.
15. See *Catholic Building Review*, Southern edn., 1960, pp. 142–4.
16. A fine original sketch of this project is in the Pro-Cathedral House, Clifton, Bristol; see also Bryan Little, *The City and County of Bristol*, 1954, plate 29.
17. *Bristol Mercury*, Sept. 23rd, 1848.
18. MS. Autobiography of Ullathorne, quoted in the Parish Magazine, Pro-Cathedral, Clifton, Oct. 1963.
19. *The Builder*, April 22nd and Sept. 30th, 1848.
20. *The Builder*, Dec. 30th, 1876; *Building News*, Dec. 8th, 1876; *The Architect*, Aug. 4th and Nov. 17th, 1877 (with illustrations).
21. Western Vicariate Archives, Vol. of 1818–37; letter of Fr. Thomas to Bp. Baines, Jan. 23rd, 1830.
22. BM Addl. MSS 35617, f. 243.
23. Western Vicariate Archives, Vol. of 1772–88; reports of 1784 and 1793.
24. *Catholic Directory*, 1842; Colvin, *op. cit.*
25. *Catholic Directory*, 1842.

CHAPTER VII

1. Pugin's drawings of 1840, and those of Charles Hansom for the undercroft, are now at Douai Abbey, Woolhampton, Berks.
2. George Oliver, *op. cit.*, section on Cornwall, p. 30.
3. See Sister Frideswide Stapleton, O.S.B., *The History . . . of St. Mary's Priory, Princethorpe*, 1930.
4. Now among the community's archives at Colwich; it is signed by Joseph Towsey of Blandford, who had worked for the Welds of Lulworth. See also, for the old buildings of Cannington Court, A. W. Vivian Neal in the *Proceedings* of the Somerset Archaeological Society, Vol. 104.
5. Western Vicariate Archives, Vol. of 1818–37, letter 53.
6. Western Vicariate Archives, as above; letter of Rev. J. J. Lyons, O.P. to Bp. Baines, Sept. 19th, 1830.
7. See *Stanbrook Abbey . . . A Sketch of its History*, by a nun there, 1925.
8. Information from papers at Stanbrook; the building is now the Chapter House.
9. Dom. Cuthbert Almond, O.S.B., *The History of Ampleforth Abbey*, 1903, p. 344
10. See *Downside Review*, Vol. X, pp. 187–98.
11. See note 10 above, also *Downside Review*, Vol. XXXIII, p. 47.
12. See note 10 above.
13. For these and the immediately following points, see Belmont Jubilee Books, 1909
14. See Harold Kurtz, *The Empress Eugénie*, 1964, pp. 321–9.
15. See A. H. Saxton, *Bygone Erdington*, 1928, p. 152.
16. *The Builder*, Aug. 16th, 1879.
17. *The Builder*, April 6th, 1878, including an illustration.
18. Preserved at Stanbrook.
19. *Stanbrook Abbey* (note 7 above), and for the completion of the first block *The Builder*, May 1st, 1880.
20. For the competition for the combined church and monastery, see *The Builder* March 25th, 1893; the competition is said there to have been a limited one for architects who were old boys of the school or who had worked on Ampleforth missions. For Smith's scheme for a church, see p. 179.
21. Information kindly given to me by the Prioress.
22. George Oliver, *op. cit.*, p. 42 gives the designer of this "convenient and respectable" church as "the late Mr. Peniston"; he was the County Surveyor for Wiltshire (see Oliver, p. 375).
23. Signed sketch of 1839 at St. Augustine's Priory, Abbotskerswell.
24. There are no architect's drawings, or correspondence with Joseph Hansom preserved at the Priory. Notes from Plymouth Diocesan Records have been kindly sent to me by Mr. P. J. Mowan of Plymouth.
25. Though addressed to Bp. Vaughan, Bucknall's letters are now at the Priory.
26. See *A History of the Benedictine Nuns at Dunkirk*, 1958.
27. Information given to me by members of the community and, from Plymouth Diocesan archives, by Mr. P. J. Mowan.
28. Diary of Dame Placida Selby, Abbess 1828–68.
29. Preserved at St. Scholastica's Abbey, Teignmouth.

30. Preserved at Mount St. Bernard Abbey.
31. See *La Trappe in England*, 1935 and CRS Vol. XLIII.
32. See J. B. Dockery, *Collingridge*, 1954, p. 181.
33. See note 31 above.
34. A contemporary print of the church etc., is at the head of an appeal leaflet; see Western Vicariate Archives.
35. Details from an article in the *Southwark Record*, Sept.–Oct. 1939.
36. *The Builder*, Nov. 10th, 1877.
37. For the above details, see the booklet on Hinckley by Rev. Martin Harrison, O.P., 1958.
38. Harrison, *op. cit.*; details of the chapel, attributed to Joseph Hansom, are from a print shown to me at Colwich.
39. Letter at Woodchester, from Bp. Ullathorne to William Leigh jr., of Sept. 28th, 1885.
40. Leigh-Pugin correspondence, 1846, at Woodchester.
41. See note 40 above.
42. Pugin to Leigh, Aug. 19th, 1846.
43. Pugin to Leigh, Sept. 5th, 1846.
44. For details of his scheme, see a letter from Hansom to Leigh, Sept. 5th, 1846; the architect makes it clear that he had already gone fully into a scheme for Woodchester.
45. See *Building News*, Aug. 20th, 1869.
46. *The Builder*, Oct. 18th, 1862 and Aug. 15th, 1863.
47. See C. M. Anthony, *Fr. Reginald Buckler, O.P.*, 1927.
48. National Buildings Record, Goodhart-Rendel card index colln.
49. See Rev. Geoffrey Anstruther, O.P., *St. Dominic's 1878–1948*, publ. 1948.
50. Minutes of the Bristol Society of Architects, May 6th, 1850; for an award "for accuracy of mouldings and general details", see minute of Nov. 29th, 1850.
51. *The Builder*, Oct. 23rd, 1869 (along with full details of the project).
52. See John Britton, *History and Antiquities of . . . the Cathedral Church of Peterborough*, 1828, p. 73. *et seq.*
53. These drawings are bound in a book in the library at Ushaw.
54. Milburn, *op. cit.*, pp. 178–9; see also A. W. N. Pugin, *The Description of the College Chapel of St. Cuthbert, Ushaw*, 1848.
55. Milburn *op. cit.*, and Henry Gillow, *The Chapels at Ushaw*, 1885.
56. Preserved at St. Edmund's College.
57. See F. G. Roberts in *The Cottonian*, Vol. 49, Pt. II.
58. See note 57 above.

CHAPTER VIII

1. *The Builder*, Oct. 7th, 1865.
2. National Buildings Record, Goodhart-Rendel Card Index; a short tower has recently been added as a memorial to Hilaire Belloc.
3. Details from notes kindly shown to me by Prof. S. T. Welsh; see also Nicholl's obituary in R.I.B.A. Journal, April 22nd, 1905.

4. See *St. Vincent's* (Centenary Souvenir), 1953.

5. For Taunton, see St. George's Centenary Booklet, 1960, p. 10, and for Abergavenny, CRS Vol. XXVII, p. 106.

6. See Anthony Hewitson, *History of Preston*, 1883.

7. See Colvin, *op. cit.*, and obituary in *The Builder*, Jan. 16th, 1864.

8. See Centenary Booklet, 1962.

9. Details on Wardell from notes kindly shown to me by Prof. S. T. Welsh, and from his obituary in *The Builder*, Jan. 13th, 1900.

10. For his career see the D.N.B.; obituaries are in *The Builder*, June 12th, 1875 and *Building News*, June 11th, 1875.

11. See Fr. Justin McLoughlin, O.F.M. *Gorton Monastery, 1861–1961*, and Cecil Stewart *The Stones of Manchester*, 1956, pp. 98–9.

12. See R. N. Billington and John Brownbill, *op. cit.*

13. See Rev. W. Salmon, S.M., Centenary History, 1950 and the Spitalfields entry in *Hodges' Catholic Handbook*, 1857.

14. For Maidstone see *The Builder*, Oct. 30th, 1880 and July 15th, 1882; for Market Harborough, see *The Builder*, July 4th, 1877.

15. *Building News*, Aug. 19th, 1864.

16. *The Builder*, Sept. 3rd, 1864; the tower was added in 1877 (Centenary Handbook, 1964).

17. For his obituary, see *The Builder*, March 14th, 1885.

18. For information on all of the Hansoms I am most grateful for information kindly conveyed by Prof. S. T. Welsh.

19. See obituaries in the *Western Daily Press*, Dec. 1st, 1888 and *The Builder*, Dec. 8th, 1888.

20. *The Builder*, April 28th, 1877; additional information is displayed in the church.

21. For his career, see obituary in *The Builder*, July 8th, 1882.

22. Cecil Stewart, *op. cit.*, pp. 94–8.

23. See *The Builder*, Nov. 24th, 1877.

24. See *The Builder*, Nov. 19th, 1881.

25. See *The Builder*, Jan. 20th, 1872 and July 5th, 1873.

26. See *The Architect*, Dec. 12th, 1879 and memorial tablets to the Willock-Dawes family in the church itself.

27. For the buildings in Gt. Ormond St. and St. John's Wood, see *The Builder*, Nov. 12th, 1864 and Oct. 22nd, 1898.

28. P. Whittle, *The History of Preston*, 1837.

29. Anthony Hewitson, *The History of Preston*, 1883 and *The Builder*, June 12th, 1880.

30. See Rev. Henry Tristram, C.O., *History and Guide* of the Birmingham Oratory, edn. of 1962, p. 19.

31. Preserved at the Birmingham Oratory.

32. Tristram, *op. cit.*, p. 27.

33. Preserved at the Birmingham Oratory.

34. See illustrations in *The London Oratory* (Centenary Handbook) 1949.

35. *The Builder*, Feb. 7th, 1880.

36. For a long article on the competition, see *The Builder*, June 29th, 1878.

37. Drawings are at the London Oratory.

38. See *The Builder*, April 9th, 1887.
39. *The Builder*, July 7th, 1885.
40. For his obituary, see *The Builder*, Dec. 15th, 1894.
41. See Gribble's drawings preserved at the London Oratory.

CHAPTER IX

1. For its history, see *The Church of St. James*, a booklet of 1965.
2. *The Builder*, July 18th, 1885.
3. See a long article in the issue of July 18th, 1885.
4. For Goldie's design, see *The Builder*, Aug, 1st, 1885.
5. See the booklet by P. S. Wilkins, 1955, also T. D. Atkinson and J. Willis Clark, *Cambridge Described and Illustrated*, 1897, pp. 177–8.
6. See *The Builder*, Nov. 21st, 1891 and *Building News*, June 14th and July 27th, 1889 and May 13th, 1892 (with an illustration).
7. For its history, see *A Great Gothic Fane*, 1913.
8. Nikolaus Pevsner *Norwich and N.E. Norfolk*, 1962, p. 244.
9. See the passage on this Sheringham church in *A Great Gothic Fane*, also Pevsner, *op. cit.*, pp. 314–15.
10. *The Builder*, March 18th, 1893 (with a plan and picture). This is the church whose proposed replacement by the closed Anglican church of St. John may provide a precedent of some historico-ecumenical interest; see *The Times*, May 21st, 1965.
11. Information kindly communicated by Mr. Peter Anson.
12. See Anthony Hewitson, *History of Preston*, 1883.
13. See *The Builder*, July 9th, 1892.
14. Hence Kirby's church at Llandudno; see *The Builder*, Sept. 2nd, 1893, mentioning a "late XVth-century style".
15. Here, as in many places in this book, I am much indebted, for information kindly conveyed, to Prof. S. T. Welsh.
16. *The Builder*, March 2nd, 1889.
17. Information from the Rev. Canon R. E. Scantlebury. For the foundation stone, see *The Builder*, Aug. 31st, 1895.
18. For Bentley's life and work, see W. de l'Hopital (his daughter) *Westminster Cathedral and its Architect* (with an introduction by W. R. Lethaby), 2 vols., 1919.
19. Drawings in the R.I.B.A. (V 17/ 16–17). See also W. J. Anderson, *A History of . . . St. Mary's, Chelsea*, 1938.
20. For Stokes's career, see H. V. Molesworth Roberts in the *Architectural Review*, Dec. 1946.
21. Information kindly conveyed by Prof. S. T. Welsh.
22. See *The Builder*, Sept. 15th, 1888.
23. Preserved at Downside.
24. For his obituary, see *Building News*, May 20th, 1904.
25. *The Builder*, Sept. 24th, 1904; *Building News*, Sept. 16th, 1904.
26. For this church, and the history of its shrine, see Rev. C. Wilson, *Our Lady of Light, Clacton*, 1960.

27. For many of these biographical facts I am indebted to Mr. Peter Anson.
28. See *The Builder*, Oct. 12th and 19th and Nov. 16th, 1895.
29. *The Builder*, Aug. 12th, 1882.
30. Information kindly conveyed by Mr. J. A. Williams. For earlier alterations, see *The Builder*, Jan. 26th, 1895.
31. See note 20 above.
32. It is mentioned by Herman Muthesius in *Die Neure Kirkliche Baukunst in England*, 1901, p. 51.
33. See *The Builder*, May 4th and 11th, 1889.
34. In the R.I.B.A. (U. 3) and dated 1895.
35. See the issues of June 1st, 1889 and Jan. 25th, 1890.
36. The resulting discussions are recorded in papers at Woodchester.
37. See Ian Nairn and Nikolaus Pevsner, *Surrey*, 1962, p. 219.
38. See *The Builder*, Sept. 10th, 1892.
39. *The Builder*, May 10th, 1902; *Building News*, Oct. 9th, 1903.
40. *The Builder*, July 21st, 1906 and July 18th, 1908.
41. See *Downside Review*, Vol. XXIX.
42. Preserved at Downside.

CHAPTER X

1. See *The Builder*, Dec. 22nd, 1877.
2. *The Builder*, Sept. 4th, 1880.
3. See note 1 above.
4. See *The Builder*, Sept. 20th, 1879.
5. CRS XLIX, Portsea Registers, p. 9.
6. Information from notes kindly shown me by Prof. S. T. Welsh.
7. See the sketches illustrating *The Builder*'s article of Sept. 20th, 1879.
8. For his cathedral at Leeds, see *The Builder*, of March 9th, May 18th, and June 22nd, 1901. For Eastwood's obituary, see *The Builder*, Jan. 24th, 1913.
9. For many of the details which follow on the Westminster project, see J. G. Snead-Cox, *Life of Cardinal Vaughan*, Vol. II.
10. See *The Builder*, Oct. 16th, 1875.
11. His designs were exhibited in the Academy of 1907. See also *Building News*, April 6th, 1906 and *The Builder*, May 25th, 1907.
12. Snead-Cox, *op. cit.*, p. 331.
13. See Rev. R. C. Fuller, *Warwick Street Church*, 1956, pp. 28–9.
14. For the Basilica of Maxentius, see D. S. Robertson, *A Handbook of Greek and Roman Architecture*, 1929, pp. 261–3 and fig. III.
15. For their relationship, see J. Arnott Hamilton, *Byzantine Architecture and Decoration*, 2nd. edn., 1956, pp. 256–8. For a detailed technical description of Westminster Cathedral, see *The Builder*, April 20th, 1907.
16. E. S. Purcell, *op. cit.*, Vol. II, p. 212.
17. F. R. Rolfe, *Hadrian VII*, 1904, p. 36.
18. R.I.B.A. drawings, U 3/ 8.

19. See the issue of Oct. 15th, 1892.

20. For a sketch of Stokes's proposed interior, see R.I.B.A. Journal, Jan. 8th, 1927 and Cecil Stewart, *op. cit.*, p. 113.

21. Cecil Stewart, *op. cit.*, p. 112.

22. Henry Gillow, *op. cit.*, pp. 57–8.

23. Milburn, *op. cit.*, p. 284.

24. See note 22 above.

25. Henry Gillow, *op. cit.*, p. 68.

26. See *The Builder*, Nov. 10th, 1877.

27. Seen in sketches at Hawkesyard.

28. See R. Willis and J. Willis Clark, *The Architectural History of the University of Cambridge*, 1886, Vol. I., p. 447 (in the passage dealing with Eton).

29. See *The Builder*, Aug. 1st, 1891.

30. See note 29 above and, for the Observants, Dom David Knowles and R. N. Hadcock, *Mediaeval Religious Houses, England and Wales*, 1953, pp. 194–5.

31. See Dom Cyprian Alston, "The Story of the Abbey Church" in *Downside Review*, XXIV, pp. 268–85 and, for a more extended study, Dom Augustine James, *The Story of Downside Abbey Church*, 1962.

32. Nikolaus Pevsner, *North Somerset and Bristol*, 1958, pp. 71 and 183.

33. See illustration opposite p. 24 of the *Downside Review*, Vol. I, and a ground plan opposite p. 356.

34. *Downside Review*, Vol. I, opposite p. 180.

35. Dom Augustine James, *op. cit.*, pp. 27–8.

36. Dom Augustine James, *op. cit.*, p. 41.

37. Dom Augustine James, *op. cit.*, p. 47. The ground plan is illustrated opposite that page, and Garner's interior elevation is reproduced on the bookjacket.

38. Thomas Garner in the *Downside Review*, XXIV, pp. 266–7.

39. Dom Augustine James, *op. cit.*, p. 49.

40. Preserved at Downside.

41. See *The Builder*, Oct. 6th, 1894.

42. Details from a manuscript history, of 1903, at Douai Abbey.

43. For these points see Very Rev. F. C. Doyle, O.S.B., *History of St. Edmund's*, 1917 p. 128 *et seq.*

44. They are preserved at Douai Abbey.

45. Reproduced in *The Builder*, Oct. 30th, 1886.

46. Information kindly conveyed by Rev. Dom John Stéphan, O.S.B., F.R.Hist. S.

47. Walters's original drawings, reproduced in the *Historical Guide* of 1923 by Dom John Stéphan, show a simple tower of only two storeys.

48. The drawings are preserved at Downside.

CHAPTER XI

1. See *The Builder*, Aug. 3rd, 1861.

2. For an article on the exhibited designs, see Christopher Hussey in *Country Life*, April 30th, 1932.

3. Preserved at Mount St. Bernard.

4. The community's first contact with Scott was made in 1919. For this, and many other points on the church as finally completed, see Dom Edward Corbould, O.S.B., in the *Ampleforth Journal*, Oct. 1961.

5. The drawings are preserved at Douai Abbey.

6. Preserved at Douai Abbey.

7. He died in 1936; for his career, see an obituary notice in the R.I.B.A. Journal, Sept. 5th, 1936.

8. Two sketches, and a ground plan, are reproduced in *Douai Abbey* (descriptive handbook) 3rd edn., 1953.

9. Drawings are preserved at Colwich.

10. See Dom Augustine James, *op. cit.*, p. 74.

11. See J. A. Williams, *op. cit.*, p. 91.

12. For these details, see Rev. Canon R. E. Scantlebury, *The Catholic Story of the Isle of Wight*, 1962, pp. 79–83.

13. Information from the Parish Priest, Very Rev. Canon R. W. Meagher, D.D.

14. See *Art Notes*, V. 1 (Jan.–Feb. 1938).

15. See D. S. Robertson, *op. cit.*, pp. 59–60 and Plate 11 (b).

16. See Peter Hammond, *Liturgy and Architecture*, 1960, pp. 68–71, also Peter Anson, *Fashions in Church Furnishings, 1840–1940*, 1960, pp. 359–60.

CHAPTER XII

1. Information kindly conveyed by Mr. Gerard Goalen, F.R.I.B.A.

2. Information from the Parish Priest, Rev. M. Lecluze.

3. See the *Catholic Building Review*: (later referred to as CBR) Southern Edn., 1962, pp. 180–1, and 1963, pp. 157–8.

4. For the Nonconformist and Catholic history of this church see the Victoria County History of Warwickshire, Vol. VII, pages 409 and 475.

6. See *The Times*, May 21st, 1965 and *Catholic Herald*, May 28th, 1965.

7. See Mr. Craze's article in the 2nd edn. (1961) of the Cathedral Souvenir and Guide.

8. CBR Southern Edn., 1960, pp. 142–4.

9. CBR Southern Edn., 1962, pp. 199–201.

10. Information kindly conveyed by Mr. Stanley Kerr Bate, L.R.I.B.A. and by the Abbot of Ealing. See also CBR Southern Edn., 1962, pp. 51–3.

11. See Dom Edward Corbould, O.S.B., in the *Ampleforth Journal*, Oct. 1961.

12. See *Architect and Building News*, July 10th, 1963.

13. For these particulars, and for other details, I am indebted to the Abbot of Prinknash (Rt. Rev. Dyfrig Rushton, O.S.B.) and to Mr. F. G. Broadbent, F.R.I.B.A.

14. For this, see *Architect and Building News*, Nov. 21st, 1962.

15. CBR Northern Edn. 1953, pp. 134–7.

16. CBR Southern Edn., 1964, pp. 134–5.

17. CBR Southern Edn., 1964, pp. 134–5.

18. CBR Southern Edn., 1962, pp. 215–17.

19. CBR Southern Edn., 1962, pp. 65–6 and 1963, pp. 70–1.

20. See Stephen Joseph in his own introduction to *Actor and Architect*, ed. Stephen Joseph, publ. Manchester Univ. Press, 1964, pp. 1–29. Also his article on "Proscenium Madness" in the *New Theatre Magazine*, publ. Drama Dept., Bristol University, July, 1962.

21. See *Architect and Building News*, Oct. 23rd, 1963.

22. For the church already completed at Combe Down, see Bryan Little in *The Catholic Herald*, Oct. 8th, 1965.

23. Information kindly conveyed by Mr. Gerard Goalen, F.R.I.B.A. For the church, see *Architect and Building News*, Sept. 23rd, 1964.

24. CBR Northern Edn., 1954, pp. 36–7.

25. CBR Northern Edn., 1959, pp. 117–21.

26. CBR Southern Edn., 1962, pp. 56–9 and 1963, pp. 35–7.

27. CBR Southern Edn., 1964, pp. 125–31.

28. CBR Southern Edn., 1964, pp. 186–7.

29. CBR Southern Edn., 1963, pp. 91–7; for Horley, see pp. 108–113.

30. *Architect and Building News*, July 28th, 1965.

31. CBR Northern Edn., 1961, pp. 41–3. For Fitzwilliam House, see *Cambridge New Architecture*, ed. Hughes, Lewison, and Wesley, 1964, pp. 102–5.

32. For an important discussion on this church, see Dom Edward Corbould, O.S.B. in the *Ampleforth Journal*, June 1964.

33. e.g. in the Comments on the Instructions (dated Sept. 26th, 1964) of the Sacred Congregation of Rites, issued by Cardinal Lercaro, Archbishop of Bologna, President of the Commission for their implementation. These have been circulated to clergy in England. See also Rev. J. D. Crichton, *Changes in the Liturgy* (Consideration on the Instruction of the S.R.C.), 1965, pp. 90–104.

34. See the Pastoral Directory of the Montreal Liturgical Commission; translation printed in *The Furrow* (publ. from St. Patrick's College, Maynooth, Ireland), Oct. 1965, pp. 639–58.

CATHEDRAL EPILOGUE

1. For a critique of the winning design, and for illustrations of some of those rejected, see *Architect and Building News*, Aug. 31st, 1960.

2. CBR Northern Edn., 1961, pp. 76–7.

3. For a photograph of this model, see the title page of *Ely*, with an introduction by Geoffrey Webb, 1950.

4. For a recent progress report on this Cathedral, see *Architect and Building News*, June 16th, 1965; see also *The Times*, Nov. 1st, 1965.

INDEX

A

*Figures in heavy type refer to illustration plate numbers, e.g. Newport, Mon., **12a**.*

SB 12/66